COLD BLOODED

A TRUE CRIME STORY OF A MURDEROUS TEENAGE VAMPIRE CULT

FRANK STANFIELD

WILDBLUE
PRESS

WildBluePress.com

COLD BLOODED published by:
WILDBLUE PRESS
P.O. Box 102440
Denver, Colorado 80250

WILDBLUE PRESS is registered at the U.S. Patent and Trademark Offices.

ISBN 978-1-952225-60-4 Trade Paperback
ISBN 978-1-952225-59-8 eBook

Cover design © 2021 WildBlue Press. All rights reserved.

Interior Formatting by Elijah Toten
www.totencreative.com

Book Cover Design by VilaDesigns

COLD
BLOODED

Other books by Frank Stanfield.

Unbroken: The Dorothy Lewis Story
Vampires, Gators and Wackos, A Newspaperman's Life

TABLE OF CONTENTS

INTRODUCTION

Faded vampire

Rod Ferrell lowered his head on Nov. 18, 2019, as he walked across the courtroom. It was not from shame. He was watching where he stepped, so he would not tangle the chains of his leg irons. It is the kind of thing you learn in prison after more than twenty years if you don't learn anything else.

The former teen vampire cult leader was wearing a faded orange jumpsuit. At thirty-nine, he looked faded, even with a prison yard suntan. His formerly long, dyed black hair was clipped to a gray and red stubble. His tongue, once used for tasting blood and preaching occult sermons, was silent.

When he finally did speak, he apologized to his victims' families.

"I know nothing I say or do can bring them back. I hope you know just how sorry I am."[1]

His defenders, including a woman who identified herself as his fiancée, said he had changed. He seemed sincere, even emotional, but his bid for a lighter-than-life sentence had come with blood-red memories and echoes of a crowbar crushing the skulls of two unsuspecting people.

"The pain will never go away," Jennifer Wendorf said about coming home as a seventeen-year-old to find her parents, Richard Wendorf and Ruth Queen, bludgeoned to death.

Nor will the questions that haunt her and the rest of her family ever go away.

Ferrell, in his second-grade school picture, looked like a mischievous little character in a 1950s TV sitcom. Years later, in 1995, a former high school classmate described him as "kind of dorky, I guess. Just a regular kid, a regular ninth grader."[2]

The next year, he was dressed in all-black clothing and looked like the kind of villain you might see in a horror movie.

It was not just about appearances, of course. One of his mental health experts at trial testified that behavior is the result of a person's thought pattern. So, what was Ferrell thinking? Did he really believe he was a vampire?

Prosecutors insisted that vampirism had nothing to do with the crime. Defense lawyers looking for mitigating circumstances in his death penalty trial argued that he was under the influence of the occult.

Ferrell was a sixteen-year-old artist. He was also smart enough and charismatic enough to form a cult.

Prosecutors described Ferrell as a master manipulator, but his attorneys argued that he was tricked by Jennifer Wendorf's fifteen-year-old sister.

Heather "Zoey" Wendorf, who dangled a Barbie doll from her backpack with a noose, was arrested with the cult three days after the murders but was never prosecuted.

The crime scene was textbook explosive rage, yet he had never met his victims. Was he out of control, or could he have stopped himself? Was there some traumatic event in his life that triggered the frenzied murders?

Psychologists at Ferrell's resentencing hearing would claim that the magnitude of the crime is not necessarily a reliable indicator of rehabilitation.

Yet, as a fellow journalist remarked, "How do you get past THAT?"

Oprah Winfrey famously urged people not to blame their mothers, but one of the most experienced forensic psychologists in the state said, "This is one of the most dysfunctional families I have ever encountered."[3]

Sondra Gibson, who was also involved in vampirism, claimed she was haunted by a demon and raped by a rival cult leader during an orgy. She was arrested for trying to solicit a 14-year-old boy for sex during a vampire ritual.

Rod claimed he was raped when he was five years old by his grandfather's friends during a satanic human sacrifice.

Gibson allowed him to be kicked out of school and turned a blind eye to heavy drug use while allowing him to stay out all night playing vampire games.

"Crazy," said people after seeing the news stories that flashed across the globe. Yet, Ferrell was not insane.

Psychologists argued that he suffered numerous personality disorders. Prosecutors said he knew right from wrong, that he was faking, and that he chose to follow an evil path.

Cold Blooded takes readers on a dark journey through interviews, transcripts, and through my eyes. I lived it every day and I am still covering the case more than 20 years later. The book also examines the Constitutional struggle between a free press and a defendant's right to a fair trial and changes in how the law deals with juveniles.

"There is genuine evil in this world," Ferrell's trial judge said before imposing the death sentence. "There is a dark side and a light side competing in each of us."[4]

CHAPTER 1

"My parents have been killed"

Jennifer Wendorf slipped into her home on cat paws at 10:35 p.m., Nov. 25, 1996.

"I was late. I was supposed to be home at 10:15 p.m. So, I kind of just walked right past the couch with my head down…and I just looked at the floor," she told a detective.[1]

"I could hear that the TV was on, and I could see my dad's feet on the couch, you know, laying on the couch, but daddy always fell asleep. I just figured that he was sleeping, and I could sneak by. So, I just snuck back into my room, and I went into my room to use my telephone…."

The phone cord had been ripped out of the wall.

That was odd, she thought, but her sister, Heather, had been on a rampage lately, so she figured she probably destroyed it in a fit of anger. She walked into Heather's room to use her phone to call her boyfriend to let him know that she got home safely.

"…I was going to the kitchen 'cause I was gonna get something to eat, 'cause I was hungry, and I saw a blood trail by the breakfast nook, almost in the living room and on the way to the kitchen. And then I saw a blood spot on the kitchen floor, and then that's when I saw my mom. She was laying there, and then I ran to the living room to see what my dad was doing, and he wasn't asleep. He had already been attacked."

She ran back to the phone and called 911.

"My parents have been killed. Please send ambulances!"[2]

"How do you know they have been killed?" the operator asked.

"There is blood everywhere. Please, as fast as you can," she said, her voice quavering.

Asked if she was alone, she replied, "My sister is gone. She should be here. She's only fifteen and she's gone."

CHAPTER 2

Is this for real?

As a long-time editor and reporter for the *Orlando Sentinel,* I thought I had heard and seen it all. Not only had a popular cheerleader lost her parents and possibly her sister, but the crime scene was horrifying. Richard Wendorf and Ruth Queen had been beaten with a crowbar so savagely he was unrecognizable, and some sheriff's deputies wondered if she had been shot or attacked with an ax.

Detective Al Gussler asked Jennifer who might have killed her parents. "Without hesitation, Jennifer responded by saying, 'My sister, Heather.'"[1]

She also named Heather's friend, Rodrick Ferrell, a former classmate who had moved to Murray, Kentucky. Gussler called Kentucky authorities, who said Ferrell was missing, along with a handful of followers in his blood-drinking vampire cult.

Reporters are insanely competitive. I was on vacation and taking care of an ill family member when the story broke, so I was twitching.

"There's plenty for everyone," said Lauren Ritchie, the bureau chief for Lake County.

"No there's not," I complained. The paper had already unleashed some excellent reporters, and the story was making international headlines.

I need not have worried. Because I was the court reporter in the Lake County bureau, the lion's share would fall to me.

I come from a family of rural storytellers, so I grew up hearing all kinds of tales. Many were humorous, like the time the community drunkard found himself racing downhill backwards when his car's brakes failed. "I knew I was going to hell," he said, recalling the sound of horse weeds banging against the fenders.

Many stories were tragic. They involved people who were killed in accidents, a World War II veteran who suffered psychological trauma, and a woman who tried to commit suicide by drinking Drano.

A history buff and a voracious newspaper reader, I was moved by tragic stories and baffled by man's inhumanity to man. Crime stories have always fascinated me, especially murders. I spent my early boyhood years in Indianapolis, where famed 1930s bank robber John Dillinger is buried. Stories of "Baby Face" Nelson, "Machine Gun" Kelly and "Pretty Boy" Floyd inflamed my imagination.

It was the assassination of President John F. Kennedy, however, and the live TV coverage of that tragedy that pushed a 13-year-old boy over the finish line to become a journalist.

Journalism is not easy. Yes, you can take notes and dump your notebook into the computer, but there's so much more to being a reporter. Cops, judges, and other lawyers are afraid that you are going to blow their case. They ask, "Can I trust you if I tell you something off the record?" All the while, they wonder if you are fair, have an agenda, are honest, if you are a hard worker, sensitive, tough, curious, whether you are an idiot, or if you have fried the last brain cell in your head while working in a field that has an ink-stained, besotted reputation from the sensational 1920s days of "Yellow Journalism." Most importantly, they wonder if you are accurate.

Believe it or not, journalism has a set of ethics, including separating advocacy and opinion from straight reporting.

TV news, forced to tell a big story in 30 seconds, has always struggled with this one, but now, with around-the-clock cable news, the lines have been blurred into obscurity. Politicians like President Donald Trump have used the term "fake news" as a cudgel while taking to Twitter and campaign rallies to tout their own message.

The Society of Professional Journalists calls for reporters to "identify sources clearly. The public is entitled to as much information as possible to judge the reliability and motivations of sources."[2]

It is not always possible to name names. Some sources must be protected from bosses who are trying to obscure the truth and protect their bureaucratic nests. However, unnamed sources almost seem to be the norm in Washington. And in a city where backstabbing and lying is an art form, it is no wonder the public is skeptical.

The 2020 presidential election further damaged journalism's reputation, with its obsession with poll numbers, which were often misleading, or just plain wrong.

The straight-forward approach is best. However, even when you're honest and accurate you might find yourself doing bizarre things sometimes, like climbing a tree to get a look at the body of a murder victim behind a police barricade, trespassing to get to a mobile home park ravaged by a tornado, or letting a source think you know more—or less—than you really do.

At my first job, in Augusta, Ga., where open-meeting laws were terrible, a columnist was putting her ear to the door of a county commission meeting one day when someone on the other side opened the door and sent her sprawling into the room. "Come on in!" the official boomed.

Sometimes deception is accidental. I once sat within a few feet of rescue workers trying to free a man who had fallen into a grain auger in a horrendous accident. They thought I was a police officer because I was holding a hand-held police scanner.

Another time I found myself talking to the witness of a police shooting inside the roped-off crime scene because I happened to be wearing a black windbreaker like ones the cops were wearing.

The job can be dangerous sometimes. Once, I found myself locked down in a jail riot. Another time I beat the cops to a murder scene. People were outraged and looking at me, wondering who I was and what I was going to do about it. I was never so happy to see the police arrive.

In my rookie year, I walked through a darkened back yard to take pictures of a house fire only to have a firefighter point out that the area was covered with live, downed power lines.

Another time, I got caught up in the excitement of a car chase and foolishly followed only to stop abruptly when an unmarked sheriff's vehicle did a U-turn in front of me.

Then, there are the hurricanes. In 1984, while working in Wilmington, N.C., I sent my family inland while I stayed at the newspaper to cover Hurricane Diana. The building, which is built like a windowless brick fortress creaked and groaned like a ship at sea.

Four hurricanes lashed Central Florida in 2004. On the last day of the last storm, a massive tree limb snapped and crashed near the spot where my photographer had just been standing.

These types of risks are nothing compared to the journalists who cover wars, of course.

You must be a little crazy to be a journalist, and it shows because the business attracts characters.

One of the rivals I had on the vampire case dug himself a hole by eavesdropping, and then writing stories as if he had interviewed the people. A judge and a defense attorney wanted to roll him down the stairs for that inexcusable behavior.

The same guy made remarks in front of a prosecutor suggesting I should be subpoenaed, which would have taken me off coverage of the trial. I was furious. I am sure he did it with malicious intent. I am a peace-loving guy, but the thought suddenly occurred to me that perhaps I should place my size-9 shoe on his backside, and I said so. It was one of those "did I say that out loud?" moments. Fortunately, the prosecutor laughed. He was no fan of the man either.

The same reporter had a way of giving women the creeps. One trial involved two women who testified that their father had raped them as children. They had a courageous, emotional story to tell, and they wanted readers to hear it. With their permission, I let the other guy sit in on the interview, something I would ordinarily never do, but I did not want him bothering them later.

A reporter is only as good as his sources. I genuinely like people, and I guess it shows. I knew the names of the secretary's dog, the clerks' children, and I shared tidbits with them from the latest rumor mill.

Much of the work is routine, especially on newspapers, which covers school board and city hall meetings. It is important. People deserve to know how their tax dollars are being spent, or misspent. Your proudest moments come when your work makes a dramatic difference.

"I thought you might want to know," a tipster told me one day, "the Mount Dora Police Department has classified a homicide as a natural. That is not right. This is murder."[3]

The department, already beset by a crime wave in the pretty tourist town, had tried to sweep the last straw under the rug. A race walker had been stabbed, a woman victimized by a home-invasion burglar, and an elderly man was murdered in his house. In the newest outrage, the body of an elderly man was found dead in his home in an awkward position, a knife and a pillow on the floor nearby. It was in the same neighborhood where the other elderly man had been murdered.

The victim's girlfriend wasn't buying the cops' explanations, and neither was I. He was old. He had a pacemaker for atrial fibrillation. Case closed. But after I wrote a series of investigative stories, the state was pressured into exhuming the man's body. He had been suffocated. It led to a confession and a murder conviction.

It is a reporter's job to the answer "the five W's and H" in news stories: who, what, where, when, why and how. The "why" question is the one that always drives me to keep digging, but even the setting was off in the vampire murders.

The Wendorfs lived in a quiet, rural subdivision of five-acre lots a few miles outside Eustis, Florida, population 12,967, about 40 miles north of Orlando.

The brick house and swimming pool, bound by a ranch-style fence and gate, was the picture of tranquility for the family, two dogs, and Ruth's pet rooster.

Nor was it a whodunit, at least not in the conventional sense. The big question initially was whether Heather was a victim or a killer. Three days after the murders, the *Sentinel* headline screamed: "Murder warrants name all 5 teens." The subhead read: "The victims' daughter, who has been linked to human-blood drinking rituals, is being called a suspect by police."[4]

My hands hovered over the keyboard for a moment the first time I wrote the phrase "teen vampire cult murders." *Is this for real?* But as the story unfolded, it was not only real but surreal, with accounts of blood-drinking, occult worship, drugs, orgies, and murder.

"This is not the [Charles] Manson case," a defense attorney told reporters, referring to the 1969 cult murder of Hollywood actress Sharon Tate and others, but there are many similarities.[5]

It also offered a glimpse into what Christians call spiritual warfare.

Ferrell's mother complained that she was stalked by a demon. At the same time, a young Christian girl was suddenly reluctant to run away with the cult, and her mother seemed to be guided by a mysterious, protective spirit.

The case would also turn out to be a tough legal battle, pitting the First Amendment's freedom of the press against the Sixth Amendment's right of a defendant to have a fair trial.

Ferrell was no ordinary criminal. Intelligent, imaginative, and artistic, he was a charismatic cult leader, tough guy, stone-cold killer and little boy wrapped into one freaky package.

CHAPTER 3

"Dark and dreary things"

Ken Adams is a big, bald man with a soft voice, quick laugh, and a self-deprecating sense of humor.

A thoroughly decent family man, he and his partner were once assigned to show photos of a Jane Doe homicide victim in dozens of strip joints in Orlando in hopes of learning her identity.

He blushed when colleagues teased him about the "tough" assignment.

"It's a dirty job, but somebody's got to do it," he laughed sheepishly.

He was the perfect father-confessor, offering a sympathetic ear to suspects and encouraging them to repeat their stories until he caught them in a whirlpool of contradictory lies.

He was also genuinely sympathetic to crime victims like Jennifer, gently leading them through the fog of shock and horror while gleaning crucial information.

"I thought that I was dreaming," Jennifer told him. "I just thought, I'm not seeing this, this can't be my life, 'cause I just saw my mom at three. What? Less than seven hours previous, I'd seen my mom. And my dad woke me for school. It's just, I didn't think it was happening to me."[1]

Jennifer said Heather had been furious with their parents. "…it just seemed like friction that a teenager would go through, but the only thing is, she got really agitated with it. If mom would tell her to clean her room, she'd just get extremely agitated and blow up."

Her mother put her on restriction.

"When she couldn't go out with the people she wanted to, at the time she wanted to, she would get pissed, very angry," Jennifer said.

There was also a war of words over Rod Ferrell.

He had been a classmate of Heather's until he moved to Murray, Ky., the year before.

"… he called our house collect and Heather would call up there," Jennifer said. "So, we'd always get the charges, and she ran up big bills, like $60 and $80 bills, just calling Rod. And dad, I mean, that's going to agitate a father because he'd ask Heather whose number it was.

"She'd be like, 'I'll pay for it. It's none of your business who it is.' And she'd get really nasty like that, and so dad was just like, 'OK, well, you've lost your phone privileges.' And she got so angry. I mean, what should she expect?"

She said her mother began answering the phone and if it was Ferrell she would yell, "Get off the phone!"

Ferrell gave off some scary vibes.

"I had an old boyfriend that was really angry with me," Jennifer said. One day, Heather said, "You know, Jen, if you ever wanted [him] dead, just tell me, and the next time Rod's down, he can do it."

Heather asked Jennifer if she ever thought about running away.

"Yeah," she replied. "I feel like running away sometimes when my problems just seem like they're too heavy to bear."

"But I've always told her, 'You have to suck it up, and you have to face what you have to face.' I've told her that I've walked off and I've blown off my steam and came back, but I told her that I would never run away."

Heather also told her she had an imaginary friend.

Heather, however, harbored much darker fantasies.

"...she had told me before that she was a vampire. I just thought that that was nonsense. And I knew she read vampire books. She read novels about vampires. At one time I saw a witches' bible in her room, and she had all kinds of just dark and dreary things in her room."

Some of the dark things were letters from Ferrell to her best friend. That wasn't the most chilling thing, however.

"... one night, late at night, we just started talking in my room, and I said, 'Well, Heather, you wanna spend the night with me tonight? Just stay in my room, and when dad wakes us up, we'll just both get up? That way, we can talk.' So, we turned out the light, and we were, you know, getting ready for bed, and we were just talking. It was kind of quiet, and Heather said, 'Jen, have you ever plotted mom and dad's death?'"

CHAPTER 4

Mark of the clan

Within seconds of Sheriff's Deputy Jeff Taylor arriving at the Wendorfs' home, Jennifer ran out of the house. No longer forced to stay calm on the phone, she was crying and hysterical.

"Are your parents alive?" he asked.[1]

"They're dead."

"Is anybody else inside?"

"No."

Taylor turned to an ambulance crew that had just arrived and told them to hold her. He pulled out his handgun and walked into the house looking for suspects.

Finding nothing but the two bodies, he shouted out the code for homicide on his radio, "Signal Five! Signal Five!"[2]

It was no wonder he was shouting. The new deputy would later testify that Richard Wendorf's face looked like "hamburger."[3]

Soon, Taylor was joined by another deputy and a sergeant.

"We searched the property. We got up by the pool area and we noticed the back, master bedroom doors were ajar. All the back doors were ajar. It looked like alarm wiring had been pulled down from the back doors.[4]

Suddenly, a door slammed inside the house.

"It sounds like somebody entered the house," he told the sergeant.

With the hair standing up on the back of his neck, Taylor and the other deputy were ordered back inside to check it out. A draft had caused the bathroom door to slam shut.

Within minutes, the house at 24135 Green Tree Lane was bathed in the headlights of patrol cars. Blue strobe lights bounced off the walls, and yellow crime scene tape gashed the yard.

Such a scene was not unheard of in Orlando 45 minutes away. Watching the news on Orlando TV stations is like watching a cop show, but it is atypical of the quiet Eustis neighborhood.

The inside of the house was enough to make even veteran investigators flinch.

The couch that Richard was lying on was soaked in blood. Ruth was lying face down in the kitchen, her head resting on carpeting in the adjoining dining room. Her little white poodle was growling and refusing to let anyone get close to the body. A big golden retriever was wandering aimlessly outside.

Ruth had been beaten so severely that her brain stem was exposed. One deputy speculated that she had been shot in the back of the head. Pieces of her skull were found in the dining room. The walls were covered in blood splatter. Experts would later testify about "cast off" versus "high impact" patterns, but there was plenty of both, and there was transferred blood as well. The killer had straddled her body and kept hitting her, leaving bloody shoe prints on the floor.

"A French door leading to a patio was ajar in the master bedroom. A curtain on the door appeared to have a spot of blood near the doorknob. Jewelry boxes and drawers were open in bedrooms and some jewelry was scattered on the floors."[5]

The front door was open.

"The door jamb was damaged, and a long piece of the wood appeared to be propped up against the exterior wall. The wood was rotted and appeared termite-damaged."

Crime scene technicians gloved up and donned white coveralls and shoe coverings while poring over the scene, burning up rolls of film and taking video, dusting for fingerprints, and gathering bone, teeth, and hair fragments. They collected 435 bits of evidence, including blood samples that did not belong to the victims. They also put bags over the couple's hands in hopes of finding a killer's DNA beneath their fingernails.

Several footprints were located in the sandy driveway, and these were secured.

Crime scene investigators found cigarette butts outside, which can contain a sample of the smoker's DNA. They turned out to be of no use for crime lab analysts, however. The same was true of two boots found in the yard. They were chew toys for the dogs.

A butcher knife found near the front door was an exciting find until investigators learned that the Wendorfs used it as a gardening tool. Crime scene technicians also found a pocketknife near Richard's feet, but it had fallen out of his pocket.

The medical examiner, Dr. Laura Hair, arrived the next day. She was escorted into the house by crime scene investigators who made sure she walked in their footsteps to prevent crime scene contamination.

She wanted to see the position of the bodies. She looked at the wounds, emptied pockets, and turned the bodies over. With the help of the evidence technicians, she placed the bodies on a sheet, and then into body bags. The bodies were then taken to the medical examiner's office for autopsy.

She did not bother trying to estimate the time of death.

Investigators would learn that the killer or killers had entered the house from the garage, not the front door. They also found an intriguing bit of evidence. It appeared that someone had used their finger, moistened with water, to write the Satanic number "666" on the door leading to the laundry room from the garage.

"Don't get too excited," a detective told me. "We don't know how long it's been there." Not every investigator was even certain that the markings were 666.

Even more intriguing were V-shaped marks on the couple's bodies. Dr. Hair would note in her autopsy report that the marks appeared to be cigarette burns.

A cultist in Kentucky would later claim that it was a sign of Ferrell's vampire nickname, "Vesago," and dots outside the V matched the number of followers in his clan. If true, it would be the first direct link to vampirism in the double homicide, but the marks would prove controversial.

While the crime scene techs were sifting for clues, detectives, with Jennifer's help, began making a list of names and compiling other information that might be helpful. They also put out a "BOLO," or a be-on-the-lookout bulletin for Heather, Rod, and the Ford Explorer.

It wasn't too long before a law enforcement officer found a 1987 Buick Skyhawk in neighboring Seminole County parked along a road not far from Interstate 4. Someone had switched tags. It now had the Explorer license plate attached to the car.

Interstate 4 cuts horizontally across central Florida, from Daytona to Tampa, goes through the heart of Orlando, and intersects Interstate 95 on the east coast, and Interstate 75 toward the west.

Adams and another deputy drove to the spot, marked the car, sealed it with tape, and had it towed to the sheriff's office. Early the next morning, sheriff's crime scene technicians, Ron Shirley and Jim Binkley, took measurements and photos of the car and began looking for evidence.

Several cigarette butts were removed and a nickel. Shirley also took into evidence a pair of boots and a floor mat that was wet. They also used a hand-held vacuum in hopes of catching fiber or hair evidence in the filter.

Shirley also dusted for fingerprints, and when he found some, he "lifted" them with tape and placed them on evidence cards for a fingerprint analyst.

"I found one of value on the interior driver's door window. It was almost center ways near the bottom of the window, and one on the interior passenger door window for the bottom right corner," he reported.[6]

The two technicians also removed the back seat and examined the area with a Luma-Lite, which can detect blood and other fluids when technicians set the light to different wave lengths.

Shirley noted that they got a "hit" on a spot in the center of the back seat.

"It was a small spot and at the time didn't appear to be blood of any kind, but we took out the seat..." It was not blood.

Later, they heated super glue and water in the vehicle. The process creates a vapor and makes fingerprints stand out.

When they went back to the house, they dusted for more fingerprints, this time using a fluorescent dust.

Detectives were eager to search Heather's bedroom but waited until they got a search warrant.

"A search of the northeastern-most bedroom of the above residence is authorized," the warrant stated. "You are authorized to search for and seize any and all correspondence between Rod Ferrell and Heather Wendorf and any hammers, axes, or other tools capable of inflicting blunt trauma."

CHAPTER 5

A warning too late

As an army of cops swarmed over the property, a baffled visitor drove up saying she had to talk to the Wendorfs.

Suzanne Leclaire could not, in her wildest guess, have imagined that the Wendorfs were dead, so she wondered if Jennifer had come home, possibly after drinking, and wrecked her car in the driveway. It was on a steep hill, the driveway was washed out, and there were a lot of trees.

"This is just what went through my mind, and I thought, oh my God, they may not even realize Heather's gone."[1]

She saw Detective Adams and told him that she needed to speak to the Wendorfs.

"Why?" he asked.

"Heather's running away. Is Jen all right?"

"Yes, she's OK."

Leclaire told him that her 16-year-old daughter, Jeanine, was Heather's best friend, and that Jeanine told her that Heather was running away with a former classmate named Rod Ferrell.

Without giving her any information, Adams told her to go home and bring Jeanine back to the house.

Suzanne hurried home, her mind filled with thoughts of Ferrell, each one more disturbing than the last.

Suzanne had first become aware of Ferrell exactly one year earlier at Jeanine's birthday party.

They had a bonfire at their home and Suzanne and her husband, Pete, were keeping watch through the window and bringing out refreshments.

No one introduced him to the family.

"That looks like a bad character," Pete said.

It was the image that Ferrell had carefully cultivated for himself. He liked to carry a walking stick and wore an inverted cross, a common sign of devil worship. He later dyed his reddish hair black and wore it long.

"I never figured him out," said Shane Matthews, a resource officer at the school. "In August, here in Florida, it's very, very warm. It would feel like 100 degrees, even in the shade. Rod would sit out there in the sun and would wear a black trench coat or something and would just watch people walk by and I thought, 'This is just a really different kind of behavior.'"[2]

Heather liked to attract attention, too. She dyed her hair pink and purple, wore fishnet stockings, and a dog collar.

"Heather was a new student at Eustis High," Matthews said, "and I remember her walking by, and she had a hangman's noose hanging from her backpack, and in the hangman's noose was a Barbie doll, which I thought was kind of strange."

She was featured in an *Orlando Sentinel* "Rave" youth section story that year with her hair colored pink and blue.

"I'm always trying to do something different," she said.[3]

"She'd have purple hair one day, then pink the next," said Eustis High Principal Jim Hollins. "She did the new-wave thing, but you can't fault her for that at all."

Suzanne couldn't help but notice Heather's outlandish fashion statement on a trip to an art festival and later told Jeanine that she was the worst-dressed kid on the trip. As an art teacher, she was used to seeing kids with pink hair and black fingernails, but Heather's clothing was bizarre and "practically indecent," she said. She was especially bothered by the bondage chains.

Although she tried not to interfere with the girls' friendship, Suzanne worried sometimes. "She was a strong influence on Jeanine, and Heather would have to push Jeanine pretty far before Jeanine would back off or tell Heather off or whatever."[4]

Jeanine was an introvert; Heather was "brilliant and extremely talented and more outgoing," she said.

Jennifer had a different take. Before Heather met Jeanine in the seventh grade, she dressed more like her. "She was more outgoing, and she didn't dress in all black, and then, she met Jeanine, and she started changing, I guess, into her person, and she'd wear the cringe clothes, and she'd dye her hair, and her thing was just to be different."[5]

She also said that Jeanine was a "depressed person," and it sometimes brought Heather down.

***

Suzanne's anxiety was a stark contrast to just a few hours earlier when the family celebrated Jeanine's birthday at home with dinner, presents, cake, and ice cream.

Heather called at one point.

"No, I can't," an annoyed Jeanine said. "I'll call you back later. I can't talk right now. I'm busy. I'll call you back later."[6]

After cleaning up the kitchen, Suzanne went to her bedroom for a while, but her husband was snoring loudly. She got up and noticed that Jeanine's bedroom door was open, and that Jeanine was not in her room.

She's angry, Suzanne thought. Jeanine's dad told her during dinner that she couldn't get her driver's license until she improved her grades in school. *She's probably walking to Heather's house.*

"So, I got in the car and I was going to drive over to Heather's house. I figured I would pick her up on the road. I saw our puppy out at the lane, and I picked her up. And the further I drove away from the house, the more feeling that I had that I was going in the wrong direction. And I kept getting this feeling, stop and turn back. And then the puppy started whining the further we got from the house, so I turned around."

She parked the car facing the driveway.

"I had a very strong urge to walk around behind the car, and I stood behind the car staring into the trees that were in front of our lane and Jeanine stepped out of the shadows."

The two walked down the road, then sat down to talk. They could hear a lot of sirens in the distance, which was unusual.

"Jeanine, it's not safe for you to be out here on the road by yourself after dark. You know, bad things can happen, and you ought to be aware of that."

"Well, I wasn't going alone."

"Well, I figured Heather was involved in this. I figured you were going to Heather's house."

"We weren't going to go by ourselves."

"Oh."

It was at that moment that she realized that Ferrell was involved.

"Come on, Jeanine, we have to call her parents."

"I don't want to get her in trouble."

"Well, if she's run away, she's already in trouble, and the sooner we find her the safer she'll be."

She told Jeanine to go into the house and finish her homework assignment on Edgar Allen Poe.

Suzanne tried but could not get through on the phone. She even called the operator and told her it was an emergency, but the operator said the phone was out of order.

***

The Leclaires had done everything they could to block Ferrell's relationship with Jeanine when he moved away, or so they thought.

He tried calling Jeanine collect late at night a few times, but Jeanine's father picked up the phone and refused to accept the calls. Her parents told Jeanine she was not to accept such calls.

"And I know they corresponded for a while through letters, which we eventually occasionally intercepted and told her she was no longer to have any connection with him," Suzanne said.

The letters had been thrown away in a thorough bedroom cleanup, except for one, which was turned over to detectives the night of the murders.

"The first couple of letters that I had picked up in her room were kind of sweet. You're so pretty, you're such, you know, an interesting kind of person kind of thing. I care about you kind of stuff, you know. Actually, the first one I picked up I thought it was just a sweet puppy love kind of thing and I thought the boy was very good with words. I thought he must be very bright. You know, I didn't see anything about that.

"I don't remember anything specific in any other letters except that it seemed to be getting dark. Didn't feel right. Specifically, I can't remember anything except that last letter talked about his mother, and it sounded like violence and blood and murder. And I think he wanted to convert his mother to vampirism and wanted to watch her as she crossed over. He wanted to delight in her crossing over, is basically what I remember it saying."

She and her husband had what Southerners call a "come to Jesus meeting" with Jeanine—literally.

"This does not go with our religious beliefs and you're not allowed to participate in any of this stuff anymore and you're not to have contact with Rod," they told her.

They also talked to Heather's mother.

"We told Ruth about the letter and we told her that she may not want Heather hanging around with Jeanine for a while. Ruth was a very quiet and shy kind of person, and she said yes, she noticed that there were some problems that she had seen. I don't know whether she actually read the letters, or whether it had just been artwork she found in Heather's room or whatever. But she agreed that it beared (sic) watching. But in the end, I guess she didn't do anything about it."

CHAPTER 6

"No, you're not going to kill my parents"

"I know a real vampire," a friend of Jeanine's said.

"Oh really? Give him my phone number and have him call me," she said.[1]

A week later, Jeanine introduced Ferrell to Heather.

"As long as Jeanine and I have been friends, we've always dreamed of a vampiric life," Heather confided to a friend in a letter.

Detective Ken Adams wanted to know what Jeanine and Rod talked about.

"Talked about feeding, places that he's supposedly been to, stuff along those lines."

"When he talked about 'feeding,' in what aspect?"

"Drinking people's blood."

Exactly a year earlier, she agreed to let Ferrell cross her over to become a vampire at her bonfire birthday party. "He said I would become a vampire if I drank his blood. So, I did. I was basically kind of humoring him."

Ferrell told Heather and Jeanine that they would gain powers if they drank blood.

"So, Heather and I would drink each other's blood," Jeanine said. "But it wasn't a lot or a very constant thing. It was if we were kind of stressed out and stuff like that. We would basically cut ourselves and drink. But it wasn't like gallons or anything. It was just like if you get a small cut or something like that, you bleed a little bit, or you prick your finger you drink some. It's not much."[2]

The stressors weren't major, Jeanine said. "My parents nagging at me. School. Just stuff like that, usual teenage stuff."

Adams asked her if she believed he was a vampire.

"It was one of those things like, every time I asked to see his fangs it was like, 'Oh well, gotta wait until we're feeding' or something like that. Something would come up. So, I just said, 'Yeah, right, whatever.' It was probably more of a game to me than it was to him. I was starting to figure that he was probably a pathological liar, and I wasn't sure he was believing it or not, but it was kind of a ticket out of my lifestyle."[3]

One of the harder stories to swallow was Ferrell's claim to be five-hundred years old. Jeanine had seen a photo of a younger Ferrell when he was in middle school just a few years earlier. She was still afraid of him, however. "Be sure not to look in his eyes," she later warned her mother.[4]

According to tradition, the vampire who crosses a mortal over to become a vampire is the "sire." The "progeny" is obligated to do what the sire commands. "He never made me do anything," Jeanine said.

Ferrell had written letters to her, and the lawyers at her deposition were clamoring for answers.

Q: "What was in the letters?" Ferrell's lawyer, Candace Hawthorne asked.[5]

A: "Stuff about vampirism."

Q: "What stuff about vampirism?"

A: "I cannot remember."

Q: "Killing?"

A: "He might have mentioned some of that."

Q: "Taking over your soul?"

A: "Some of that also."

Ferrell also asked Jeanine "to become his mate forever through eternity."

Sometimes they stayed in close contact, usually with Ferrell calling the girls when they were together, and always promising to come and pick them up. Other times he would drop off the radar for weeks at a time.

Shannon Yohe, a former classmate, was as surprised as anyone when Ferrell appeared at her house with his friends on Sunday, the day before the murders. Ferrell asked her to call Jeanine so he could get on the line. "Her parents don't like me," he explained.

The message was simple: He had come to get her and Heather, but Jeanine was suddenly hesitant. She had just joined a church youth group, "and I was becoming a major Christian, and he was not, and Heather was not either and it was kind of upsetting me."

Regardless, hours later, at midnight, Ferrell and his friends met Jeanine on a dirt road outside her house. Howard Scott Anderson, whose vampire name was "Nos Feratu," Charity Lynn Keesee, and Dana Cooper stayed in the car.

Ferrell talked about the group running away to France. He also talked about how Keesee "liked" him. "We kissed, stuff like that," Leclaire told Adams.[6]

They had talked for about 45 minutes when Anderson walked up and said that Keesee was angry about something. Anderson started walking back to the car, but he came back and asked Ferrell if they were going to Daytona Beach.

"He smelled bad. So did Rod," Jeanine said, "like they hadn't taken a bath in months. Like they weren't wearing any deodorant. They hadn't been brushing their teeth, and they hadn't been taking any showers or baths. Nasty."[7]

But if Ferrell smelled bad, it was nothing compared to the shock that came next. "He mentioned about how he was going to have to kill my parents and take everything out of the house, and I said, 'No, you're not going to kill my parents and take everything out of the house!' He said, 'Fine, we'll tie them up and take everything out of the house.' I said, 'No, I'll empty my bank account, but you're not going to do that either!'"

Ferrell told Jeanine she had a week to decide if she wanted to leave with the group.

"I wasn't sure. I wasn't sure what Heather wanted to do."

She talked to Heather on the phone the next evening after school, and Heather had some big news. She said she had crossed over to become a vampire that day in a large cemetery near the high school.

They talked about leaving with Ferrell, but Heather was reluctant. "Well, she put it as it might be easier for me to leave my parents because I always get into arguments and fight with them and stuff, but she loved her parents," Jeanine said, but that wasn't all. "She said something about he was mentioning about killing her parents, and she told him not to," Jeanine said.

While the two were talking, Ferrell beeped in on the call. Heather put Jeanine on hold to talk to him. When Heather beeped back in to talk to Jeanine, she was panicked. She said they had to leave that night. Ferrell didn't offer much of an explanation, but he said there had been some type of emergency, that the Kentucky authorities had tracked him down somehow.

Jeanine was about to eat birthday cake and ice cream with her family, so she told Heather to call her back. Heather said they all had to leave in 15 minutes. Jeanine told her to stall. It was still early, and she knew her parents might walk into her room and see her packing.

At about 8:30 p.m., Heather tapped on Jeanine's window. "I told her that I had to wait until my parents were asleep and to go see her boyfriend because she wanted to do that. I didn't know that she had already seen her boyfriend. But I told her to go do that and she said they needed to leave now. And so, she went back to the car with them. And I quickly threw my stuff together and walked out the door. And they were gone." `

CHAPTER 7

"A liar type person"

Among the many law enforcement officials who rushed to the crime scene that night was Bill Gross, an assistant state attorney who handled all homicide cases in Lake County.

At 5-foot-7, the bespectacled career prosecutor joked that he was the only one in the courthouse who could say that he bought his suits in the boy's section of department stores.

A fan of *"The Simpsons,"* and a sometime practitioner of acerbic wit himself, he was respected for his relentless work ethic but resented by defense attorneys because he had a long, almost completely unbroken record of convictions.

He brought out the figurative long knives if he had a chance to cross-examine a defendant who took the stand, especially if he could get them to touch the murder weapon. In one trial, Gross put the unloaded revolver in the defendant's hand and stood in front of him so that the pistol was pointing at him.

The man claimed the gun went off accidentally, even though a crime lab technician testified that the gun had an unusually hard trigger pull at seventeen pounds.

"So, you're telling this jury that this gun, which is like picking up three 5-pound bags of sugar with your finger, went off by itself?"[1]

The jury got the picture, and so did the *Sentinel* with a photo on the front page of the Lake County edition.

Unlike some prosecutors, Gross liked to go to the scene of the crime. Not only could he see the lay of the land, but he made sure evidence was handled properly. The last thing he wanted was for law enforcement to create an opening for defense attorneys.

Once, he went searching for a .22-caliber revolver that had been used in a homicide. The owner of the gun said he had used it for hunting raccoons until it was stolen. It sounded not only strange but suspicious, even when the man showed him raccoon meat in the refrigerator.

Gross noticed a commercial-sized trash bin outside the home. On a hunch, he climbed into the bin and started moving trash around. He jumped back when he found a dead raccoon staring back at him.

After learning of Jennifer and Jeanine's statements, Gross set out for Yohe's home.

It was 4 a.m. when Gross and Sheriff's Detective Ron Patton knocked on her door.

Yohe, a thin, intelligent, pleasant girl with strawberry blonde hair, would turn out to be an important witness in the days and years to come.

Yes, Ferrell and his Kentucky friends had visited, she said. They first came Sunday afternoon, and then again on Monday shortly before the slayings.

"One girl was tall, about five-six or five-eight.... She had long black hair, and she was really thin," said Yohe, describing Keesee. "And according to Rod, she was like a month pregnant."[2]

"Who's the baby's father?" Gross asked.

"Rod."

She described the other girl, Cooper, as "kind of short. She had short black hair, and it had like red in it. She was kind of on the heavy side." Cooper, who was five-foot-five, weighed 205 pounds.

Yohe didn't know Scott's last name, but described him as 5-foot-11, "maybe six foot," thin, with black hair, "and it's like shaved underneath, and it's kind of wavy, and he has glasses." Anderson's arrest affidavit listed him as 5-foot-10, 160 pounds.

She also gave a very brief description of his car, "and he said that Rod kind of kidnapped him and took his car to bring him with him, and he was willing now or something. I didn't really understand this."

Ferrell had Yohe call Jeanine. Once she came on the line, he set up a rendezvous for midnight. Afterword, he talked to Yohe about how he wanted to hang out in Florida for a while. "Nothing bad or anything. He just wanted to see his friends."

Rod and his friends unexpectedly returned to Yohe's home the next day at about 5:30 or 6 p.m., and he made another call, this one to Heather.

Ferrell told Yohe that the girls were going to run away from home, and they were all going to New Orleans. He also said that they were going to steal Heather's parents' car, because there was something wrong with Scott's vehicle.

"I didn't believe him, because I thought he was just kidding around."[3]

Though she didn't ask any questions about stealing the car, she did ask Ferrell about cuts on his arms. He said he cut himself because he was "bored."

She was stunned by how he had changed. "...he used to be very nice and kind, sweet, and he would never like run away with people or steal somebody's car. He didn't smoke when I knew him. He didn't cut himself."[4]

Later, in a deposition, she said the group, which had been in the living room, drifted into the kitchen where there was more conversation about Scott's car.

"And then, I don't know how it came up, it just went from the car and then Rod said something about he was going to kill them." She asked him why. He said he was going to take their car. "And I didn't think anything about it because Rod's a liar type person."[5]

A few minutes later, Ferrell backed up to the dishwasher, used his arms to lift himself up and began swinging his legs. "He said if they had this at their house, [he] could jump up and crack their necks...."[6]

He continued: "My favorite way to kill somebody is by decapitation."

"And that really grossed me out," she said.

Scott chimed in, though Yohe could not remember what he said. Then, Dana said: "I want to be a part of this, I want to help."[7]

Ferrell then reached into a drawer, pulled out a knife and cut his arm. Dana came over and began sucking the blood. "And then she commented that it tasted better off the neck, or something like that."

Ferrell tried to take all the knives from the drawer, but Shannon stopped him.

The conversation turned to New Orleans where he wanted to go and experience Mardi Gras. The celebration was months away, but he intended to stay in the city until then, she said.

Ferrell tried to hug her as he left, but she hung back. She claimed she wasn't scared of him, but the talk of stealing cars and killing made her "uncomfortable."

"...he was fun before. And he was nice and sweet and funny, and not psycho," she said.

CHAPTER 8

"Rod might kill her parents"

Gross and Detective Patton were also eager to interview Heather's boyfriend of six weeks, Jeremy Hueber.

"What has Heather told you about this gentleman?" Gross asked, referring to Ferrell.[1]

"She says that he is, I think, an evil person, I guess I should say. She didn't really specify how she meant by evil, but she said that he believed himself to be, I guess, immortal, a vampire type person."

She described him as not completely a Satan worshiper, "but something to that effect," Hueber said.

"She said that he would do whatever he feels like, whenever he feels like it. He doesn't have to listen to anyone. He's kind of a father figure to Heather and her friend, Jeanine."

Hueber said he asked her how old Ferrell was, and she replied, "whatever age he wants to be."

He said Heather bought into Ferrell's vampire beliefs, "and she goes along with Rod and they're kind of like a family, sort of."

Heather liked drinking blood, he said, and she had cuts up and down her forearm where she cut herself with razor blades.

Hueber said Heather called him Sunday after he got off from work around 8:30 p.m.

"Rod's back,' she said. "You know, I'm planning on going with him, and we're gonna take off, if you want to come with us.'

And I said, 'Why are you doing this?' And she said because she has to."

The next day at school she told Hueber that she was going to see Ferrell after school.

"She said that she wouldn't leave unless Jeanine left also, and that if Jeanine stayed, that she would stay, 'cause she doesn't want to leave her best friend, Jeanine."

That night, he said she called him sometime between 7:45 and 8 p.m.

"She said that Rod wants to leave that night, and she was gonna try to get him to stay a couple extra days, and she then asked me if I wanted to go with them, and she was like, 'Do you want me to go with him?'

"I told her no. I said that's a stupid idea to just up and leave, and I told her not to do it, but she had her mind made up."

About 30 minutes later she called again. "She said that Rod was there." She also said she was coming by to see him.

That wasn't all, he would later recall. "She said she had to go because Rod might kill her parents."[2]

"Did she tell you whether she wanted her parents dead?"

"No, she did not want her parents dead."

When she showed up at his home, she was with Cooper and Keesee in Anderson's car.

"I'm sure you must've been curious by this point, since the subject had been brought up on the phone," Gross said. "Did you ask her, you know, what happened to your parents, how are they doing, is this guy going to kill your parents?"[3]

"No. I asked her like how she had gotten out of the house. She said that she kind of like snuck out of the window with some stuff. That's what she told me, and she said that Rod was over getting her friend, Jeanine, so she could come with them."

"They asked me if I was going with them. And I told 'em no, and they said, 'You better come now, because when we leave now, we're not gonna come back, you know.'

Heather said the group was going to Mardi Gras.

"Did anybody ever point out to her that Mardi Gras is three months from now?"

"No."

As for the absurd idea of cramming seven people into the little Buick, Hueber said he thought Rod had a car, too.

Scott Anderson's attorney, Mike Graves, was curious about Rod's influence during Hueber's deposition. "Do you think Heather would go with just about anybody who said, 'Hey, let's go to New Orleans?'"[4]

"No."

"Did Rod appear to have more influence over her than other people?"

"Yeah."

"Did she ever explain what she saw in Rod?"

"No."

"Did you ever ask her about it? You know, what is so cool about this guy? Anything like that?"

"Yeah, I asked her about it, but she didn't want to answer me."

Hueber would end up giving a lot of thought about the way things turned out.

"She didn't know much about life. Then she got so involved in it that the fantasy became reality. She didn't believe in any kind of God. I worried about her."[5]

CHAPTER 9

"Demure little girl"

"You've got one wild bunch on the loose," said Sheriff Stan Scott of Calloway County, Ky.[1]

Ferrell was a suspect, with other teens, in a horrific abuse case at an animal shelter, Scott told Florida detectives. About 40 dogs had been beaten and mutilated, including two puppies, one stomped to death and another who had his legs ripped off. Four dogs were never found.

The savages had marched around in a circle in a grassy area in some type of bizarre ritual.

The teens were among about 30 members of a group that call themselves "The Vampire Clan," Scott said. They used razor blades to cut themselves and drink each other's blood.

Authorities were also investigating a report that Ferrell and other teens were making gasoline bombs just before he left to come to Florida.

News of the double slaying was an even bigger shock than the animal abuse case. "When we got the teletype, it just beat anything we've ever seen," Scott said.

Sgt. Mike Jump of the Murray Police Department was also stunned. "I don't know if they've been watching *Natural Born Killers* or what," he said of the movie starring Woody Harrelson. It's got us scared to death."

"These kids are serious," said Calloway County prosecutor David Harrington.

Kentucky law enforcement officials were serious, too, including how they were dealing with Ferrell's mother. They had charged Sondra Gibson with solicitation to commit rape and sodomy after a 14-year-old boy's mother found a letter she had written to him. Sex was to be part of a vampire initiation, prosecutors said. The boy was a friend of Rod's.

Information was coming in fast and furious, and reporters wasted no time in talking to friends of the Wendorf family, including students and administrators at Eustis High.

Despite the shock over the murders, people generally had good things to say about Heather.

"She dressed differently but had the same outgoing personality as everyone else," said Chris Boggs, an 18-year-old senior.[2]

"It's all rumors, and I think it stinks," said Brian Cass, a ninth grader. "Nobody was there to know what happened."

Hollins said Heather was not a problem student, though she did skip a few classes and come to school late sometimes.

Students and staff alike described Ruth as a friendly, helpful volunteer at the school.

"She was a very sweet lady," said Jennifer Parker, 15. "She had a big smile for everybody."

Hollins said he spoke to Ruth shortly before she went home for the day, and she seemed fine.

"This is very earth-shattering," he said. "It takes the wind out of our sails."

People had nice things to say about Jennifer, too.

"Jen is really bubbly, a crazy kind of fun," said BethAnn Crow, 17. "I hope she realizes she has a lot of friends, and we're all praying for her."

About 100 students gathered in the school auditorium to pray for the family.

Richard's coworkers also had nice things to say about him, describing him as an excellent worker and storeroom manager at Crown Cork & Seal, a Winter Garden container manufacturer, where he worked for 23 years.

One man disclosed that Richard had been worried about Heather.

"He did talk to me at one time and said he thought she was in with the wrong crowd," said Max Hargrove. Richard didn't seem too concerned, however.

"All of us have problems with our kids at one time or another," Hargrove said. "Those girls were highly intelligent young people. The oldest girl got a scholarship..."

The girls' grandfather, James Wendorf, 75, a retired lawyer who had once worked for the Billy Graham organization, described his son's household as a "loving, loving family."

He had played golf with his son on Saturday. "I was so blessed that we had that time."[3]

After playing 18 holes, he went to the family home and was greeted by Jennifer after she got off work.

"She came in and hugged her grandpa. And she asked her dad, 'Did you tell him?'"

Richard told her to relay the news, and she told him about her scholarship.

"There was nothing but future in her mind," he said.

He said Richard and Ruth bought Jennifer a new Saturn when she turned 16, and Heather was due to get one, too.

The family was close, James said. Richard had a twin brother, William. The boys moved from Wisconsin to Winter Park in the Orlando area with their mother when they were teenagers. Richard graduated from the University of South Florida in Tampa.

"It's absolutely appalling and unbelievable to those of us who knew them," he said. "We are utterly flabbergasted."

He said that Heather's disappearance was so unbelievable, "I'm almost believing that she's a victim."

He had no knowledge of Heather being involved in any occult activities. "Heather's so quiet. She's a demure little girl. I never saw any evidence of anything like that."

James would become the family spokesman. He would also become Heather's staunchest defender, but it would not be easy.

CHAPTER 10

Trapped

Sheriff's deputies in two states couldn't find the missing cult members, but it wasn't for lack of trying.

Lake County investigators received several tips, "but nothing that's panned out for us," Lt. Chris Daniels said.[1]

Meanwhile, rumors were running rampant in Murray. Among the red herrings was a report that Ferrell had been spotted at an area high school.

Another dead end was that the teens had supposedly ditched the Wendorfs' Explorer in exchange for a white Chevy Blazer. A radio station erroneously reported that police chased the Blazer, which crashed.

Police exuded confidence, however, including Dewayne Redmon, the assistant police chief in Mayfield. "They can't hide much longer," he said.

On Thursday, Nov. 28, on Thanksgiving Day, three days after the slayings, Keesee called her grandmother, Joyce Commer, in South Dakota while trying to reach her mother.

She was not the first to call home. Rod called his grandfather Tuesday. "Grandpa, it's me," he said.

Harrell Gibson said Rod sounded nervous and claimed not to know where he was.

"I said, 'Rod, please turn yourself in.' Then, he hung up."[2]

Charity told her grandmother that she was with Rod and some others. Commer said "she sounded either tired, high, or drunk." She said she heard laughing in the background, that Charity kept telling someone to 'stop it.'"[3]

Commer told Charity to call back, and that she would try to get hold of her mother. She then contacted Detective Adams.

"…when I asked for a phone number, she at first said Charity didn't give her a phone number," Adams said. "Just prior to her hanging up, Ms. Commer gasped, and said that she did have a number. That she looked at her caller ID box and that there was a phone number on it as to where she had called from. It was still on the box."

Adams checked the number, found out it was a Baton Rouge area code, and called the police there.

Cpl. Dennis Moran, a 17-year veteran of the Baton Rouge Police Department, and a member of the homicide-robbery division, had seen a teletype about the homicides.

The call had come from a pay phone at the Centraplex Center, he told Adams, noting that there were two motels nearby.

Officer William Clarida III went to the Howard Johnson and began questioning the clerk. Almost immediately, Cooper and Keesee walked into the office.

"They were very, I guess the word may be somber, very quiet," Clarida said. "The younger female appeared to be very afraid, almost in a shock-like state. And the older female had her arm around her and was comforting her."[4]

Tommy Dewey was one of the detectives called to the motel. Once there, he was told that Ferrell had already been read his rights, and he was ordered to take Ferrell to the police station.

"…he began to initiate conversation with me. And he told me that he was glad that I was transporting him because of my age. I appeared younger than the other detectives out there. He advised he was happy to be caught because he had been on the run for seven days."[5]

"I'll tell you everything you want to know. I just want to see my girlfriend," Ferrell said.

"If I remember, he said, 'I'll make you famous,' and all this other stuff."

Dewey urged Ferrell to be quiet, read him his rights again, and said he could not make any promises.

Ferrell had one more request: "Tell her I love her."

One of the officers was a uniformed patrolman, James Welborn. Like the other officers, he didn't know anything about the case. He was asking a few questions in the parking lot, including where they came from. He noticed that one of the girls, who he learned later was Heather, was "real nervous, kind of scared and shaky."[6]

"Do you think your parents are worried about you?" he asked.

"She was nervous already, but she just started shaking pretty much uncontrollable (sic). It wasn't that cold. I mean, it was pretty hot. I thought about needing to call EMS but she kind of calmed down after."

Welborn immediately noticed that Ferrell was the leader. "…they all looked towards him. It was just about at all times. He seemed like he was the one in control. They were kind of just, 'yes sir,' 'no sir,' no eye contact. I can remember him looking me in the eye and never, never blinking."

CHAPTER 11

"Mentally disturbed"

There's no telling how many bodies Sgt. Ben Odom has stepped over after barroom killings, street corner drug deals, and kitchen-knife stabbings in bedrooms. The gravel-voiced detective didn't just have twenty years' experience on the street, but was a graduate of the FBI National Academy, a police instructor, and robbery-homicide supervisor.

He tucked his reports in a secure metal clipboard holder, but the cover was decorated with cop humor. It was adorned with a cartoon of a door to a homicide department with lettering that read, "Our day begins when yours ends."

With the Lake County sheriff's detectives still making their way to Baton Rouge, Odom, Moran, and Dewey rolled up their sleeves and walked into the stuffy interrogation room, with its carpeted walls and a camera lens hidden in the light switch. Ferrell was seated, or rather slumped, at the table.

After reading him his rights, Odom how asked how far he had gone in school and whether he could read and write.

"I've lived more knowledge than school ever thought of."[1]

"I understand," Odom said, as if he did.

"The reason why I did this bullshit," he said.

"Well, we'll see. Um, have you had any controlled dangerous substances or alcohol within the last three or four hours?"

"Probably about an hour after I had some."

Odom then asked if he was seeing a mental health expert.

"I was seeing a psychiatrist. Don't know what for. Never paid attention."

"Who sent you, your parents?"

"The school, the sheriff's office, my mom. Basically, the whole city."

"But you are not under a physician's care for anything."

"Not drug-wise or anything, just going to the psychologist."

Ferrell said he agreed to talk if he could see Keesee.

Odom asked if he could take notes.

"I really don't care. I guess I'm mentally disturbed. I don't know."

"Rod, you should never get to that point son. Even if you are in trouble, you know."

"It's not because of the trouble," Ferrell said. "It's because I don't have any concern for life anymore. My own, especially."

"Perhaps you say that, but you know, I'm not inside your head. I don't know what's going on, but I know you're still a young guy and you've got a lot of living in front of you."

Ferrell said the group left Murray at 12:30 p.m. Friday. He had gone to Charity's apartment "because her and I've been seeing each other for 11 months now and are engaged and she's pregnant and all, and I told Shea beforehand that I was going to take her with me and just take like a half-ass road trip because I was sick of Murray because all the cops were bugging me there for something I didn't do," he said as he began to get choked up.

He said he gathered up Dana and Anderson and asked them if they wanted to go.

Anderson was supposed to pick up his brothers from the skating rink at midnight, so Ferrell had Charity go in and tell them that Scott had been kidnapped by his vampire mentor, Steven "Jaden" Murphy.

He told the detectives about meeting up with Jeanine once they reached Eustis. "After that I got hold of Zoey after school...and she was wanting to leave with us 'cause we really had no idea where we were going. That was on Monday, whenever I got hold of her."

The plan was to give Heather and Jeanine time to prepare, but Anderson's Skyhawk had a flat tire Monday afternoon, and while he was putting on a "doughnut" spare, a Lake County sheriff's deputy pulled up. The deputy asked for Anderson's identification. What the teens did not know, was that they were near the home of Sheriff George Knupp.

Ferrell panicked, even without knowing the car had broken down near the sheriff's home. He was sure the Florida authorities would check and find out that the teens were missing, and that he was a suspect in the animal abuse and bomb-making cases.

The teens went back to Yohe's house, called Heather, and told her they had to leave right away. Ferrell made arrangements to pick up Heather on the road that runs in front of her house.

Once they were there, Keesee and Cooper left with Heather to go see her boyfriend and to pick up Jeanine. He told Heather that he and Scott would walk to Jeanine's and meet them there.

After they left, he said he and Anderson "walked up the driveway, looked around the house just to check the perimeters. They left all the doors unlocked. Went to the garage, looked for special items, found special items."

"What kind of special items? Weapons?"

"Yeah. That's all I was concerned about, weapons, food, and cash."

"Okay."

"Went into her house, her mother was taking a shower, her father was asleep on the couch, so I took the liberty of rummaging through the house and getting something to drink because I was thirsty."

"Okay."

"Scott was following right behind me like a little lost puppy and then, before her mother got out of the shower, I went to her dad and smacked the [expletive] out of him until he finally quit breathing. So yes, I'm admitting to murder."

"Okay."

"Actually, it took him about 20 [expletive] minutes to stop. I swear I thought he was immortal or something."

"What did you hit him with?"

"A crowbar. I was going to use a machete or chain saw but that was too messy, just nasty."

"Crowbar's pretty messy, too, you know."

"No, it only got a little blood spot on me surprisingly. But anyway, so after that I basically picked his body up, screwed him around and looked for his wallet and stuff, and that's where we found his Discover card."

All right."

"And about two minutes after I flipped him back over the way he was, the mother came out of the shower with a nice hot cup of coffee that she spilled all over me. She asked me what did I want, 'cause she thought I was just robbing them."

"She hadn't seen her husband yet?"

"No, I made sure that he was hidden."

"Okay."

"Didn't want her to freak. Like I said, she just basically looked straight at me and said, 'What do you want?' By that time, you know, it was pretty obvious. I had blood on me and a crowbar in my hand.

"I was fixing to say, 'Yeah, I want to have coffee with you, you son-of-a-bitching smart ass,' but anyway, that's when she lunged at me. I was actually going to let her live but after she lunged at me I just took the bottom of the crowbar and kept stabbing it through her skull and whenever she fell down, I just continually beat her until I saw her brains falling on the floor 'cause that pissed me off. That's how I got these," he said, pointing to scratches on his face.

He said after making sure she was dead, he rummaged through the house looking for car keys, money and other useful items. He said he found the Explorer keys in the master bedroom. Another set was in the ignition.

"Thought about waiting for Zoey's sister, but decided, nah, why bother? Let her come home, have a mental breakdown, call the police, which I was correct, she did."

Ferrell claimed that Anderson wanted to dump the bodies in the swimming pool. "And I was like… that's just sick, and for another, no."

He said he wanted to leave as soon as possible to avoid police. "Didn't want to deal with cops because they are a lot more hostile there than you ever seem to be here. That's why I'm cooperating with you. You didn't beat my ass or anything."

"Why would we do that, Rod?"

"Because the Murray cops have done it, the Florida cops have done it, and whenever I see a cop car, I got a night stick upside of my head. That's why I've had such a lack of faith in law enforcement."

Odom asked about Scott's involvement.

"Oh God, he totally froze. He's never seen people get killed before. He was hyped about telling me how he was going to kill them, so basically he is just an accessory," Ferrell said.

"He took one side of the house and I took the other. The most he did was move the bodies a little bit."

Odom also asked what they took.

"We took her mother's pearls, which were around her teddy bear's neck. We took her father's knife. I don't know what kind it is," referring to the brand.

He said it was a hunting knife with a seven-inch blade.

He said they drove the Explorer to Jeanine's house to look for the girls. "...they thought we were only getting the girls to run away with us, which was very far from our minds at that point in time 'cause I didn't want to be followed..."

He said when Heather realized what happened to her parents, "she flipped out for about 100 miles or so."

"Heather did?"

"Yeah, she goes by Zoey."

"Okay."

"She looks to me as her father or something."

Odom also asked about the girls' involvement in the case.

"Those three were basically just the ones we kind of kidnapped. We weren't accompanied."

"But they went along agreeably, right?"

"Shea had no choice. I told her either she agreed, or I'd hogtie her, take her with me. Dana came along with Shea because she was worried about Shea. Zoey came along 'cause she's been planning to come with me for about a year because we had planned on whenever I moved back into Eustis her and Jeanine were going to come up here and we were just like going to go somewhere 'cause I still have a lot of friends in New Orleans and that was where I was going to live."

The stop in New Orleans was a bust, however. They had started walking around a bad neighborhood. "That's when Shea freaked out because she's never been to a big city and she's never seen black people carry around AK-47s in their back yards. So, we left there and came here and were like flat broke, had no food...," he said.

"And if Shea didn't freak out that's where I would have been right now. What can I say? It's a bitch living in the big cities. You learn to be good friends with the cops and the crime lords."

"We got pulled over by the cops there, too (unintelligible). We got pulled over five times on this whole trip and never got caught 'til now, 'til we checked into a hotel."

He said it was because Charity called her grandmother. "She was freaking out and she's basically the only thing I care about in this world..."

"Bingo, that's who she got when she made the phone call," Moran said.

"Oh, I know," Ferrell said. "That's when I told them, 'Get out of town now,' but they didn't listen to me. See, they never listen to the leader."

"Where were you going to go?" Odom asked.

"Don't know, don't care." He said he was going to ride around until he found "a nice forest area," ditch the Explorer in a lake, "and start going through the ... woods, killing deer or whatever I could find for meat."

"Did you ever discuss these homicides prior to the day you went over there with anyone that you can remember?"

"We never thought about it until about 10 minutes before we did it."

He said he had never seen Heather's house before. "Hell, I went to the wrong house first. Didn't kill anybody though, 'cause I looked in and saw there was little kids, and that's my rule. I don't kill anything that's little. Now adults, that's perfectly fine, 16 and up."

Odom remembered Ferrell's comment about Anderson never seeing anyone being killed before, and asked Ferrell to tell about his experiences.

"I've [expletive] seen murders all my life, ever since I was five, because my grandfather, for one, he's never been caught either," Ferrell said.

"He's part of an organization called The Black Mask. Whenever (sic) I was five, they chose me as the guardian of the Black Mask, and the guardian has to become one with everybody. In other words, they raped me, and they have to sacrifice a human to the guardian, so they sacrificed someone right in front of me."

"These guys that are with you, are they… have you indoctrinated them into the ways of the cult, or are you just their friend that you run with?"

"No, I never became part of them," Ferrell said, either apparently thinking the question was about whether he had been a member of a cult, or he was ducking the question.

"Kind of tough, even when you're hard core, isn't it, man?" Odom said.

"Two things bother me: What happened whenever (sic) I was five, and the fact that I will never get to see Shea after this. I've been hanging around gangs and cults and all that… all my life, so I've seen sacrifices and drug buys…"

"I'm just asking, Rod."

"Killing is a way of life. Animals do it, and that's the way humans are, just the worst predators of all, actually."

"How old is Shea?"

"Sixteen…she's carrying around my kid. She's almost two months pregnant. Like they say, shit happens."

Odom told Ferrell that he wasn't going to "sugar coat this thing."

"Is it actually possible for someone my age to get like, a death penalty?"

"It depends. I don't know what the laws are in Florida. When you're 16 years old in this state you can be tried as an adult and you're subject to adult penalties."

"So, I was kind of hoping, you know. I was like, please go ahead. Ha!"

"To be straight up with you, yeah, it's probably going to entail the death penalty."

"I'm sorry. This is like a big [expletive] joke. My life seems like a dream. My childhood was taken away at five. I don't know whether I'm asleep or dreaming any more… For all I know, I could wake up in five minutes."

"Rod, I can assure you it's not a dream."

CHAPTER 12

"Don't worry about me"

Ferrell was sitting on the floor of the interview room staring at the ceiling when Charity rushed into the room. Standing up, he had to brace himself for her fierce embrace.

"Everything's okay," he said.[1]

The room, with its carpeted walls, muffled some of the conversation, but the grainy images on the video speak volumes.

The two engaged in long kisses and he reached up and tenderly touched the side of her face.

"I love you," she whispered.

Mostly, they talked about their capture.

"Your mother's the one that got us caught," he said, referring to the phone call she made to her mother.

He told her that he told the police that he had kidnapped her and the others.

She was crying and wiping her nose with a tissue when he said, "Don't worry about me."

He told her he might be sentenced to seven to eight years in prison with a parole hearing in three months. It is not clear where he got that idea, or if it was simply a blatant lie. There is no record of anyone in Baton Rouge telling him that.

However, he then said, "Right now, I'm this close to being tried as an adult, and that means the death penalty."

He told her he loved her, then said: "We'll find some way out of this."

He tried to ease her fears. "You haven't done anything," he said.

"They kept asking me the stupidest questions," he said. "They asked if I felt any remorse for killing them."

He expressed concern for her health (she was either not pregnant or would soon have a miscarriage), and he tried to get her to sit down.

"Take care of the [expletive] kid," he said.

He returned to the subject of a possible execution.

"I don't think the death penalty works," he said, but he did not explain what he meant.

"If I do not survive, then I want you to come to my grave once a year."

He brought up the idea of suicide.

"I can use this Coke can right here," he said, grabbing it off a table and pulling it toward his stomach.

Clearly, however, he was thinking of Florida's electric chair, "Old Sparky."

"They cranked it up last year," he told her. "I know because I was there."

Eventually, a police officer came in and took Keesee away.

Ferrell walked to the corner of the room, sat on the floor, and reached up to the table to grab the soft drink can. He began sobbing as he crushed the can, then reached up and put the can back on the table.

His eyes were dry by the time the guard came back into the room.

CHAPTER 13

"I don't want to lose him."

Lake County Detectives Al Gussler and Wayne Longo were exhausted by the time they got to Baton Rouge, but as soon as they checked into a motel, they threw their suitcases down and headed for the police station.

They made an interesting team. Longo, who would later be promoted to lieutenant before retiring, is a serious-minded, quiet man. Gussler, a veteran detective, had good instincts, a touch of country and a wry sense of humor. He would be promoted to sergeant.

Homicide detectives sometimes get into the habit of leaving their handguns in their desk drawer or in their car. After all, the first person they see in an investigation is dead. After that, they interview witnesses, who are nearly as harmless. In one case, however, a witness acted suspicious and had a fishy-sounding story. Not only that, but his nightclub office was packed with firearms. Gussler said he looked at the man who was his partner at that time, and his partner looked at him with a look that said, "Did you bring your gun?"

It didn't matter if Gussler's tale was real or fiction. He had his listeners laughing by the time he finished.

Charity Keesee could have benefited from a funny story when Gussler and Longo showed up. Her nerve endings were jumping like frog legs in a skillet, and she started talking before the detectives were ready to start listening.

"Told me to tell the cops when they pulled us over."[1]

"Pardon, now?" Gussler said.

Keesee had just confessed to using her stepsister's name, Sarah Remington.

"I got one question. Why are you guys questioning me? I didn't do anything."

"Well, that's what we are here to find out, okay?" Gussler said.

"I just don't want to be separated from Rod. That's all that's wrong with me, is I don't want to be separated from Rod."

"We're going to answer all your questions, too, okay. Just relax. We'll help you the best way we can, okay. Is that fair enough?" Longo said.

"There is just one more question. Why is everybody like so messed up about that?" she said, pointing to cut marks on her arm.

"Does that mean anything particular?"

"No, it's just how, if I get mad, I cut myself because then the anger goes away," she said.

"I've done that for a lot of times."

Gussler fiddled with his tape recorder and told her that they were going to explain her right to remain silent. He then asked her if she had anything to eat.

"I ate two bites out of a pancake."

"Don't feel a whole lot like eating?"

"No. I can't believe they'd take Rod away from me."

When he asked her name, she said, "Rod calls me Shea. That's what all my other friends call me."

"Okay."

"I'd prefer to be called that."

"Well, we're your friends…"

Keesee took the detectives back to December when she first met Ferrell. He and another boy started talking to her at school. "And then I called him and then we ended up talking for six hours and I was hooked from there."

Keesee, who said she didn't talk very much, began talking a lot, even to the point of running her sentences together. She talked about how she and Rod planned to get married next year, how Rod wanted to visit his friends in Florida, how he wanted his mother to take them to Mardi Gras in February, and how Scott came over to Dana's house the night they left.

"Just take a deep breath, it's all right," Gussler said.

Her story would jump around, and so would the detectives' questions. Sometimes she shaded the truth to shift blame. Sometimes she was candid. The detectives would occasionally apply pressure to drive a wedge between the young lovers. In the end, it would not be "all right," and the investigators were not her "friends."

"Don't you realize that he has already been interviewed?" Gussler asked when she began to try and cage her answers.

"I realize that 'cause he told me that…"

"And he has cooperated 100 percent. The stuff he whispered in your ear…"

"He didn't whis…"

"…doesn't mean nothing."

"He didn't whisper too much. All he said was that they told him something about getting the death penalty or seven to eight years in jail or something like that."

"Ah, he's just laying some big-shot bull crap on ya."

"What did he tell you that happened?"

"He told me that, ah, they were questioning him about Zoey's parents and that somebody got killed and that they were gonna question me about it. And that, something about me being an accessory to murder. And that he didn't think that they were going to do anything to me because I wasn't there. That, you know, I didn't have anything to do with it so they really couldn't do anything to me. And then he sat there and all he did was told me he loved me."

"So, he's a qualified lawyer that you're gonna put your life in his hands? Is that what you're doing?"

"No."

A few minutes later Gussler said, "I'm trying to help you... I ain't trying to scare ya. I ain't trying to be mean with ya. I'm just trying to say don't sink yourself."

"I'm not. I've told you everything. I mean that's what I know. I mean he had been talking about killing people. He always talks about killing people, but he's never done it."

"Guess what?"

"What?"

"Yes, he has."

"Has he before?"

"He is a stupid idiot. That's what your boyfriend is. I'm gonna tell you exactly what he is. Yes, he has. It's as simple as that. He's been charged with first-degree murder. Scott has been charged with first-degree murder. Heather has been charged with first-degree murder. You haven't heard this? You have been charged with accessory of first-degree murder. Dana has been charged with accessory of first-degree murder."

"How come Zoey and Dana and I did, I mean, when we weren't there? We were at Jeremy's house. I mean, ask Jeremy where we were. I mean, we went there, and we went to..."

"We heard a lot of conversations," Gussler said.

Ferrell had talked about killing throughout the trip to Florida, she admitted. "He's like, 'I want to kill something. I want to kill something. I want to kill somebody. I want to kill something.'"

At one point he turned to her and said, "Well, who could I kill? Who could I kill?'

"And I sat there and told him, 'Nobody. Shut up! You know you're not going to touch anyone.'

"And he goes, 'Oh, and you're gonna stop me?'"

"And I'm like, 'Yeah, I will.'

"And he goes, 'You can't. I'm sorry, you can't.'

He later said, "Well, maybe Zoey's parents."

He also talked about killing Jeanine's parents.

"No, all they have is a hoop-dee for a car. We'll definitely kill Zoey's," he said.

The first time she knew for certain of the murder plot was on Monday afternoon at a park.

"At one time, him and Scott went off and were whispering and I couldn't hear them. They told me to go away. So, I went for a walk and I went down on the bridge and sat on the bridge. And then he came down and sat beside me…"

He told her that if Heather wanted to leave, she had to leave now.

"And I asked him why, and he goes, 'You don't need to know. You'll find out later after we get down the road and stuff.'"

The group then headed to the home of Rod's former classmate, Audrey Presson. She was interested in witchcraft. "…it had something to do with weapons. A spell for weapons," she said.

When the group eventually parked near Heather's house, Scott and Rod got out of the Buick to greet her. "And then, Zoey like started screaming, so we got out. Dana and I got out of the car to see what was the matter with her. And she sat there screaming, 'No. You're not gonna do it! You're not gonna do it!' And Rod was like, 'Fine, we won't.' And then he's like, 'Just go get your stuff. Get your clothes.' We will be back. So, she went down there to get her clothes …"

Charity said she and Dana climbed back in the car. "And then, they come back to the car and they told us to get out. So, we got out and we went and sat in front of the car on the grass. And he (Ferrell) was like, 'We're gonna go ahead and kill them. We're gonna sneak in there and stuff.'

"And they had a big stick thing, and it had black electrical tape wrapped around it. It's in the car. They snapped it in half and Scott had one. Scott had one part of it in his hand when they left, and Rod had his like up in his shirt. You know, just the top of it was like sticking out of his shirt right in the back and stuff. And then Zoey started coming back up the road and stuff and Scott's like, 'Don't tell her what we're gonna do. Just take her to Jeremy's…"

Keesee began having a panic attack while telling the story. Gussler asked her why she was so frightened.

"Because I don't want to lose Rod, and I don't want to get in trouble with all of this stuff, because I didn't do it."

"He's not gonna hurt you, okay?"

"No, I'm not scared of him. I'm just scared of what's gonna happen to him. You've got to realize I love Rod more than anything. And if anything happens to him, I swear…"

She also talked about seeing Ferrell and Anderson drive by in the Wendorfs' Explorer.

She said she had rolled down the window in the Buick when Scott pulled up beside her and yelled, 'Come on!'" She was so startled she almost hit a mailbox.

"And Zoey seen the Explorer and she's like, 'Oh my God! That's my parents! That's my parents! They stole my parent's car, they stole it!' I'm like, 'I don't know, Zoey.' Because I didn't think they'd actually kill them. I mean, he's always talking like that, so I figured, oh, maybe he killed a dog or something, you know, and maybe he just stole the car."

"Why are you still thinking that?" Longo asked. "You just got done telling us you knew what they were going there for?"

"No, I said this is what I *was* thinking. I'm not thinking it now, but I got to thinking, and like, well, you know, he just killed a dog or something, or maybe he didn't even do that. Maybe he just walked up and stole the car, you know, or threatened them and took the keys or something."

Later, the two vehicles came to a stop and Anderson motioned for Keesee to get out and approach the Explorer. "So, I went over to the side of the car and Rod goes, 'I'm not getting out.' And I said, 'Why?' He's like, 'Because I don't want Zoey to see me like this' He had already changed his shirt."

"See him like what?" Longo asked.

"He had blood splattered," she said, indicating the face. "It wasn't like solid. It was just like little polka dot drops like a Dalmatian puppy or something like that. And he's like, 'Well, I don't want Zoey to see me like this because she'll know I did it.'"

She got back in the Buick and followed the Explorer. After a while, Heather started demanding to speak to Ferrell.

"She's like, 'I need to talk to him. I want to know if they stole this.' I'm like, 'Zoey, you can't.' She's like, 'Why? Why?' And I'm like, 'Because you don't need to see Rod how he is right now.' And she's like, 'He killed them. Rod killed my parents, didn't he?' And I'm like, 'Yeah.' And then she started freaking out and trying to crawl over me to get out of the car. And Dana told me to lock the door. And so, I locked the door and stuff and then we went..."

The Buick soon broke down. "And he [Ferrell] said, 'Come on. We're getting into this. We're driving this. So, we drove that to New Orleans and stuff, and we freaked out and all that."

Longo asked why she followed Ferrell's orders.

"Because he told me to. I mean, if I told him no sometimes, he'll like grab my throat and stuff... I didn't want to go with him to kill those people, and I didn't want to see it, and I didn't want to hear about it."

Ferrell was determined to go New Orleans, she said.

"He knows somebody named 'Chicken Man' that lives there and he's a voodoo priest. And he wanted to go and talk to him or something. And then we wanted to go to Mardis Gras. And so, we went there, and when we got there we went for a walk and stuff and...we were going down this like little sidewalk by a school and these cops come up and told us not to go down there. He asked us if we had any weapons or anything, and all we had was like a little knife or something that Rod had. And he showed him the knife. And he's like, 'Well, just don't do anything stupid with it.'"

The officers told them that the people down the road had "really big guns or something, and they'd kill Rod and they'd rape me and all this stuff. So, I freaked out and Rod said that we could go back to the car even though he was mad at me because he said I was chicken."

She said they left New Orleans and spent the night behind a gas station at "a little spot in the road" and later at a rest stop.

"...Scott woke up in his sleep and he didn't, well, he didn't really wake up. He thought he was awake, and he grabbed the keys and he put them in there, and instead of putting the car in reverse to back it up, he didn't have his glasses on, and he pulled forward and he hit a picnic table at the rest area and missed the pavilion and went through the center of the pavilion..."

After that, they drove to a truck stop and Heather put the keys in her poncho pocket, 'so that he couldn't get the keys and try to kill us again."

The next day they parked in a heavily wooded area. Ferrell was playing with a hunting knife the group had purchased at a Wal-Mart in Tallahassee with the stolen credit card. Scott walked up behind him and startled him, and Rod cut his thumb. "He said he could see the bone in it."

She said the group wrapped it in a shirt to stop the bleeding.

"Let me ask you something. Was he scared because that thumb wouldn't quit bleeding?"

"No, he was just sitting there, and he was looking at it. And then he would look back at me, and then he would look back at his thumb again. And then he would like, look at me funny. And then he'd look at his thumb and unwrap it and start laughing at it. He's got this fascination with cuts. I don't know why."

"He likes watching stuff slice. I mean, it doesn't matter if it's his skin or what it is."

She said he also liked "watching stuff break in half…"

After going to a store to get a drink for Ferrell, the group parked in the woods. "And we was (sic) like playing tag and talking… Zoey and Dana and I were looking at a lot of his pictures and stuff that he has drawn. You know, a lot of his poems and stuff. And she wanted to see this one picture that he had drawn of me one night when I stayed over there. So, we found it and we were talking about it for a long time."

Earlier, they had spotted a house ripe for burglary. Ferrell took Heather and Dana with him, while Scott and Charity stayed in the vehicle. They stole some food, a shotgun, a bow and arrows, and a plastic water jug containing $20 in change.

The next day they were headed down a back road when they ran out of gas.

Rod and Dana decided to walk to the nearest gas station, which was seven miles away.

"And so, they went down to the store and got like a gallon of gas and stuff. And on their way down there some guy, some drunk guy stopped and picked them up. And he asked them if they had any weapons with them. They didn't have anything with them, and they patted down their pockets. And he opens up his trench coat and he's got like guns and knives in the inside of his trench coat. And Dana was like sitting there saying how crazy she thought he was, but he was drunk."

She said the two sat in the man's vehicle for 10 minutes before the man started driving. They had to walk back with the gas, however.

As they prepared to put gas in the Explorer, a man drove up and advised that they should pour slowly. "And then he left and like right as he left the cop come up and asked, or he had said that somebody had reported that we had car problems. And he seen that we were just pouring gas in there and he's like, okay, 'So you guys are okay then?' And Dana's like, 'Yeah.' So then he left, and then we sat there and tried starting the car a couple of times and then it finally started."

They drove into Baton Rouge and to the waterfront where they sat on a slope and talked. It was Thanksgiving Day, but they were tired, dirty, broke and not feeling too thankful. She told Ferrell that she had to call her family.

"And we got up. We were getting ready to go use the [pay] phone and I noticed like all these fountains and stuff, and it amused me. So, we had to walk through all the fountains and all that."

She called one of her grandmothers. She tried calling her mother but got no answer. She called her other grandmother, who lives in Rapid City, S.D., and got into an argument with her, so she returned to the fountains. She went back and made another call, this time reaching her mother at her house in Piedmont, S.D.

Her mother asked Charity where she was.

"Why was your mom wanting to know where you were?"

"Because she said that she was going to come down here and get us," meaning all of them.

"…she told me to go find that road sign and then call her back as soon as I found one. So, I went back and called her back and she told us to go to the Howard Johnson. That she would have my grandmother wire some money with her credit card so we could get a motel room until she could get down here. Because she said she'd be down here tonight and stuff. And she wanted us to stay there. And then when we got to the Howard Johnson there was cops everywhere."

Longo asked if she wanted to help Rod.

"No, I think if he did it, he needs to get his little butt out of it. He deserves it."

"What do you think about him doing that?"

"It's sick. He knows I don't like stuff like that. And I've yelled at him and told him not to talk about it, not to do it, and not to even think about it. So, I think that he if did it, then he can just like suffer for it himself instead of trying to drag me into it."

"Well, he's dragged you into it."

"I know."

And the end of the interrogation, Gussler said, "Let's take a break."

"You feel better, though, don't you?" Longo asked.

"Except for about him, I don't know."

CHAPTER 14

"Jokes and stuff"

Dana Cooper was 19, just three years older than Rod, but it showed. She was a lonely, overweight, young woman, in a dead-end job, in a dead-end world, and she knew it.

She had only known Ferrell three or four months. She met him through Charity.

"What I can you tell you about him is nobody liked him. He always kept to himself. Everybody kept going around calling him things like "freak" and "vampire" because he liked to be out at night."[1]

She said she didn't believe he was a vampire, and she told a conflicting story about whether she considered herself to be one.

She admitted she had "crossed over," for example.

"From what Rod told me, cross-over is when they make a human one of them. The reason I crossed over was because, for one, it would give me somebody to be with, somebody to hang out with. As it was, I was alone by myself in my apartment. The only people that came over were my parents. Nobody else. And once I crossed over, and through Rod, I had people calling me, checking on me, coming over, coming to pick me up and take me out places, just general stuff like that."

Longo ran through the list of cult members, including Heather, asking if all had crossed over. She said yes, including Charity, "as far as I know."

He looked at the cuts on her arm and asked, "Is that the normal markings?"

"I only had three," Cooper said. "They're just about gone now."

"And what's the other one, on your other forearm?"

"...these are for feedings."

"If someone gets weak in the group you make two incisions on one arm. One on your hand, one on the arm. Both of these are just about healed up."

She said the procedure was supposed to give the recipient strength.

"Okay, what were you getting weak about a couple of days ago?"

"We haven't been eating properly. We haven't been getting hardly any sleep. We've been traveling day and night."

Longo asked her about the visit to Shannon Yohe's house and Ferrell talking about stealing the Wendorf's car. "Okay. And Mr. Ferrell, Rodrick Justin Ferrell, was telling Shannon and everybody else that was present something else he was gonna do."

"He was going to kill her parents," she said. She claimed to have no idea why and said she thought he was "joking around."

"I thought the original plan was just to sneak her out of the house and get gone. The original plan was to go to Florida, pick up Heather...and go back to Spokane to Charity's grandparents and stay there."

However, the group quickly went through her $100 cash and Heather's $60, which led Charity to eventually call her mother. Dana admitted signing Richard Wendorf's name on the stolen credit card two or three times.

Asked if she overheard Anderson talking about going into the Wendorf home, she said: "He just asked Rod if he could go. He goes, 'Yeah, I might need some help.'"

Longo then asked her what happened the night of the murders.

"We parked a ways from the residence and we waited for Zoey to come out. Once she got out, me and Charity got her into the back seat and put her stuff in the back of the car, and Rod told us to take her to see her boyfriend Jeremy, and to go and see a girl named Jeanine. So that's what we done."

The boys said they were going to kill Heather's parents. "Me and Shea did try to convince them not to do it. They was (sic) like, 'Well, there's no other way.' It was like talking to a brick wall."

Rod had mentioned the idea of killing the Wendorfs two or three times on the way to Florida, she said.

She said the idea of stealing the vehicle wasn't planned. It came up because Scott's car began having mechanical problems.

After going to Jeremy's and Jeanine's homes, they drove back to Heather's neighborhood.

"We got to the stop sign and a vehicle pulled up behind us. Zoey looked up and she said that it was her parents' vehicle, so she slid back down 'cause she thought they were looking for her."

Scott and Rod yelled for them to pull over. Rod wasn't wearing a shirt. When the girls left them near Heather's house, he had been wearing an olive-colored T-shirt emblazoned with the slogan, "Get Over It."

"...Charity told me that he took it off on the other side of the vehicle so that Zoey wouldn't freak out." She said she thought he threw it out the window along the Interstate.

Charity told Heather her parents were dead as they were leaving Lake County. "She started freaking out real bad, and I got her quiet and I got her to lay down."

Longo asked Dana how she felt about it.

"I felt sorry for her. I still do."

"Okay. It appears that she was, after a little while, maybe enjoying herself. How long did it take her to come back to, you know, her normal self, enjoying herself?"

"About a day-and-a-half."

"About a day-and-a-half she was back pretty well back to normal?"

"She was talking and laughing and..."

She had initially been in shock, Cooper said.

"But she got over it in a day-and-a-half?"

"I don't know if she'll ever get over it, but she did start talking to us and started laughing."

"Laughing about what?"

"Jokes and stuff. We was (sic) listening to the radio and we was (sic) cutting up listening to it."

"Later on, you know, after the day, day-and-a-half that the murders were mentioned, what was her reaction?"

"She'd just get real quiet. Sort of space out."

Longo asked Cooper if she could have walked away, and if so, why didn't she?

"I could have but where would I have went (sic)? I had no money and no place to stay."

Gussler asked if there was anything else she could think of, and she said: "The only thing I can say is that I didn't plan on her parents getting killed."

"How long do you honestly believe it would have been if you hadn't been caught last night or today or tomorrow... before he would have killed somebody else?"

"I honestly don't know."

"Do you think they have any remorse about it?"

She shook her head.

"...did they seem to enjoy it?"

"They just acted like it was done and over with."

CHAPTER 15

Heather: "I didn't know"

With Ferrell already confessing to the murders to the Baton Rouge detectives, and Charity and Dana filling in some of the blanks, Gussler and Longo were still eager to interrogate Heather. The burning question was, did she in any way suggest, encourage, or aid in the murders of her parents?

Police interviews begin slowly, starting with the reading of the defendant's rights.

It might seem routine, but mistakes made during this process have led to more confessions being thrown out by judges than anything else.

Gussler began by asking Heather if the Baton Rouge investigators had explained her Fifth Amendment rights.

She said she had asked one officer if she could stop answering questions, "and he said no, because I was a minor."[1]

That was a red flag, so Gussler explained she had a right not to incriminate herself and to have a lawyer present.

"Having these rights in mind, do you wish to talk with us now?" he asked.

"Sure, or is there a lawyer here right now?"

"No."

"Well, what the hell, okay."

He asked if she and Rod had ever corresponded. She said she had talked to him only on the phone. She said she did write to Ferrell's good friend Matt Goodman, and talked to him on the phone a few times. "Seemed a little strange to me," she said, adding that he was always trying to "hype" himself up to her.

"Would that be when he was trying to hype himself up to make you believe he was a vampire?"

"Yeah, I don't think he had to hype me up to do that."

"Okay, did you believe him?"

"I always liked to believe in supernatural things."

She claimed she got along with her parents "real (sic) good."

Gussler asked if Richard was her biological father.

"Yes."

"Okay," Gussler said. "So, you liked daddy?"

"Uh-huh."

"Did you love daddy?"

She nodded her head.

"Yeah, was he hard or strict on you?"

She did not answer.

"No. Alright. What about mom?"

"Mom (unintelligible). She's the one that usually set the rules."

"Yeah, and so it was just you and your sister at home?"

She did not answer.

"Okay. That's pretty natural sometimes that momma will set the rules…"

Heather then began to cry.

"Okay, take a couple of deep breaths. Paper towel. Did you feel sometimes that mom was a little too strict?"

"Well, sometimes I felt she didn't understand the (unintelligible) that's just typical teenage youth, right?"

Gussler said he was sure he probably felt the same way when he was young. Then, unexpectedly, he dropped the bomb. "…did you ever have a conversation with your sister that, a few times, it had crossed your mind to plot their deaths?"

"No."

"No?"

"Did you ever ask your sister if she had ever thought about plotting..."

"No."

"...their deaths?"

"No."

"No, okay, just asking. Okay, got plenty of towels there," he said, switching the topic to her boyfriend, Jeremy.

When Gussler named the apartment complex where he lived, she said, "You talked to him already?"

"We've probably talked to the world already, okay? Most of the questions, I'm gonna be honest with you, straight up front, I'm not trying to lie to you, blow smoke or anything else. I don't need to, okay. And there's no reason to, but on the other hand, just be the same way with us. Deal?"

"Okay."

Gussler asked her to explain "crossing over."

"I don't know, just I guess, you would it call it basic vampire stuff, and he drinks from you and you drink from them."

"What do you drink? Pepsi, Coke?"

"Blood."

He assured her that they were not "trying to make fun," but just wanted to understand. "You just cut yourself..." He then pointed to cuts on her arm and asked about them.

"Yeah, some of it's just, that's what this one was, the other ones were just 'cause I got mad."

"Can I see? So, you cut yourself here, and then what happens?"

"You drink from it."

"I mean, they just drink from your arm?"

"Just, no, just suck on it, you know, just drink the blood off, lick the blood off as much as they need and then you do the same to someone else."

She admitted crossing over on Monday.

"Who convinced you to do that?"

"No one convinced me."

She said Rod crossed her over.

Everyone else in the group had already crossed over. She said Jeremy had not. "I don't want to bring him into that."

"What happens when you cross over? I mean, do you feel different, or…?"

"They say you can see and hear and smell things different (sic), more acute (sic). That's just in the beginning."

"Who says that, Rod? Books?"

"Yeah, Rod and Dana and Charity and Scott. All of them."

"Can you?"

I guess, a little. I don't know. I never really tried it out."

Gussler asked why Jeremy didn't leave with her and the others.

"Well, he wanted to finish school, which was understandable. He didn't like the idea of depending on Rod, you know. So, he stayed there."

Asked why she didn't stay, she said she had promised Rod that she would run away.

Gussler returned to the subject of blood.

"You like to see blood?"

"No more than I like to look at a flower."

Gussler told her the whole thing with Ferrell was "fascinating," but he could not understand it.

"What's so fascinating about a guy that does absolutely nothing but harm people and run and get caught. Where's (sic) his powers? His power wasn't strong enough to get him out of two, three states before he got caught. His powers weren't strong enough to get him out of the state of Florida before we knew who we wanted… What kind of power is that? If I had a leader, you know, when I was in the Army, or if I had a leader in this business that told me things that wasn't (sic) true, I certainly wouldn't follow him, you know. I wouldn't follow him into no battle for Pete's sake, from what you just said."

"I know."

"He's laid a big line on ya, but he's (unintelligible). He's a little scared boy that's here with big tears in his eyes and told everything that happened, everything that happened, and tried to blame it on everybody that he could."

"What do you mean, blamed it on everybody he could?"

"Everybody he could. Why go down by yourself when you can take everybody?"

Gussler then asked if she knew why she was in trouble.

"Well, 'cause I was with Rod and he got caught."

"Got caught doing what?"

"Being with him at least. He's an outlaw, I know that now."

"And this is the kind of life that you wanted to follow this guy for?"

"I didn't know he was gonna kill my parents."

All she knew, she claimed, was that they were going "wherever we wanted to."

Gussler asked her about crossing over and whether it meant that she had to kill or steal.

She said no.

"You have talent. Maybe, some of the other young ladies out here have some talent. I don't know. I haven't seen their drawings or their writings or their grades or anything like that, but you have talent, this I know," he said, and then he suddenly switched gears: "But at no time you ever had a conversation with your sister, have you ever plotted to kill your parents?"

Her answer was unintelligible on tape, but she would deny again later.

"How are you feeling right now?"

"Well, I don't know."

"Are you upset with Jeremy?"

"No."

"Are you upset with Rod?"

"A little."

"Just a little?"

"Actually, a lot, yeah, a lot."

"Not enough to leave?"

"I don't have anywhere to go."

"You have a sister, you have a grandfather, you have aunts, you have uncles. I just named five places. Why do you say you have nowhere to go?"

"Because they probably don't love me anymore."

"Why?"

"Because I left."

"Why did you leave?"

"So I could go out and see things."

"You realize in three years you could have went and seen anything you wanted, you know. Let me ask you something. How long, like I said…we've already talked to Rod and everything else, a lot of what we're asking now is…to see who's going to sit there and tell us the truth, you know. Who is big enough to tell us the truth and who isn't. That's what it is all about. That's what questioning and interviewing is all about, okay. I know you know what an interview is. How long did you and Rod plan on stealing the blue Explorer?"

"I didn't plan on it."

He then asked a question that investigators thought was a surefire gotcha. "Okay. Who would have sent a sketch of the inside of your house to Rod?"

"Sketch? I never did."

"You didn't tell Rod that all the doors were unlocked on your parents' home?"

"No."

"He said you did, that's how he knew."

"Well, you can also know by opening them up, too, and seeing."

He asked her about the sketch again.

"Jeanine knows the inside of my house," she said.

"Did she send it?"

"I don't know if she did or not."

Jeanine, in fact, had drawn the floor plan.

Gussler asked her about a statement that Dana had made. "…when they told you about your mother and father being murdered that you were very upset."

"Uh-huh."

"For about an hour-and-a-half."

"Longer than that," she said.

"I'm still terribly mad at him. So sad."

"But you wouldn't even try to get away from him."

"Because I didn't know where to go. I couldn't get back."

"Why certainly, why did you even go to start with?"

"Because I didn't know he was gonna do anything like that."

Gussler pressed the point, asking why she stayed when she knew shortly afterward what had happened.

"Because we were already on our way. We were already in the car. We were already gone."

He then pointed out that the group stopped several times. Why didn't she leave then?

"I thought you all were going to blame me, that I did it."

"No, we're trying to understand why you didn't stay and defend your mom and dad who are no longer here to do it theirselves (sic), but you chose to go with the man who killed your parents. We're trying to find out why. You don't seem to think that there is anything wrong with that other than hour-and-a-half being upset, or a day."

"You don't know how upset I am inside."

The Baton Rouge police officers had done their best to keep the teens separated. They would be chained to a chair, in the case of Ferrell, locked up in an interrogation room, and all of them rotated from time to time.

"We had to keep Ferrell and Keesee separate...kind of out of sight of one another because they kept doing the little hand signals and batting the eyelids, and stuff like that," said Baton Rouge Detective John Colter.

However, Gussler noticed that Rod and Heather had a way to entertain each other.

"...you sat there and made funny faces at Mr. Rod sitting across the room making his funny faces."

"Just bringing a little levity to the ground."

"Pardon?"

"Bringing a little levity to the ground. If I didn't, I probably would of (sic) gone crazy in there."

"Oh yeah. He, at least, he's got a brain up there (unintelligible). Sergeant, I've got nothing else. As far as I'm concerned, I've heard a whole bunch of lies and I don't want to hear no (sic) more. Ms. Lady, when we see you again, you know where it's going to be?"

"Where?"

"It's going to be in Lake County, Florida at our place, okay?"

Gussler then left the room.

"Heather, is this how you want to leave this thing?" Longo asked. "You want us to leave here and you come back to Florida being charged and offering no explanation to any of our questions? If you have nothing to hide why will you not offer any explanation...? Why? I would be furious if an individual did that to my parents, but yet you two consider it a joke out there, eating pizza across the room from each other."

"Who's considering it a joke?"

"How can you stand to be in the same room with him and laugh and joke and smile at each other? Do you know what he did to your parents? Tell me, tell me."

"He killed them."

"No, tell me what he did to your parents."

"I don't know."

"Yeah, you do."

"He just killed them."

"No, you know what he did because they told you what occurred. Tell me what they did."

"I think he used a crowbar, didn't he? I don't know."

"You tell me."

"I don't know. That's all I know. All I know is he killed them, and he used a crowbar."

"How do you know that he used a crowbar?"

"Because they said, and they had it with them."

"Who did he say that to?"

"He said it to me."

"Who said it to you?"

"I think Rod did."

"Rod told you he did it?"

"Yes."

"Where did he get the crowbar from?"

"From my garage."

"Did you recognize the crowbar?"

"No."

"Did you see the crowbar?"

"Once."

"Where was the crowbar?"

"In the car."

"Which car?"

"In the blue car," she said, referring to the Explorer.

"In the blue car. Where is it now?"

"I don't know. I don't know where you guys put it."

"Is it still in the car or is it in the lake where they threw it?"

"I don't remember. I don't know if they threw it out or not."

"If you had to do it all over again, what would you do?"

"I wish I had never seen Rod in my life. I wish I had never met him."

"What can I do for you? How can I help you?"

"I don't know. I don't know what you can do."

"Do you want our help?"

"Yes."

"Or do you want to remain crossing over with him and his group?"

"I don't want to be with him anymore."

"Were you allowed to leave if you wanted to?"

"I don't think so, no."

"Why?"

"Because he wouldn't let me."

"How did he keep you there?"

"He just told me that I didn't have a choice to go or stay. I was afraid to leave. I was afraid if I tried to leave, he would hurt me."

"There were times that he wasn't even there with you? He was with Dana and Charity. Why didn't you leave?"

"He might find me."

"At least you'll tell me that you stayed there because you wanted to stay, right? Maybe you were confused? You were afraid. Okay, dry your tears, relax. Do you have a problem if we look through your parents' Explorer?"

"I don't think so."

"You don't think so? You don't want us to look through it?"

"If it will help you, you know."

Longo acknowledged that the questions were tough.

"It's a situation you're going to have to live with for the rest of your life, and you're going to have to realize that you're the only one who can help yourself, because you're the only one who put yourself in that situation, you understand, and sometimes things like this does hurt, but you need to soul search, and if you are keeping anything from us, you need to get it off your chest, and you need to talk to us. You're the only one who can fill the picture in what happened out there. We weren't there, you were. No matter how big your part was or how small it was, you're the only one that can fill in that puzzle for us, and right now it sounds like you don't want to, for whatever reason it may be."

"I remember flat out telling him flat out, don't even go near my parents."

"Why would you tell him not to even go near your parents?"

"Because he asked me not too long ago if I wanted my parents dead or alive, and I said straight out I wanted them alive."

"When did he ask you this?"

"On Monday...after school.

"So, on Monday after school he talked to you about killing your parents?"

"Yes, and I said no. I said I wanted him to leave them alone."

"Why didn't you tell us about this before we were asking you about it? You played dumb with us? These are the type of things we're talking about. Do you understand where we're coming from?"

"Uh-huh."

Longo asked where the conversation took place.

"We were at the cemetery," she said. It was just the two of them. The others were back at Scott's car.

Later in the interview, she recounted the exact conversation.

"He said, 'Question. Do you want your parents dead or alive?' And I said, 'Alive. I don't want you messing with my parents. I don't. Just leave them alone. I want them alive. I don't want them dead.' He said, 'I just want to ask 'cause I ask everyone that.'"

She said she asked him if anyone ever said yes. "...and he looked down at the ground and looked up and he says,

'Now that I think about it, no. Nobody ever says that they want them dead.'"

Longo asked her to recall the first time he mentioned killing her parents.

"I mean, maybe there was (sic) small accounts when we talked on the phone but whenever he talked on the phone or whatever he tried to mention something like that, and I told him I didn't want them bothered. I didn't want him to come near them."

She said Ferrell made what she called "small insinuations."

Ferrell would say things like, "It's (sic) so much easier if your parents weren't there."

She said she replied: 'No, it wouldn't. It wouldn't be easier for me.'"

"Why did he have an obsession of (sic) killing your parents?"

"I don't know. He probably…because he knows if, if he kills my parents, then I'd probably come to him, I probably wouldn't have anything to stay in Florida for."

"But you did go with him, so why did he kill your parents?"

"He likes killing people."

"Has he killed people before?"

"He's told me he has."

She said she didn't know details but said, "he likes killing people. He enjoys it. Didn't he tell you that?"

"You told us you knew nothing about your parents and now you're telling me that Monday and on numerous other occasions he's brought up to you about wanting to kill your parents."

He asked her why he wanted to kill her parents and Jeanine's.

"Because he wanted to break the ties, we wanted to break the ties to Florida."

"To have you all to himself and Jeanine?"

"Yeah."

She said when she saw Ferrell and Anderson in the Explorer, "It made me really upset. I didn't know what they had done. I didn't know if they had just knocked my parents out, or just snuck in and got the keys and then drove off, or if they had actually killed them."

She said she couldn't remember the exact words Charity used but quoted her as saying: "To put it bluntly, they killed your parents. Your parents are dead, to put it bluntly."

"...and I started giggling, that's when I lost it, and we were already down the road."

Longo wondered why she didn't ask for help, or tell anyone, "Hey, this man is gonna do this, he's talked about it several times?"

"Because...I thought if I told him no enough that he wouldn't. I thought I could get through to him. I thought he cared what I want because he was coming down to get me."

"Are you afraid to admit that to me that you knew what he was gonna do and you couldn't stop him?"

"I didn't know what he was gonna do. I didn't know he was gonna kill my parents. I thought what he meant, when we were gonna break the ties, I thought that just means to leave, just go, not actually kill them."

At the end of the interview, she asked: "Is he out there?"

"He sure is."

"Do I have to be in the same room with him?"

"Not if you don't want to."

"I don't want to."

Longo asked if it was because he didn't abide by her wishes not to harm them. "You feel that you are to blame for part of this (unintelligible), being involved with him?"

"I'm afraid that I'm gonna get in trouble for killing my parents. I thought that you were gonna blame me."

CHAPTER 16

Killing was "a rush"

"You still hanging in there, Rod?"[1]

"Same as it was when I last left," an exhausted Ferrell replied.

"I've got a pack of cigars," he told Ferrell as the two detectives sat down. "I'll show you. I never lie to anybody…." He then showed him an actual tape recorder.

"Just figured you would like (sic) put it on tape. That would make it a lot easier," Ferrell replied.

He asked how far Ferrell had gone in school.

"I was in tenth before I got expelled."

"What did you get expelled for?"

"Being a little asshole."

He asked what kinds of grades he had been getting.

"When I actually did work, A's and B's."

"Okay."

"Whenever I stopped, F's."

Gussler then asked if he knew why he was there.

"Let's see, the murders of Heather Wendorf's parents."

"Okay, did you know their first names by any chance?"

"Uh, no."

"Okay, Mr. and Mrs. Wendorf."

"That's the most I knew."

He said he didn't care if his mother was present for questioning.

"Okay, I want to ask and make sure you're comfortable with us and everything else."

"Well, my life's [expletive], so…"

He said the plan was to pick up both Heather and Jeanine. "It didn't quite work out the way we planned."

"Okay."

"Because we weren't supposed to do what we did."

"We had planned on taking a car down from Kentucky to go pick her up. She was gonna run away."

Stealing the Explorer was not the in the original plan either, he said.

He talked about meeting Heather at the cemetery near the high school on Monday.

"What did you talk about while you were at the cemetery?"

"About her running away, asking her if she was sure, asking her where she wanted to go, asking her just about her personal life, like her boyfriend, Jeremy."

"Did you discuss with her about her parents at that time?"

"We didn't think anything about her parents at that time. We didn't think about the parent thing until 10 minutes before we did it, so that was kind of spontaneous. It wasn't premeditated."

"You didn't mention anything to her and ask her about if she wanted her parents killed?"

"Ah, within the year I jokingly said it once, but I never thought I would do it."

"She's mentioned that you said it several times," Gussler said.

"Is that true?" Longo asked.

"Just like throwing it in," Ferrell said.

"Well, like, well, I mean, what's your version? Is that true or…"

"Well, I'm saying she didn't point (sic) out ask me. She didn't say, 'Oh please, kill my parents.'"

"No, I'm asking you. I'm telling you she's telling us…"

"That I've said it," Ferrell said.

"That you asked her, 'Do you want your parents killed?'"

"Like I said, I said it once because she kept throwing the hint to me and then I just go, 'What? Do you want me to kill your parents?'"

"How was she throwing you a hint?"

"Like she was saying, you know… like both my parents have a misfortune or an accident or something it would make it a lot easier to run away.' Things like that."

"Did you say anything to her at the graveyard about that again?"

"Like I said, I was just asking her if she was sure she wanted to leave, because I knew it had been a year and she'd gotten a steady boyfriend. The only thing she was flunking in school was French, you know, it seemed like a halfway good life at least, so I was asking her for sure if she wanted to leave with us."

"Nothing about hurting the parents, though?"

"Nothing about death or anything besides just running away."

He recounted moments leading up to Keesee and Cooper driving off with Heather and talking to Anderson.

"…I pulled Scott to the side because I got to thinking about how Heather's parents would probably react, and I didn't want to be found for one thing…and I said, 'How do you feel about taking someone out?' And he's like, 'No problem.' So, we decided that we would go into the house, at least hogtie…her parents. Didn't exactly plan on beating them to death."

He said he did not tell Charity and Dana about his plans. "I don't know if Scott told them or not, but I didn't tell them anything because I wanted to keep them out of it."

He said he broke a bow staff in two and gave half to Anderson, though he realized it was not much of a weapon.

"What were you planning on doing with it? I thought you were just going up there just to hogtie?"

"I was saying, just in case they attacked me."

"Okay."

"Because I didn't know how her father, like how big he was or what."

"And you found?"

"A crowbar."

"Okay."

"I figured it surpassed wood by far."

He said he saw machetes, chainsaws, and axes in the garage. "Notice I didn't use them because I didn't plan on killing anyone..."

He claimed he was just going for the Ford Explorer and money. "That was it."

He said he guessed they had money. "I mean, Heather's sister owns a cell phone. They own, you know, like a big Explorer, and they own the house. I was pretty much guessing."

He said he needed the bigger vehicle because the Buick was too small.

"So obviously you thought about it before you got there, then. You didn't just decide when you got there. You thought about it before getting to the house. Follow what I'm saying?"

"It only took seven minutes to get there. I thought of it two minutes before we got there."

"Okay. So out of the clear blue you're talking, you came up with this?"

"I'm sitting there, walking down the road with Scott beside me saying, 'Okay we do this, this, this, this...'"

"Just like that, okay?"

"I'm very strategic about it and very fast. I don't plan things out."

"Okay."

"As you notice, that's why we got caught."

Once he got inside, he said he saw Richard watching TV and told him, "Don't move or I will beat the [expletive] out of you."

Hours earlier Ferrell told Sgt. Odom that he was asleep.

"...at that point in time I was like afraid that he was going to come after me, so I had the thing propped up and ready just in case he came at me. I was going to slug the [expletive] out of him. So, what happened is, he did turn around and started to get back up, so then I did waylay his ass, and I didn't stop because he was still breathing and stuff. I just kept beating him, and beating him, and beating him, and beating him, taking pleasure in that."

He said it "knocked him cold, and while he was cool, I figured now or never, because if he gets up, I'm a [expletive] dead [expletive], so I just beat him until he died."

He admitted to also stabbing in him in the heart. "I took the bottom of the crowbar and *splack*!"

He said he then started looking for the Explorer keys before Heather's mom got out of the shower. He found van keys but wanted the Explorer's because it was newer.

"That's when her mom came out through the kitchen area holding a very hot cup of coffee and she asked me what I wanted, and I flat out told her I wanted the keys, and she was like freaking. She thought that Zoey was still in the house..."

He said she lunged at him. "She spilled her coffee on me, like all over me, then she clawed my face and grabbed my wrist, and that's when I took the straight end of the crowbar and just started bashing the back of her head."

"So, she was running away from you when this happened?"

"No, she was holding onto me."

He said he also kicked her with a "crescent kick," something he claimed to have learned in martial arts training.

"Kicked her on the ground and then continued to beat her there until she stopped breathing."

Rod said he told Scott "to quit freezing, get his ass in gear, told him to get one half of the house. I took the other half."

They found precious little cash—about $5, a Discover credit card, and Ruth's pearls. The next day, Heather asked for the pearls and draped them around her teddy bear's neck. She also asked Ferrell for her father's pocketknife, he said.

"Why would she want remembrances of her parents dead?"

"Maybe she's a sick bitch. I don't know."

He said if someone killed his parents, "I would be like, I don't want anything."

Longo asked why they didn't just wait three hours until they went to bed.

"Because I'd heard Zoey mention one time before that the keys were in the parents' room, and I didn't want to take a chance of them getting up and finding out what happened."

Ferrell also confessed to burglarizing a house off a path deep in the woods between New Orleans and Baton Rouge.

They parked in the woods while it was still daylight and cut brush for camouflage. After it got dark, they went to the house. He saw some long guns in a pickup truck but did not take them. He said he rang the doorbell "25 times," and finally kicked the door open. Heather and Dana accompanied him, he said.

They checked the entire house, including closets, to make sure no one was hiding inside. "Then we did food detail, weaponry detail, and money detail."

They found a jar with $20 worth of coins inside, took food from the pantry and refrigerator, a shotgun, a box of bullets for some other type of firearm, a compound bow and several arrows.

"Why upgrade to a shotgun?" Longo asked.

"Because at that point in time, I knew the police would be looking for us, because I knew by that time Heather's sister had been there, and since I was already a murderer, why would it matter whether I killed police or what, because we're all human."

"You would really have taken out an officer?"

"If he shot at me first. If he hadn't shot at me, I would have cooperated like these guys. They didn't shoot, so I didn't shoot, because that's one thing I didn't tell them. That I had the shotgun in my hand when they pulled up."

"I thought you were going to get rid of it. You still had it then?"

"I'm talking about whenever they pulled up, they had patrol cars going through the harbor where we were at."

"Oh, okay."

"There were five of them that day, and whenever they came up, I had the shotgun sitting in my lap just waiting for them to stop us, and I have precise aim. I could have blown their head from there to the waterfront, no problem. But I was going to give them a fair chance that if they didn't shoot, I wouldn't, because I didn't want to kill anything else. But anyway, what happened is come nightfall, Shea was freaking out because we had no money and stuff, so she was like, 'Let me call my grandparents and my mom so that way we can have a place to stay.'

"She called her mom. Her mother was asking way too many [expletive] questions. I knew she was going to turn us in. I told Shea to hang up right then and get the [expletive] out, don't tell her where the [expletive] we were, because I knew she was going to turn us in."

He said she made the call while he was ditching the shotgun and bow and arrows. Within a half hour, patrol cars rushed to the Howard Johnson's where they had pulled up. "I just walked straight to the cop car and put my hands behind my back and said, 'Okay, let's go.' And then I came and slept in this room and on goes the story, and that's it."

Longo noticed cuts on Ferrell's arm and asked if they were injuries from the murders.

"No, it's self-infliction."

"What are they for?"

"Physical pain to override the mental."

He said Charity did the same thing.

"I don't know about the others because Zoey is kind of a freak chick and Dana, she's just Dana."

Longo also asked if Ferrell was familiar with the term "over the edge, or over the other side, or over."

"Cross over?" Gussler asked.

Ferrell said, yes, that he had heard it from his friend, Steven "Jaden" Murphy.

"It is supposed to be where you go from human to vampire."

"And how is that supposed to occur?"

"You cut yourself, let them drink it, it runs through their veins for a few moments, and then your blood becomes tainted and you drink from them and become the untainted. You go around feeding on humans."

"Do you do that?"

"All the time."

"Seriously, seriously, do you?"

"No, I have never killed anyone in my life."

"No, I'm talking about your saying you're making cuts on you and you drink each other's blood."

"I cut it to watch the blood roll down. Sometimes I cut to hope I can die."

"Uh-huh."

"Suicide has never worked for me, so that's why I was kind of hoping at this rate now I could maybe be tried as an adult and get electrocuted or something. Not that I'm throwing a hint."

"You want to die?"

"Yes."

"You do?"

"Oh yes, definitely."

"Why?"

"Because I know otherwise I won't be able to see Shea within the Lord knows how much [expletive] time, which means by that time she can find another guy, which by that time my child will be born, and by that time my whole [expletive] life is screwed, so I might as well [expletive] die right now. And if I had something to do it, I would."

Longo asked why he didn't just stay in Kentucky.

He said Charity's father was being unreasonable. "He called me an A-class freak, and the cops in Murray were hazarding (sic) me about what was on the news about the animals."

He said they blamed him because he was a cult leader.

He claimed that two other teens had committed the animal abuse.

He said his mother did not want him to marry Charity. "So, I just told her you have a week to get all your shit together and we're leaving so we can stay together."

He said before he met Charity, he wanted to kill himself. "And when I met her, I wanted to live. Now that she is being taken away, I will find a way to kill myself. No matter if it's a little padded room or what."

He said he thought about resisting arrest "in hopes that these Baton Rouge police would actually shoot me in the heart or head or something. Something that would actually give me a fatal wound, but I knew I could see Shea like after I get done talking to you, and that's why I cooperated so much, 'cause like I said, she's all I care about, and as long as I can see her, I will cooperate 120 percent."

Gussler returned to Ferrell's statement about "taking pleasure" in beating Richard with the crowbar.

"There was a rush..."

"A rush, okay."

"To feel that fact that I was taking a life, because that's just like the old philosophy about if you can take a life you become a god for a split second, and it actually kind of felt that way for a minute, but if I was a god, I wouldn't exactly be here, would I?"

"How many times did you hit him?" Longo asked. "I mean did you actually count or are you approximating...?"

"Around 50."

"Together, total, or each."

"Total for him, for her about 30, really (expletive) hard hits because his face was just, it looked like a rubber mask. It didn't even look real, and her head, her brains were just like oozing out of her skull."

"Uh-huh."

"So that's when I basically knew, yeah, they're dead, so I got nothing to worry about."

"Did Scott do anything, stop you from doing it, watched you...?"

"He just watched and smiled."

"He got a rush, obviously, too, then? Is that what the kind of smile you are referring to?"

"He was like, just really like a happy, almost like a kid at an amusement park for the first time."

CHAPTER 17

"I froze"

Maybe it was because they were tired, or maybe they sensed a weak link, but Gussler and Longo were in no mood to let Scott Anderson ramble on or try to lessen his culpability, so they cut to the chase.

Within a few minutes, Gussler asked: "Okay, what happened Scott?"[1]

"We went to Heather's house."

"Uh-huh."

"We saw her and then the three girls left, and me and Rod entered their house, and then I froze up, and he beat them to death."

Gussler asked about the sequence of events. "And he had never before mentioned, Scott, about killing these people?"

"No."

"Okay. Do you know a Shannon who lives in an area, we refer to there in Lake County, Florida, as Pine Lakes?"

"Yes."

"Okay. There was a phone call made from Shannon's Tuesday night, probably about 7:00, do you recall what that call was all about? (He was referring to the call made Monday)."

"No."

"Okay. Then do you recall the conversation that was being held at Shannon's when it was being discussed the different ways of killing these folks, meaning Mr. and Mrs. Wendorf?"

"I wasn't paying attention to the conversation."

"Okay, the conversation was going on like that and you don't pay attention to them?"

"Not really."

"Sit up in your chair," Gussler said.

"Okay."

Gussler then confronted Anderson about Yohe's account of him showing his pocketknife to everybody and saying, "I want to get my licks in too, and I'm gonna do it with this…"

"I've never done that."

"You've never done that, okay?" Gussler said.

"Hey, Scott. Before you start lying anymore. You know that you are the last one that has been interviewed, right?"

"Yes."

"We knew the story before we came here, and the four other people has (sic) confirmed everything. Okay. So, before you're going to sit there and insult our intelligence and lie to him, think about it," Longo said.

"The questions he's asking you, he's already got he answers to. Now we are going to start over. Do you want to start over again and get the story straight, 'cause we're going to give you one last chance…."

Gussler asked Anderson if he knew what he was facing. "You have been charged with first-degree murder," he said.

"Two counts," Longo chimed in.

"It's not a game," Gussler said. "It's not a board game. It's not a bullshit game to sit and lie and play silly games with. It's a very serious situation. Two human lives are gone for some stupid reason. Can you understand that?"

"Yes."

Gussler said investigators had probably talked to "40 people if they have talked to one." He also said, "Your big leader has sat here and told the truth. And, of course, the girls have."

There was one thing, though, he said. "The only reason we don't have is why. Other than, you know, I've heard, well, so they wouldn't tell on them for taking the car. Well, that's no reason. No jury or no judge in the world would ever buy that. You don't take two human lives because you don't want them to tell on you for taking the car, okay. Okay. You came to Florida. How much was it discussed between Rod and yourself about taking these people's lives?"

"I never knew about it until he called over from Shannon's house."

He then insisted that he couldn't recall all of the phone conversation, but said they were going to get Heather and leave.

"I didn't know we were gonna end up killing her parents until we got over to the road in which she lived on."

"So, Shannon or any other people out there that has given us sworn statements…"

"They probably knew before I did."

"Were you in the house with them when they were talking about it?" Gussler asked.

"They went outside."

Gussler went into a bit of a tirade, calling the murders to cover up a vehicle theft, the "weakest, weakest, weakest, weakest excuse I've heard in my life. Twenty-three years in this business."

He also relied on the pressure tactic, saying "…we can leave here with two things in mind: the guy tried to help us, he tried to explain to us, tried to get us to understand this happened, or we can think all he did was sit up here and bullshit us and go for the jugular."

Anderson was stubborn, however.

Without mentioning her name, Gussler recalled Charity's statement about Ferrell wanting to kill someone while the group was traveling to Florida. "And you ain't heard none of that?"

"I heard. I was trying to concentrate on driving as well. I didn't want to kill us all."

There was no working radio in the Buick, Gussler noted. "Then your ears were focused, your brain was focused on a conversation going?"

"Somewhat."

"Uh-huh. What was the conversation?"

"He was tired of sitting, and everyone was agitated, and he just wanted to kill someone."

Anderson admitted that besides Heather's parents, he had also mentioned killing Jeanine's.

"What made him choose Heather's versus Jeanine's?"

"I don't know. I promise, gentlemen. I don't know."

With his defenses beginning to crumble, Anderson admitted he went into the house to help Ferrell kill Heather's parents. "…but then, when I saw him make the first blow, I knew I couldn't."

"And how were you going to assist?" Longo asked.

"He was going to go after the father and I was going to go after the mother."

The two agreed to that scenario after the girls left with Heather.

"Did they know about this, what you were doing?"

"Two of them did."

"Which two?"

"Dana and Charity."

"Did they try to talk you out of it, Scott?"

"No."

"They wanted you to do it?"

"They didn't really want us to do it. They knew they couldn't stop us."

The detectives, armed with Jeanine's drawing of the house plan, had Anderson explain what happened when they entered the home.

Richard was asleep, Scott said. Rod hit him in the head with the crowbar he found in the garage about 15 times.

He said Ruth came out of the bedroom. "She goes, 'What do you want?' But Rod didn't answer. He just hit her."

He talked about Ruth fighting back.

"Okay. And what were you doing during this time?"

"I just froze. There was nothing I could do."

Gussler later asked Anderson if he enjoyed seeing the couple being killed.

"I was scared."

"Did he seem to be enjoying himself?"

"I guess he did, I don't know."

"Was he making any comments, or…?"

"No."

"No comments or sounds or anything?"

"Just sounds of anger."

"And what did they sound like?"

"Like a, like it was growling or something, like a dog or a bear growling."

CHAPTER 18

Murky Mississippi

The Mississippi River is dark, murky, and covers a multitude of sins, especially at night, but Anderson was willing to show the Baton Rouge investigators where Ferrell had disposed of the murder weapon and items taken in the Louisiana burglary.

It was about 9 p.m. Friday by the time Anderson, Moran, and some of his fellow officers made it down to a pier and a levee near the Interstate highway bridge.

Anderson pointed an area near higher ground where he said the shotgun and a bow and arrow were thrown into the river. The murder weapon was tossed in an area where the riverbank is low.

"Did he actually use the words 'murder weapon?' Ferrell's lawyer, Bill Lackay, later asked Baton Rouge Officer Moran in a deposition.[1]

"Yes sir, he did."

Lackay also asked, "Did he say what weapon that was?"

"He said it was a tire tool, crowbar, or some type of iron object that he had tossed into the river."

"When he said 'he' threw it, who?"

"Ferrell."

The next day, the police dive team returned to the area and recovered the shotgun and bow and arrow, but the crowbar was never found. "They pulled up some iron and stuff, but it wasn't a crowbar or tire iron," Moran said.

Anderson described it as a small crowbar, about four or five pounds, with one end designed for use as a nail puller.

While watching the dive team, Moran made a discovery of his own.

"I noticed this tree limb and it had some initials…"

A willow tree had the initial "R" and Z-O-E carved into a large branch, about 100 yards or so from the river.

CHAPTER 19

"They're children"

Finally, after all the teens had been interrogated—Ferrell twice—the bedraggled, smelly, blurry-eyed group was taken to a lockup. Cooper was taken to jail, the rest to a nearby juvenile center. Outside the station, reporters gathered like "hungry dogs," according to one detective.

The teens' families were relieved that the group was not harmed.

"She basically ran away from home, but I don't think she knew what she was getting into," said Charity's father, David Keesee of Murray. "I'm just glad that she's safe and alive."[1]

"We were just relieved to know that they didn't have to gun them down," said Scott's father, Howard Anderson.

Dana's father, Otha Cooper, had been worried—about himself. He fired six rounds at a carload of teens he mistook for his daughter and her friends. He was arrested and charged with wanton endangerment. No one was injured.

Sondra Gibson and her tattoo artist boyfriend had not notified police that Rod was missing. She said she figured he and Charity had eloped.

She had a theory about Rod not being guilty of murdering Wendorf and Queen.

"I'm wondering whether they weren't already dead when they got there. If I can see him and look straight in his eyes, I'll know what happened," she said.

Shortly before the extradition hearing began, Assistant District Attorney Aaron Brooks put a black coffee cup on the judge's desk with a stuffed pig with black horns and a pitchfork. The inscription read, "You little devil."

He got some laughs, but he snatched it off the bench before the judge appeared.

Judge Jewel "Duke" Welch didn't seem concerned about having a vampire in his courtroom. "We don't get many vampires around here. They're usually all down in New Orleans," he said.

By Monday, Cooper had agreed not to fight extradition and a caravan of sheriff's vehicles began making its way to Baton Rouge. Handcuffed and shackled, her short hair hanging in tufts across her forehead, she appeared unruffled and answered questions clearly. But a Louisiana juvenile court judge ruled that the other four would stay put for two more days, so their parents could attend the extradition hearings.

"They're children," Judge Pamela Johnson told reporters. "The law allows them to have their parents present."

She said Florida had not requested their return. However, a probable cause affidavit for extradition was sitting on a nearby desk.

It wasn't just extradition that was at issue. Louisiana law restricted law enforcement officers from questioning juveniles until their parents or guardians were present.

Prosecutors in Lake County, however, insisted that Florida law prevailed since it was a case in their state.

Hundreds of miles away, in Winter Park, Fla., more than 200 mourners gathered for the slain couple's funeral.

The Rev. Peter Nordstrom urged the crowd to extend their love to Heather.

"It would be wrong not to think of Heather now…with all the speculation and rumors, we know one thing for sure: God loves her. Nothing will change that," he said.[2]

The next day, a sheriff's van transported Cooper to Lake County.

First appearance is a routine matter—unless the defendant is involved in a highly publicized case. The defendant is called up to a podium where a closed-circuit TV camera is located, raises her right hand, swears to tell the truth, and listens as the judge, who is sitting across the street in the courthouse, reads the charges, asks for the rudimentary not-guilty plea, and asks if she can afford an attorney.

Once, a suspect in another murder case started to say something, then said, "No, I'd better not."

It was one less antacid pill for a defense attorney that day.

Cooper, who was wearing an orange jump suit, sat on a bench with other women waiting for her name to be called. A gaggle of reporters, including myself, practically had our noses pressed up against a glass partition a few feet away. When one of the TV crew members raised his camera, a woman ducked her head.

"I don't care about you," he muttered, knowing that she couldn't hear him anyway.

It was over in minutes, but it was proof, if there was ever any doubt, that there was no such thing as routine as far as news outlets were concerned.

In Baton Rouge, the wheels on the justice system were turning very slowly on that Tuesday.

Judge Johnson said the reason she did not know about the Florida affidavit was because the Louisiana prosecutor had not filed the paperwork. She assigned attorneys to each of the teens, and she assigned a guardian ad litem to Heather since her parents were dead.

Lake County Sheriff's deputies said the investigation had gone "extremely smoothly," but they were becoming irritated.

"You couldn't ask for anything better, and then to have it all become bogged down in a technicality over extraditing is frustrating," said Lt. Chris Daniels.

"In fairness to the judge, this is a statute that is extremely rarely used because we don't transport juveniles that often," Gross said.

"We're doing our level best to get this stuff Federal Expressed out," he said. "We don't have forms for this stuff. We're writing this from scratch."

Sondra Gibson said she wasn't aware that she could attend the hearing in Baton Rouge. "This is the first I've heard of it. No one has told us anything. No one has called us about anything at all."

She said she had talked to Rod on the phone, "and he just said he's going to court. He seemed like he was scared, and he doesn't know what's going on. He acted like a little kid to me."[3]

She said she was in the process of going to Baton Rouge.

With each development, and with each piece of paper filed in the growing court case, we were able to give readers a good idea of what was happening in the investigation. Florida's open records law is pretty good, despite the Legislature watering it down every year, but confessions are exempt. *Sentinel* attorneys and other media lawyers would have to fight that battle another day.

In depositions, the defense lawyers would occasionally make snarky remarks about news media credibility like, "you can sure believe everything you read in the newspaper." They did not mention a newspaper by name. However, State Attorney Brad King, who was also the custodian of public records, verified that information in the stories was true.

One day, Mike Graves, who was assigned to represent Anderson, said: "I hate reading in the newspaper questions I forgot to ask."

We were also working the phones aggressively. I talked to Shannon Yohe, and it was an eye-opener.

"I didn't understand why they wanted to kill them, so I didn't believe them," she said. Ferrell lied "about tons of stuff," she said. "Nobody believed the things he said," she added, including telling others that a school computer malfunction classified him as a graduate.[4]

She said, however, that she was concerned enough to call a friend to see if he might be serious.

She did not identify the friend, but the friend said she had nothing to worry about—Rod would not kill Heather's parents. It was Jeanine Leclaire. "My mistake," Jeanine told investigators.

Yohe said Ferrell sliced his arm so that one of the teens could drink his blood and they talked about which parts of the body tasted best.

"That made me sick. I was like, 'Get out of my house.'"

On Wednesday, December 4, Ferrell agreed not to fight extradition. Anderson and Heather tried but failed to stop the process.

Martha Anderson, who came to Baton Rouge for the hearings, disclosed that Scott once had a mental breakdown in Kentucky. "Mama, I'm losing my cookies," he said. He was sent to a crisis center, but authorities "ignored his desperate cries for help," she said.

She said Scott was cooperating with authorities.

"He's taking responsibility for his part," she said. "I'm truly sorry that this happened."

Leon Harrell, the attorney assigned to Keesee, described her as "an innocent, naïve 16-year-old girl who is following a guy around. We all have idols," he said.

"She's frightened, she's scared, and she didn't do anything. And no, this is not a Charles Manson case," he said, referring to the hippie cult leader responsible for the murder of actress Sharon Tate and others in 1969.

By late Wednesday, the judge was okay with the 90-page package of legal documents that Gross had sent from Florida and approved their removal from Louisiana.

The little narrow parking lot outside the Lake County jail was a curious sight that Friday night with reporters milling around the TV news trucks. Mixed in among the professionals was an elderly woman who described herself as a "court watcher."

She had the very odd habit of trying to ingratiate herself with the families of both the defendant and the victims. Sometimes excitement got the best of her. She once climbed up on chairs in the courthouse lobby so she could hear what a prosecutor was saying at an impromptu press conference. "Get down from there," a bailiff scolded. "You know better than that."

Once, she slapped me on the back while I was pounding on the keyboard—past the normal deadline—when the verdict was announced.

The courthouse was abuzz Friday with the news that the vampires were on their way to Lake County. There was a mix of humor, too. A mobile blood bank bus had coincidentally set up shop in the parking lot, which led to a lot of vampire jokes. I couldn't resist a little bit of gallows humor myself. When the elevator stopped and I got on with a bunch of lawyers, I said, "Looks like lawyers and reporters are not going to be the only blood suckers in town."

Finally, after waiting for hours, the caravan pulled up and entered the sally port door. Newspaper photographers were waiting inside. As soon as Ferrell got out of the vehicle, he stuck his tongue out for the photo. In Louisiana, he sarcastically told a crowd of reporters, "God bless America"[5]

Inside, at the booking desk, the teens were searched before they turned to the corrections officers handling the paperwork. Outside, camera crews and reporters rushed to a tall, narrow window just in time to see Ferrell smooch a large plastic glass partition.

The court watcher stuck her nose in, too.

"You're going to be bonked in the head," I told her as she began rising up underneath a news camera.

After they were fingerprinted, photographed, and had filled out the proper paperwork, they were driven to a juvenile detention center in Ocala, about 45 minutes away in Marion County.

The next day, the juveniles had their first appearance before Marion County Judge Frances King. After being told to raise their handcuffed hand to be sworn in, she warned them that "this is not the time" to discuss their case. She read the charges and asked if their families could afford an attorney.[6]

"Not that I know of," Ferrell said. He said his mother was moving to Florida "because of all this," and waved his hand toward the other teens.

He would be represented by the Public Defender's Office, which takes on the most difficult cases. The others were assigned court-appointed private attorneys.

Unlike the previous day's antics, Ferrell was solemn and well-behaved. He cocked his head, his long, black-dyed hair falling across his left eye, so he could look around with his right. Keesee and Anderson stared at the floor.

Heather bit her lip, bowed her head, twisted her hair in her hands, and shook.

More paperwork was made public, including the results of a thirteen-hour search of the Explorer.

Among the items collected for evidence were a bedsheet and a bloody paper towel (from Ferrell's knife injury); a hunting knife; two teddy bears, one draped with Ruth's pearls; a wooden stick, 2 ½ feet long wrapped in black electrical tape; a copy of Anne Rice's novel, *Queen of the Damned*; *The Ultimate Dracula*, an anthology of vampire tales; and *Necronomicon,* a book of spells that could supposedly summon demons.

There were also several children's movies, including *The Lion King* and *Aladdin.*

CHAPTER 20

Twisted sex

"He hated it here," his mother, Sondra Gibson said of Rod in Kentucky. "When the family visited Daytona Beach in Florida, he fit right in."[1]

Ferrell stood out in conservative, small town Murray, with his long hair and black outfits. Gibson wasn't keen on the idea of moving back to Kentucky either, but with her history of broken relationships with men she had to rely on the financial support of her hard-working blue-collar parents.

She quit school when she was sixteen and went to work at a McDonald's. She became pregnant when she was seventeen in 1980. She and Rick Ferrell got married, but they separated three weeks later. They were granted a divorce the following year. He was ordered to pay $100 per month in child support, according to Calloway County records.

For a time, Rick was a regular figure in Rod's life, and the two liked to play Dungeons and Dragons. He said he eventually quit coming around because Sondra made it too difficult.

Harrell Gibson transported cars long distance. Rosetta worked in food service at Murray State University. When her 85-year-old mother needed her close by, the family pulled up stakes in Florida and moved back home.

With her gray hair up in a bun and a closet full of old-fashioned dresses, Rosetta even looked the part of the doting grandmother. She was Rod's strongest supporter.

Things started spinning out of control, however, when Sondra and Rod moved into an apartment and darkness started taking over their lives.

The two dressed in black, and neighbors thought they were boyfriend-girlfriend, when they saw them walking while holding hands. When they moved out, the landlord found a pentagram emblazoned on the floor.

Things took a turn for the worst when she got caught writing what Kentucky prosecutors called "lurid" letters to a 14-year-old boy who had moved away, trying to get him to cross over to become a vampire while having sex with her.

"While you were away before, I dreamed every night of your return. I longed to be near you, for your embrace. Yes…to become a vampire, a part of the family, immortal and truly yours forever. I only hope that one day you will once again return to Murray. You will then come for me and cross me over," she said, describing in explicit detail certain sex acts and blood-drinking she envisioned. "And I will be your bride for eternity and you my sire."[2]

Charged with misdemeanors and facing possible felony charges, authorities ordered Gibson to get a psychiatric evaluation.

"About two years ago, her then-15-year-old son became involved with some older teenagers, who she says engaged in satanic rituals," Robert B. Sivley, Ph.D., noted in his Sept. 9, 1997 report.[3]

"Her son and the others were on drugs heavily, did not attend school, and began to gather frequently at her house, and she could not control her son or the other teenagers. They were abusive to her, and she says the leader of the group, Steven, raped her repeatedly in these ritual sessions and told her that she would have to get with one of the men in the group to 'cross over,' which apparently meant engaging in sex and mutually drinking each other's blood in order to become vampires. The group was heavily involved with drugs and Satanic rituals that included group sex..."

Gibson denied using drugs voluntarily, but claimed she was drugged several times "during the worship sessions," the report said.

Gibson also said she was stalked by demons.

"Sometimes she hears fingers tap on her upstairs window and something in a gray robe swooped through her room."

Gibson told the counselor she was afraid to tell anyone about being the victim of the alleged sexual abuse because she thought several prominent people in the community were involved with the cult. She also claimed that she felt pressured by the group to cross over the 14-year-old, though she thought he was 18.

She said she was born and raised in Florida, but that she moved to Murray with her parents when she was 15 (a later report by a Florida expert listed her birthplace as Mississippi).

"She states that her childhood was unhappy because both of her parents, particularly her father, were very strict. They were members of the Baptist church, became members of the Pentecostal faith, and she describes them [her parents] as "mentally and emotionally abusive...

She said her father would yell at her but not hit her. "The mother was passive and would go along with the father."

She said she smoked pot and drank after moving to Kentucky, even though it upset her parents.

The psychologist described her in his report as a "small, slender, neatly groomed mother who appears about her stated age (35)." She has no history of psychiatric hospitalization, he noted.

"This is a woman of low average intelligence who has no history of treatment for mental illness and who gives no indication of mental disorder at the present time. She is worried about her legal status and that of her son, but these are appropriate concerns."

Gibson's court-appointed lawyer argued the mailed letters to the boy were "free speech protected by the U.S. and Kentucky constitutions."

"I don't think that will fly," the prosecutor said. He was right.[4]

In January of 1998, the Murray *Ledger* newspaper reported that Gibson pleaded guilty but mentally ill to a charge of first-degree criminal attempt to commit an unlawful transaction with a minor in return for a sentence of five years' probation.

The boy's mother, Penny Murphy, who discovered the letters and turned them over to police, was furious about Gibson's attempt to seduce her son. "In the letter, she acknowledges that she knows he is 'very young,'" she said in a Sept. 17, 1996 affidavit to authorities.[5]

"It's been said that I misunderstood the letters. There's no way to misunderstand what's written word for word, exactly what you want to do to someone, or want them to do to you," she wrote in a letter to the *Sentinel*.

"She gives an excellent performance when she knows she's being watched. For those who know Sondra for Sondra, we know the truth. God help those who do not."

CHAPTER 21

"Nothing to do with vampires"

Law enforcement and the attorneys tried to deflect a storm of international publicity as the date approached for the grand jury, on Monday, Dec. 16.

"I'm a little concerned that people are more interested in a supposed vampire cult than a double homicide," said sheriff's spokesman Sgt. Cecil Garrett. "We're not doing any press releases. "We're out of the business."[1]

Calls were coming in from tabloid TV shows and U.S., British, and German networks.

NBC News ran an erroneous report about the teens drinking the blood of the slain couple. The sheriff's office quickly denounced it as false.

The Public Defender's Office put out a press release on Friday urging reporters to refer to the crime as the "WENDORF CASE."

"This case has nothing to do with 'vampires,'" the statement read.

"People should calm down and let the grand jury make its decision," said prosecutor Gross.

Grand jury proceedings are secret, behind-closed-door sessions in which the prosecutor presents enough evidence to see if the defendants can be charged and the case continue to trial. It is a one-sided affair. Defense attorneys are allowed to watch the jury selection, but that's usually about it. Even the judge, who swears the panel in and takes their final report, is absent from the proceedings. No one can be charged with first-degree murder without the grand jury's say-so.

Florida law, at that time, allowed 16-year-olds to be sentenced to death. That was a deal-breaker for one woman during grand jury selection, who sobbed at the thought of sending a teen to the electric chair. "I can't!"[2]

Once the panel was picked and the doors closed, prosecutors called a string of witnesses, including evidence technicians, Jennifer Wendorf, Hueber, and Yohe.

Yohe, who wore jeans, sneakers, and a sweater, turned and smiled when someone called her name in the hall. Relieved when her part was over, she bounced on the balls of her feet while walking rapidly, and practically skipped out of the courthouse.

Jennifer "held up fairly well," King said.

Neither Gussler nor Longo were called to testify. It is very unusual not to call the lead investigator, and it would cause a rift between State Attorney Brad King and Sheriff George Knupp.

The next day, after only an hour-and-a-half deliberation, the panel indicted all but Heather.

Ferrell was charged with first-degree murder and other charges. Anderson, Keesee and Cooper were charged with being principals to murder in the first degree, and principals to armed robbery and armed burglary. A principal is someone who "aided, abetted, and assisted" the main suspect. There is "no legal distinction" between being charged with first-degree murder or being charged as a principal.

"I'm mad as a hornet," Knupp said of the panel not indicting Heather and not calling his investigators to testify.[3]

Heather's attorney, James Hope, described the process as a "holding pattern." He had urged the grand jury to go slow. King said it was not a "snag."

Within hours, all of the teens, except Heather, were moved from the juvenile detention center to the Lake County jail.

Ferrell's attorney, Assistant Public Defender Candace Hawthorne, said she would quickly file a not-guilty plea and ask for copies of all discovery.

With the exception of Heather not being indicted, Hawthorne was not surprised. She knew it would be a year or longer before the case went to the trial.

She had no clue, however, that her client was about to blow up her "nothing-to-do-with-vampires" press release.

CHAPTER 22

"Interview with the vampire"

Sometimes a reporter is scooped by his own team.

The note, dated Dec. 18, read: "Dear Mr. Ferrell: I am the court reporter for the Lake County bureau of the *Orlando Sentinel*, and have been reporting on some of the developments in your case. Unfortunately, much of the information we receive comes from only one source: the police. There is, however, always more than one side to the story, and I would like to meet with you to hear your version of events. Please feel free to call at any time. Jail inmates are allowed only to call collect, so please call the *Lake Sentinel* at... Ask for me, if I'm not at my desk, leave a message. I'll get back to you as soon as possible. Sincerely, Frank Stanfield."

I took the note to the Lake County jail, dropped it off, and went back to the office to wait and see if he would call. I waited and waited, then went home for the evening. Then, he called.

As County Editor Lauren Ritchie later explained, red-faced and with trepidation, she decided not to take the chance of him changing his mind, so she immediately had reporters Jerry Fallstrom and Lesley Clark take the collect phone call from the jail.

The next day's lead front-page *Orlando Sentinel* headline read, "Interview with the 'Vampire," and it landed in all editions like a bombshell on front doorsteps across Central Florida.

The subhead read: "Ferrell blames Eustis slaying on rival cult."

"I know they did it," Ferrell said of alleged rivals.[1]

Then, he said something equally strange. He claimed he had multiple personalities and "special blackout moments." He said his personalities switched when he got stressed out.

"Right now, I'm totally mellowed out," he said. "Mentally, I have no clue as to what's going on."

He claimed that a psychiatrist told him he "counted at least 10" different personalities.

Psychiatrists I later interviewed said dissociative disorder is so rare some mental health experts don't even believe it exists.

Dr. John Hogin, with Shands Hospital of the University of Florida, figured that only about .01 percent of the population has it.

"I've been practicing since 1977 and have only treated two patients with it—that's how rare it is," he said.[2]

Dr. Eddie Roce, with the University of Miami Jackson Memorial Medical Center, would not even hazard a guess at a number. "It goes up and down. It's like a fad," he said.

Like Dr. Hogin, he had only seen two cases in 20 years.

It is in the same category as amnesia, and it is brought on by severe childhood abuse or trauma. Patients try to break down events into manageable parts in their mind, and in the process, their personality becomes fragmented.

"It's almost like *Sybil*, Ferrell said of the book and movie based on the life of a woman who claimed to have multiple personalities.

It is so unusual it does not even show up in psychological tests, Roce said. It is more useful to analyze a patient's history.

Famed FBI profiler John Douglas figured that there was another reason it is so rare.

"It seems the only time you really hear about multiple personality disorder is after someone goes on trial for murder,"[3]

***

Six years later, I found myself covering a case involving a 41-year-old woman who had been diagnosed with 12 different personalities. She was not on trial; she was the alleged victim. She claimed that her psychotherapist took advantage of one of her personalities, a sixteen-year-old sex-crazed girl named Bridgett.

She described going in and out of the different personalities as "losing time."[4]

She said she "comes to herself" when she returns to her normal personality, often with no memory of what had occurred.

She lost time twice during her testimony. Once, she was answering a defense attorney's questions when she suddenly started talking seductively. "How do *you* do?" she asked.

"Who am I talking to?" the attorney asked. She suddenly snapped out of it.

In the end, the jury acquitted the doctor, but the state yanked the doctor's practice privileges.

***

Ferrell's claim about being set up by a rival clan referred to his old friend and vampire mentor, Jaden Murphy, the older brother of the boy Sondra tried to seduce.

"He was getting back at me for defying him," Ferrell said. "He was trying to get me to do "totally immoral" things, like killing animals."

"It's humorous. Rod's a delusional little kid," Murphy said.[5]

Sgt. Mike Jump with the Murray Police Department called the rival clan idea "pretty far-fetched." Murphy and his friends did not even have the means to go to Florida, he said.

King told Jaden that he needed to have an alibi anyway.

"How in the world is someone going to remember me from a couple of months ago being at a certain place at a certain time?" said Murphy, who said he had been hanging out at Hardee's the night of the murders.

There seemed to be no end to Ferrell's outrageous claims in in the *Sentinel* interview.

Ferrell denied ever entering the Wendorfs' home, despite admitting it to police. "We just went to pick up Heather."

He said Anderson told Keesee and Cooper to take Heather to see her boyfriend.

The car took off, leaving Anderson and Ferrell by the side of the road. He said Anderson borrowed his combat boots and walked down the road while he rested under a tree.

"I was just about to doze off when Scott pulled up in the Explorer. He honked and said, "Get in.""

He said Anderson assured him the couple was safe, and Ferrell, who called him "my best friend," believed him. "I don't think he is capable of killing anyone more than I am."

The story itself is a preposterous lie, an obvious effort to pin the blame on Anderson. But beyond that, did he think reporters wouldn't eventually be able to get their hands on his confession? Or at least ask investigators what he said? Did he think that investigators would suddenly buy his new story?

Jaden had called Ferrell "delusional," but there is no evidence to suggest that Ferrell was believing his own wild story. He did, however, enjoy telling stories, and probably enjoyed the mistaken idea that he was fooling reporters. The notion of publicity backfire apparently either never entered his head, or he was so confident in his ability to lie that he figured he could pull it off.

Ferrell also claimed his vampire days started when he accidentally cut his finger in a ninth-grade biology class at Eustis High. He reflexively stuck his finger in his mouth and classmates said, "He's a vampire."

The movie, *Interview with the Vampire*, was playing in theaters at the time, Ferrell said.

He claimed that he tried to ditch the vampire scene when he moved back to Murray, but his black trench coat and his growing interest in the Vampire: The Masquerade game had created a new identity.

Ferrell did clear up a couple of things in the interview. The bloody sheet found in the back of the Explorer was from his cut thumb, he said.

He was also aware of the press coverage, and he pointed out one consistent error. He and Heather never dated, he said. Letters that investigators found in her room were addressed to Jeanine. Heather was merely keeping them at her house because Jeanine's parents disapproved of him.

Reaction to the multiple personality claim was swift.

"It's the first time anybody connected with the case has heard that story," King said.[6]

"Based on what my investigators are telling me, I put no stock in it whatsoever," Knupp said.

"I don't care which personality we have in jail," Gross joked.

Hawthorne was outraged that the paper interviewed her client. "He is a disturbed child," she told me.

Hawthorne is a formidable woman. She fights hard for all of her clients, but Ferrell brought out her maternal instincts. One *Sentinel* photo captured an awkward moment when she smiled and touched his long hair during a hearing. She vowed half-seriously not to smile in court again.

She worried that Ferrell's interview and other publicity would jeopardize his chance of getting a fair trial. Change of venue is a legal remedy, but it is up to the trial judge.

In the meantime, she filed a motion demanding that any law enforcement interviews only be conducted in the presence of his legal team, and she left word at the jail not to let any reporters get near her client.

She then sent subpoenas to me, Fallstrom, Clark, the editor, and to the newspaper itself demanding all records, notes, and other materials and asking that depositions be taken. That was worrisome. Not only do newspapers have to fight subpoenas to protect their right to publish unfettered, but as editor Ritchie told me, "You can't cover the story if you're part of it."

I would have to be patient and have faith in the newspaper's legal eagles. In the meantime, I still had a job to do.

CHAPTER 23

"Prince of the City"

Ferrell's claim of a rival cult framing him for murder conjures up images from a vampire novel or an episode of *Buffy The Vampire Slayer*. In reality, it was Ferrell who betrayed a sacred vampire trust, because Murphy had crossed him over and was his "sire."

Murphy, who changed his last name and added "Jaden" from a character in a *Star Trek* episode, told Public Defender Investigator David Norris that he first noticed Ferrell shortly before Christmas 1995.

"He wore black, he...liked solitude, he was very recluse (sic) as opposed to everybody else in the school, and that attracted me to him."[1]

Murphy also wore black. "Half the students knew me or feared me 'just because I wore black'... If you wear black people tend to leave you alone because they think you're into some kind of evil shit or something like that," he said.

"People were constantly trying to get me and him (sic) to fight. We didn't even talk to each other. I was always stereotyped as a vampire or a Satanist cultist...and finally, I just said to hell with it, and went up to him and introduced myself and we became friends after that."

They shared an interest in the occult. "At one time I did practice witchcraft," Jaden said. "He told me about things he used to do, and that he used to be in demonology... It's the conjuration of demons. The studying of demons to do your bidding and stuff like that."

Ferrell's obsession with vampirism started out with role-playing in the popular Masquerade of the Vampires game, Jaden said. "I think Rod got lost in a fantasy world."

Some of the game enthusiasts were students at Murray State. Others would come from as far away as Nashville, including some who were in their 30s. They would hold events like Dragoncon, and as many as 500 might show up to play the game.

There were strict rules. "You couldn't touch another person to cause physical harm, you couldn't bring weapons," Jaden said.

Ferrell's first experience with a vampiric cult, which occurred in Florida, was not pleasant. The group labeled him as "valueless," Jaden said. "... in vampiric terms, that means food, because they were just constantly feeding off him."

Norris asked Jaden about his level of interest in vampirism, but the 18-year-old was cagey, saying it was limited to the game, which he called "improvisational acting."

Twenty-two years later, he said: "I was introduced into the path of vampirism when I was 16 years of age. To me, it reflected my soul, because the nighttime called to me and conveyed the power to me in human blood. This literally would send chills through my entire body because I finally found my spiritual haven."[2]

Jaden adhered to strict vampirism rules, like those in Masquerade. Ferrell did not, and he showed his disdain for living creatures when a stray cat walked up to him one night.

"We were walking and talking about normal, everyday [expletive], and he picked it up and was petting it, and I started petting it. And then I took a couple of steps back and I was sitting there talking to him and he's still petting the cat, and he goes, 'Look kitty, a tree.'

"And then he just threw it. Smacked it right into a tree."
Jaden was aghast. Ferrell laughed.

"This is not funny, man. Dude, what's your problem?"

"It's you, you and your holier than thou attitude that you've got," Ferrell replied.

A Lake County sheriff's deputy got a chilling insight into Ferrell's cruelty before he moved back to Kentucky.

Christie Mysinger had met Ferrell while patrolling in Eustis. One day, she was driving by his house when he stepped out onto the front porch with two samurai swords.

"He was telling me how he knew how to use the swords and how sharp they were, and then he made the comment, "You don't see any cats around here, do you?"

***

It wasn't long after they met that Murphy crossed Ferrell over to become a vampire, becoming his "sire," or leader.

"I had Rod meet me at a tombstone we called the birthplace, and we began the ritual. We just used regular razor blades. We cut the upper arm… After we cut ourselves, he would feed from me first, until his heart's content, or until the bleeding stops, and I would do the same as well. Giving blood as a gift is one of the most precious gifts you can give to someone. It's a total commitment and there's no turning back…"

Anderson immediately noticed a key difference between Ferrell and Jaden.

"When I started getting into it and learning from Rod and learning from Jaden, they both had two totally different aspects to blood drinking. Jaden's belief was you only take as much as you need to survive. Rod would take it as far as he needed to take it. He believed in that drinking the blood and taking a life, he gained life. I thought, 'This dude actually has the capability of killing somebody.'"

"There had to be some kind of change in him to cross over from thinking about killing someone to literally removing life from this realm," Jaden said.

"Everything I'd been studying before, it was darkness, it was nighttime, and it wasn't evil," Jaden said. It's just like anything can be turned into something bad. It's all in your intent and that was not my intent. That was what I was also shown. That was not what I showed Rod." He said he and Rod had started hanging out in cemeteries, "because for one thing we sure as hell wouldn't go up on the court square where a bunch of rednecks hang out. And every other place was getting boring. We didn't want to be bothered by people, so we'd go to the cemetery and sit there, because, well, nobody's going to bother you there."[3]

Ferrell sometimes placed a guitar pick or a psychedelic mushroom on top of a headstone. He was especially drawn to the black headstone of a seventeen-year-old fellow classmate at Calloway High School. The youth died in an automobile accident trying to hurry to see a friend who had been shot in Tennessee. The gunshot victim also died.

Jaden told Norris that he missed the Rod Ferrell he first knew.

"...he had problems at home. He had family problems. His mom and him always constantly fighting. ...he wanted to kill his mom."

Sondra had a problem with Jaden.

"She'd accuse me of controlling Rod, and I was like, 'Nobody controls Rod. Rod does what the hell he wants to do.' And that was the truth," he said.

"She just had this thing against me for some reason. She accused me of casting a spell over her and sodomizing her one night."

Norris asked if it was true.

"[Expletive] no that ain't true! God bless."

And then, there was her attempt to seduce his 14-year-old brother while crossing him over to become a vampire.

"She was constantly telling me stuff about him. About how he was just the sexiest man in Murray. She's 20 years older than him!"

It was probably one of the reasons he moved out of state, he said.

Jaden didn't know if she was ever interested in demonology.

"I know she was married to a satanic cultist. Just got a divorce from him. That's what she told me."

"I don't know if she was a practitioner or anything, she's constantly going to psychics and getting tarot card readings from friends and stuff like that. They were saying that all the arrows were pointing to my brother, that they were together in a former life and all kinds of whacked out [expletive] like that.

"I blame everything that happened on her. The way he was raised. Because she was constantly telling him that he had a younger brother, and he killed him. He smothered, suffocated him with a pillow."

Jaden talked to Sondra's sister on the phone, and she said that Sondra never had another child.

Tension that had been building between Ferrell and Jaden finally exploded one night.

In an Aug. 28, 1996 affidavit for a restraining order, Ferrell said Murphy accused him of having some role in another teen "messing with his girlfriend."

Ferrell said he didn't answer, and Jaden grabbed him by the throat, slammed his head against a brick wall, and said, "Don't lie to me!"

"As I was walking back upstairs, he said, 'Now you know I'm superior and you're under me.'"

Jaden told the *Sentinel* the fight started when Ferrell "started getting cocky with me."[4]

Ferrell had made death threats to his fiancée, Ashley.

Ferrell said it would be "real funny to come in and find her guts strung up in his apartment," said Jaden's mother, Penny Murphy.

"He would go to the school and sit there, outside the school, even though he was kicked out. He'd sit over at the Expo Center and sit and stare at her and watch her. Every day he would do this. At least a month," Jaden said.

"He liked scaring the hell out of people," Penny said.

Sondra Gibson told reporters that Jaden pushed Rod and said, "Now you know who's the prince of the city."

The prince is a character in the Masquerade game. If the prince is challenged, he must battle the challenger "until sovereignty is determined."

Authorities speculated that the two clashed because Ferrell was forming his own cult. Murphy told reporters that Ferrell was lying when he claimed that he had asked him to recruit vampires in Florida.

"He just wanted to control people. That's what he's done," Penny said.[5]

"This is a boy that wants to make everybody believe that he's not all there in the head. And he's very intelligent. He's very smart, he's smart, he's very articulate. He knows exactly what he's doing now," she said.

"He wanted people to surround him and worship him. He found power in that," Jaden said.[6]

He said he could see how Rod and Heather were drawn together. "We all have a dark personality," Murphy said, and that personality is "gothic."

"We don't fit in with society whatsoever. We're considered what you call freaks, it is what we're labeled as by everybody because of our views. Of society and stuff like that. And we don't try to get in with everybody because we believe in individuality."[7]

CHAPTER 24

"Nine-foot demon"

Trouble was brewing two weeks before the murders, and it spilled out into a bizarre incident.

April Doeden was entertaining seven friends at her mobile home when Ferrell and two other uninvited teens pulled up in a Ford Escort at around 10 p.m.

A juvenile named Michael got out of the car and walked up to the front steps where Jaden was talking to a girl.

He asked Jaden to get a man named Joey to come outside.

Jaden got up and went inside, but he headed straight to a phone so he could call the Calloway County Sheriff's Office. He was under a restraining order to stay away from Ferrell, and he wanted no trouble with the law.

Doeden and Ferrell had lived together for a time before he became obsessed with Keesee, and they had considered themselves to be engaged.

Like Murphy and Ferrell, Doeden also shared an interest in the occult, but she called herself a "fairy," and built an altar to nature with flowers, not skulls.

"Rod said he heard Joey and I were looking for him, although we had not been asking about him," she wrote in a Nov. 5, 1996 sheriff's report.

"Mr. Ferrell told residents that he was a nine-foot demon and he wanted someone to kill him to free him of his worldly existence and make him more powerful," the deputy wrote. "I found that this had occurred on previous occasions."[1]

Ferrell told Joey, "Well, if you don't kill me, I'll take her with me,'" Doeden said.[2]

"And I looked at him, and I said, 'You can't take me anywhere I don't want to go to.'

"He says, 'I can take you, and you know that, and you know, I'm not afraid of him.' And I started laughing, and he just looked at me all crazy, and we all started laughing and he got in the car to leave.

"I went behind the car when they were pulling out to see the license plate number... And Rod said, 'Back up,' and they threw the car in reverse and he tried to hit me. And I jumped out of the way, they ran over my foot..."

Doeden, who ended up on crutches, decided to press charges. Deputies arrested the driver, "but they left Rod alone. They kept leaving Rod alone, and if they had just arrested him in the first place, he'd never went (sic) to Florida, and he'd be fine," she said.

It was a strange thing for her to say. Before this incident, Doeden told Murphy that Ferrell threatened to kill her son. Murphy had heard a rumor that Ferrell was going to "sacrifice" her child.

"He had several people on his list to gain power, I guess. He wanted to try to control their souls or something to that effect," Murphy said.[3]

Murphy said he was on the hit list, so he was laying low at his mother's house. He said there was another teen at the high school that Ferrell also wanted to kill.

"Rod wanted to be immortal. He couldn't find immortality physically, so he got it another way. And then again, he also wanted to die," Murphy said.

"...he feels that this [expletive] world is his prison, and he wanted his soul to be released so he could become what they call a plane walker."

"Plane walking is throughout religion since the beginning of time," Murphy said. "When you dream, that's a different plane. You know, a different plane of thought, a different level. There's just other levels when you can go into other people's dreams and stuff like that."

Ferrell's defense team wanted to know if murder elevated a vampire's status. It is just the opposite, Doeden said.

"You become a murderer, and you get outcast. There are family rules. You never take a life. You never take blood unwillingly. You never embarrass anybody. And you never, never disgrace your family. Or turn on your family."[4]

Rod turned on his family, she said. "And you never talk to anybody about it. About being a vampire, you keep it low key."

Doeden said she had been angry with Ferrell "many times."

"…he'd get some stupid idea in his head, his hare-brained idea, he'd run off and get himself in trouble, and I worried about him. I was angry with him for getting me run over with a car. And I was angry with him for…Shea and threatening to kill me and my unborn child. And I'm angry with him for killing people. That is not a cool thing. This is a bad thing. You don't take another human's life. You just don't do it."

CHAPTER 25

Destroying minds

Seeing Matt Goodman for the first time was like having a favorite pine tree in a national forest. If you turned your head, you wouldn't be able to pick him out again.

He was as normal looking—right down to his work boots—as Ferrell was flamboyant.

Yet, he had a highly unusual way of thinking, and he had a story to tell David Norris, the public defender's investigator.

Goodman and Ferrell spent countless hours inventing role-playing games.

"Rod was a very good player," Goodman said. "He liked playing some of the vampire characters..." He especially liked playing one character, who did not care who he killed or how he behaved.[1]

Ferrell and Goodman's friendship went all the way back to the second grade. Goodman was repeating the grade, he said, because he had been traumatized and depressed the year before.

"They would put me in detention for the whole year...."

Teachers forced him to sit in a darkened, black box in the back of the classroom. It was depressing, but he said it had an unexpected benefit for his poor eyesight.

"I could see things that normal people wouldn't see at night because of the handicap of this eye. It strengthened the other one. Too much light gives me blinding headaches. I could see motion and gained night vision.

"And that's when I decided, as I was pretty much in darkness all my life, that I'd make a game of the ultimate creature of darkness, which would be a vampire. The ultimate evil. And that's when I started learning about games. And how you can play against a human being. And destroy their mind. You know, like a psychologist. You can do many things with darkness. ...all I wanted was for revenge for what they stuck me in that box for."

He isn't sure if teachers ever put Ferrell in a box, but he thinks it is possible.

The use of isolation boxes is controversial. A 2018 article in *Pacific Standard* magazine stated that 75 percent of the students secluded or restrained were children with disabilities.[2]

A newspaper in Great Britain reported in 2017 that "45 schools in England excluded at least 20 percent of their pupils in the last academic year."[3]

Like Ferrell, Goodman would also eventually become a high school dropout.

Months before the murders, Rod let Goodman in on a secret. "My goal is mind control. If people are in fear, they are easy to control."[4]

Goodman said Ferrell would pore over books on psychology and black magic.

Ferrell tried one technique on Goodman by walking around in a circle and repeating one phrase: "Your mother and father are not your mother and father."

Ferrell also said he was going to get Anderson in trouble, but he did not say how or why. Ferrell considered Anderson to have a weak mind because his father was an alcoholic and his family was poor, Goodman said. "Rod used his mind games to pretty much take power of him. Fear is what he feeds off of. If Rod said something and he didn't do it, he would threaten him."

Goodman said he tried to warn Scott and his mother.

"I said if he ends up getting hurt or getting in trouble, don't come whining to me, because I warned you. Because I know Rod. If he's going to start what he thinks he is, what he really thinks he is, I said he is going to finish this… He was going to bring down an army. That, as soon as he made his army of darkness, he was going to bring them down with him. "

Goodman described what sounds like classic brainwashing.

"You can just keep lying and keep deceiving and keep spreading rumors until you've completely destroyed their mind. You know, they have no self-confidence at all…"

Ferrell was able to create an us-against-the-world mentality, Goodman said. Ferrell would say, "the only friend you've got in this world is me, and I've been trying to protect you,' when actually he would be more or less betraying them."

Norris had one burning question: Did Ferrell really believe he was a vampire?

"He did get to the point where he felt he was a vampire," he said.

It played a role in Ferrell's animal cruelty.

"I had seen him abuse animals before…. So, I figured, you know, because partially in devil worshipping and sometimes a vampire will also feed off an animal pretty much to gain nourishment. You know, because being as the vampire is undead, only the blood of the living can re-heal them. In other words, they age. You know, they grow very weak…. And when they feed off the blood of the living it more or less restores their youth."

He said Ferrell also believed that if you sucked the blood of an animal, you would gain their ability to hunt and to do other things.

Rod had very specific ideas about setting up his vampire "family." Jeanine was to be his "queen." Goodman was to be his right-hand man and he was to be coupled with Heather. Goodman said he wrote letters to Heather because Rod wanted her to be his "dark mate."

"Rod traveled in twos. You know, a male and female, king and queen, that's the way he wanted it to be."

The girls were supposed to recruit new members in Florida until the cult could return on their first leg of its journey to New Orleans and Europe. The plan was for the family to eventually live in a castle. "Somewhere, some castle he was talking about in England, I don't remember exactly what it was, some ancient vampire's castle."

When Heather carelessly suggested one day that Goodman should be the cult leader, Ferrell kicked him in the teeth while sparring.

It loosened four of his top teeth, which were in an orthodontic brace. He went to a tool shed and got some vise grip pliers and tried to straighten them. He said he was very angry about it and told Ferrell he wanted to settle it "one-on-one."

Rod left, came back a couple of months later, and apologized. Then, out of the corner of his eye, Goodman saw Ferrell roll his eyes, so he knew he didn't mean it.

Goodman said Ferrell later kicked another boy in the mouth because he went out with Charity one night, but Charity had asked him out.

Norris asked how Dana got involved with the group.

"I don't know. I'm thinking maybe Rod may have threatened her. I'm not exactly sure, because Rod doesn't have no humanity. He's completely remorseless. He's completely destroyed all of his emotions. There's no emotion in him except for hate and vengeance. That's (sic) the only two he's got. There's no love, no pain. He doesn't feel pain that often. He might feel a little bit of fear. I know one thing; he'd rather die by the sword than die by a bullet.

Even though he thought himself immortal, "he wouldn't step up to a gun," he said.

"All he wants to do is destroy you. That's the main thing. And multiple personality? He doesn't possess that. No multiple personality.

"He wants to die. He thinks that he'll have a throne under Satan. He thought he's the third antichrist, or the very final one. I've heard him talk about it many times."

Goodman told Norris the clan "had planned, for about seven months, to run away together."

Ferrell has a straightforward goal, Goodman said. "He wants to do anything and everything wrong," he said.

"When he looks at somebody "he's thinking how he can kill them. And what he can do with them. And how the ultimate punishment would be torture. Anything he can do to torture them. He likes thinking about stuff, morbid thoughts," he said.

"People called him a freak. When people started fearing him, he became more intelligent. He figured, 'I can destroy them by playing with their minds and turning their friends and their best friends against them, and if I [convert] them into this vampire clan, their mind will go to the complete dark side, you know, to evil and they will be thinking morbid thoughts and everything all the time, you know, death, and everything about it. And eventually when you do that, then you have no friends.'

"That's when I was hanging around him, the only friends I had was him and Scott Anderson."

"When I see Scott on the news, I've seen the way he looks. The way he was standing and the way his face was turned sideways, and I could tell that his eyes were dilated to a fixed position. And when I knew (sic) that, I knew that Rod had more than likely scared him into a zombie, so that way he'd do everything Rod said."

CHAPTER 26

"It wasn't supposed to go this far."

Heather glanced up at the window in her juvenile detention cell in Baton Rouge, but there was nothing to see but a black square. In the daytime, at least, she could look out and see a big maple tree.

Nighttime was the worst time, she said in a letter to Jennifer.

"The kids in the other cells bang on the doors constantly and they took away all the pictures and letters I kept from you, Jeanine, and Jeremy. Now, when I am so lonely at night, I have nothing to read and look at to remind me of you all. Maybe they'll give it all back to me."[1]

She worried about what people were thinking about her.

"I never got to see any papers or news shows about us at all, so I don't know what trash they're saying about us. Since I've been kept away from anyone, I have no idea what anyone is saying or thinking. You all probably think I'm crazy or something. How couldn't you with all this talk about vampires and such? I bet they're even trying to say that I'm some sort of devil worshipper. Well, I don't worship the devil, so I hope that eases you a little."

She said she wished she could tell her about everything that had happened, but her lawyer told her to keep quiet.

"I don't know how to express to you how sorry I am that all this has happened. It wasn't supposed to go this far. I was going to go and leave everything and everyone untouched. No one was going to be hurt. However, Rod wanted it another way, and he had it. I was so afraid to get away from him for fear he'd hurt or kill me as well. I can only hope you believe me and wish that you don't hate me for what has occurred. I already hate myself enough.

"I suppose you all are getting a lot of ridicule because of me. I bet all of the ones I love are. I wonder how Jeremy is handling all of this. If you ever get the time could you do me a favor? Call him up and tell him I am so terribly sorry for everything, and I don't know if he loves me anymore, but I still love him. If he loves me no more, then he won't ever have to worry about me ever again....

"It goes the same for you. If you love me no more, you shouldn't have to worry about me. But just remember I still love all of you.

"Of course, you can guess that I'm always thinking of Jeanine and how she is handling everything. She already had enough problems before any of this started."

She worried about upcoming court appearances and hoped there would be no news cameras. She said she had to bite her lip to keep from screaming at the photographers that gathered outside the police station.

"Ever since I got to this detention center all the people here have been calling me 'vampire girl' along with Shea. They knew everything about me before I even got here. I wish the media would just leave me alone. They can't even get the information right."

Back in Florida, on Dec. 9, 1996, she wrote to Jeanine from the Marion County Juvenile Detention Center. "I am just so glad that we didn't come to get you that night. I wouldn't want you to be in the same mess I am."[2]

She complained about being locked up in her cell all day, "but it does give me a lot of thinking time."

She said she was worried about her case, the news media, and "that I might never again get to see you or my family. And I miss all the ones I have lost because of my naivete and troublesome actions. And every night I cry myself to sleep wishing I had only stayed at home. I know that a lot of people are praying for me and I appreciate all of it. The only thing it can do is help, but I don't see how things are going to get better at this point."

She asked Jeanine to write and promised that "if I ever get out of this, I'll be sure to accompany you to the very next Happenings," referring to Jeanine's church youth group.

On a separate piece of paper, she traced her hand and wrote: Whenever you miss me just hold onto my hand and remember me."

Heather wrote to Jeanine again, on Dec. 15. "Unfortunately, I haven't received any letters from *anyone* (her emphasis) which extremely depresses me. So, I'm still in the dark as to whether Jeremy, you, or any of my family hates me or not."[3]

She also complained that she had not received any visitors, though she did receive a phone call from her stepsister, "Sam," in Texas.

"That lasted for about five minutes. And afterword I went back to my cell crying.

First of all, the call was a very hard thing for me considering she is the *first* (her emphasis) family member I've spoken too since I've been gone. Also, it didn't help that where I was talking was right in front of the cell where Rod was being kept. Not only could I see but also feel his cold and evil stare as he watched me the entire time."

Heather also shared what would be normal teen gossip in the outside world, but with a pinch of pixie dust.

"Some strange things have been going on. Do you remember how Rod was going out with Shea? Well, obviously they are history."

She then went on to explain that Scott had asked Rod to put a love spell on her. "Well, to say the least, I still feel nothing for him, just as before. But now Shea believes the spell did work but on her. This confuses me because I know, and she knows, that Scott and her (sic) will never be able to see each other, let alone have a relationship. Strange isn't it?"

It was obvious she was not as depressed as she had been in Baton Rouge.

"Now that I think about it I only have about nine or 10 days left until Christmas. The worst part is, I haven't done any of my shopping yet! Ha ha, just a little joke to put a smile on your face."

Her last letter from detention, dated Jan. 7, 1997, was even more upbeat. She had some news. Jeremy had written to her.

"He still loves me! Now and forever he says."[4]

She was even allowed to do some artwork, by creating a poster for Juvenile Department of Justice. "I know it's a little cheesy but hey, I get to draw it out and I get to paint! Wa-hoo!"

Living conditions had improved overall. "No bread and water but a lot of milk and a snack at 8 p.m. We have nap time like in kindergarten." She said they also gave them books and magazines to read. One book that she was reading was *Schrodinger's Cat,* "which is about quantum physics and quantum mechanics. I was supposed to start chemistry honors anyway and I figure this is close enough."

She said she was trying to make the best of the situation.

"I always have new songs popping into my head and when I go to sleep thinking about them, I dream in MTV. Yeah, I have music videos for dreams sometimes. It's really neat 'cause I don't get to listen to any music here. Here's one:

Angel mine, my left side
she watches me as I do my time.

Angel mine my right side
he does the same to ease my mind.

Bye and bye I go through.
Time and time again it's true.
In my mind and all I do,
again, again I see both of you."

She also said that she was reading the Bible.

"I realized something. My mother's full name was Naomi Ruth Adams Wendorf and she was named after the two people in the Book of Ruth. Naomi means sweet in Hebrew. Cool, huh? In your letters it's okay to talk about my parents and family. Even though I'll never forget them. When I hear people telling me about them, I love to remember them. When I hear others speak of them, I know they will forever live in the hearts and memories of the people whose lives they touched.

"My mom was always doing something for someone else. If it was volunteering at the high school, sewing me some new clothes, or knitting me an afghan to keep me warm at night. My dad was always a softy at heart even when he had a long day working hard for his family. Always the father figure but still had the spirit of a young person such as ourselves."

She mentioned that it was Sunday and could hear a Christian hymn. She said she usually went to the church service but was locked in her room for telling another inmate about her "situation."

She said the girl was sympathetic, and even offered to give her a place to stay when she got out. She said her sister Sam offered to let her live with her in Texas, but it was too far from Jennifer and all her friends.

Her letter skipped around. At one point she returned to the Bible. "Sometimes I feel like Ecclesiastes 1:1. Look it up."

The verse in the NIV translation reads: "The words of the Teacher, son of David, king in Jerusalem...." Apparently, she was actually referring to the second verse: "Meaningless! Meaningless! says the Teacher. Utter meaningless! Everything is meaningless!"[5]

She apparently had not read the final two verses, 12:13-14, where Solomon wrote about the true meaning of life, as he saw it: "Now all has been heard; here is the conclusion of the matter; Fear God and keep his commandments, for this is the duty of all mankind. For God will bring every deed into judgment, including every hidden thing, whether it is good or evil."[6]

"Sometimes I do want to be Christian," she wrote, "but the times I don't I can't ask God about it. I'm too alone. I can't do it by myself. I don't know how. So, I'll wait."

CHAPTER 27

"No more chains"

James Hope is a short, solid man with a broad, impish grin. An ex-prosecutor, he is both experienced and smart. As a former magician, he has an engaging, entertaining way

with jurors and a sense of the dramatic. He might, for example, hold his index finger up to his

lips while shredding the credibility of a witness and say, "Isn't that interesting?"

He once generously tried to teach me how to juggle, a hoped-for skill that was on my bucket list until I found out that I couldn't juggle a single ice cube in an empty glass.

In 1997, he came to the defense of a career game warden who had been charged with battering his wife. Her sister discovered her lying nude in bed with a broken collarbone and 80 percent of her body covered in bruises.

"I've seen dead people who haven't looked this bad," the assistant state attorney told me.[1]

The house was trashed, and food had been yanked out of the refrigerator and thrown on the floor.

Her husband said he locked himself in his bedroom while she went on a rampage and demanded unlimited access to pills. The next morning, he said he picked her up and put her to bed. He said he didn't know her collarbone was broken, only that she had red marks on her body where she had fallen.

She was taken to the hospital by a family member and interviewed by a sheriff's detective. She said she didn't know how she got injured.

"Is it possible someone did this to you?" the detective asked.[2]

The woman said she didn't know, and that the only person who had been around was her husband.

When she was asked to describe him, she said he was, "A very loving, kind person."[3]

"Does he have a mean side?"

"Not that I've ever seen."

She also said she didn't want her husband to lose his job and for her to end up as a "bag lady."

The problem was, she was bipolar, sometimes wildly out of control, and addicted to pills. Her sister conceded that she once fell asleep at dinner. Her husband said he tried having her hospitalized, but her doctor kept prescribing the pills that were destroying her ability to live like a normal person.

Prosecutors offered a plea deal: Take anger management classes and agree to probation. He refused, telling Hope he was willing to risk going to prison for five years rather than admit to a crime he did not commit.

"I've got to win," Hope told me.[4]

The man took the stand to testify in his own defense. Hope ripped into the detective, accusing her of taking advantage of "a mentally feeble and pitiful, drugged up woman."[5]

The jury deliberated for an hour-and-a-half, then came back with a not-guilty verdict.

The next day, the *Sentinel* carried a photo of the couple kissing in the courtroom. Two years later, she was dead of natural causes, possibly caused by the effects of the pills she took to try and control her mental illness.

Heather was clearly in trouble and in need of a good attorney, if not a rabbit pulled out of a hat.

A girl had called the crime tip line and told them that she saw Ferrell at Heather's house in October. She said she knew Heather and had been to her home.

"I knew some of her friends. I knew that she was in a vampire cult. I knew that in her past she thought she was a demon, and that she was in the tenth grade," she told detectives.[6]

"...I don't know how to explain it. She just really kept to herself unless she knew you. She looked really evil,"

She said Heather was always talking about how she couldn't stand her parents. On Nov. 16, she said she talked to Heather on the phone and she said, "...we're finally gonna do it."

She said she met Ferrell at Heather's house.

Heather wanted her to join them on their trip, she said, "but I didn't want to go. I didn't want to spend the rest of my life in jail. That's not what I want to do with my future."

The problem? It was all a lie. The girl didn't even know Heather.

It was a mess the investigators would clean up with further checking, but it was not the only problem.

Sondra Gibson told the *Sentinel* in November that Heather "was saying she was going to kill her parents for a long time."[7]

Jennifer didn't know what to think. She was hoping that Heather was telling the truth when she wrote to her from Baton Rouge blaming Ferrell.

"I want to believe that that's true because she's my little sister, and I love her to death. "Maybe she's just putting all the blame on Rod just so she...won't get in trouble. She could also just be saying this just to get my support, and it could all be a lie."[8]

Hope was undaunted. "I read the newspapers, too," he told me. "I think the grand jury is an excellent forum for a person who wants to tell the truth and does not fear the truth."[9]

The move is unusual and risky. Although Hope would be allowed to go into the room with his client, he was not allowed to present a case.

It only happens one-in-a-thousand cases, said Anthony Musto, chairman of the criminal law section of the Florida Bar. He added that while it was a risk, it was a calculated gamble.

"A lawyer knows what his client is going to say."

Heather's desire to leave home had less to do with problems at home than a desire for Mardi Gras excitement, Hope said.

He also talked about what he considered to be a key piece of evidence. She left a greeting card in the hall bathroom next to a small porcelain figure. It read: "To my dad, the best father any daughter ever had. Love, Heather." The base of the porcelain figure read: "Dad, Friends Forever."

Prosecutors would later release her handwritten note. "I don't have much time, but I must say that *I love you all so very much.* You must understand that I have to stay with Jeanine and she's leaving to search for her new-found religion. I have to watch out for her. Remember, I didn't leave because of anything other than that. Again, I say that I love you. I will be fine. Please don't try to find us."[10]

The headline in the *Sentinel* on Jan. 29 read: "Heather goes free." The subhead read: "Grand jury says witness made up story."

Heather was released to a family member, while her grandfather, James Wendorf, exclaimed: "She has no more handcuffs, no more chains! She's a free girl."[11]

Heather was "incredibly frightened" and sometimes broke down while testifying for more than two hours, Hope said.

Key to her release was the testimony of the teen who recanted her earlier statement that she had seen Ferrell at Heather's house. The girl's testimony at the first grand jury was "inconsistent" with the other four teens and with Heather's statement to police, the grand jury stated in its presentment.

The other reason for the grand jury's decision was a lack of trust in Sondra Gibson.

"Ferrell's mother, in her polygraph examination, stated that she had no recollection of the statements earlier attributed to Heather Wendorf. This being so, we deem her to be unreliable as a witness," the panel noted.[12]

"We recognize that we, as the Grand Jury, are the 'guardians of all that is comprehended in the police power of the State of Florida. We have as much an obligation to protect the innocent as to pursue those who may have violated the law. In this regard, we must find that there is NO LONGER PROBABLE CAUSE to believe that Heather Wendorf was a knowing participant in the terrible acts that occurred at her home.

"While she certainly acted inappropriately in planning to leave home, and arguably so in remaining with the others after learning what had been done, we acknowledge that these acts are not crimes. We also wish to unequivocally state that these actions were wrong.

"Heather Wendorf, her sister, and the families of both Richard and Naomi Ruth Queen, will live the rest of their lives with the consequences of Heather's choices of associates and activities. Nothing that anyone can say or do will change the loss they have suffered. We wish them God's mercy and grace in the recovery that must follow."

Hope said Heather would need time to "decompress."[13]

"She was orphaned by murder. For 60 days, the world thought she was a murderess."

She could not be located for a comment; she was freed from jail while the panel was writing up its conclusion.

The decision left many with a sense of "what now?" There was speculation that she might testify against the others.

Anderson's attorney, Michael Graves, was diplomatic— and grim. He said he was "looking forward to reading her statements."

James Wendorf said, "I never lost faith in her, and her grandmother and I are just overjoyed—we're just overjoyed. Our faith was proven true even in the face of these accusations."

Paula Queen, Ruth's daughter from a previous marriage, said, "It's great. We all knew that she was innocent. My family didn't have any doubts."

Ferrell's grandfather, Harrell Gibson, thought it showed the state didn't have much evidence against anyone. "I figure what's good for her is good for the rest of them."

David Keesee, father of Charity, had a much different take.

"That figures. That's American justice. That's all a lie," he said.

CHAPTER 28

What did Heather say?

The grand jury's decisions to free Heather had the defense attorneys scrambling. The first thing Hawthorne did was to ask for a transcript of the grand jury proceedings.

Grand juries operate behind closed doors to protect people who are accused but not charged by prosecutors. Brad King, who argued against the release of transcripts, called grand juries great "investigative tools." Witnesses are also protected. They can make statements knowing their comments will remain secret.[1]

In Florida, no one can be charged with first-degree murder unless they are indicted by a grand jury.

A judge can rule that the transcripts can be released, but only if there is reason to believe that someone has lied, and that the transcript can be used to impeach that person's testimony.

Hawthorne saw it as a "catch-22." How can anyone know if a person lied if the transcripts are kept secret?

"The accused's right to confrontation provided by the Constitution…outweighs the public interest in maintaining the secrecy of the testimony of a codefendant," she argued.

Graves put it another way. "No one in the world" knows more than Heather why Ferrell and his friends drove to Eustis from Kentucky, he said.

Hope said Heather might not want it released for privacy reasons.

Hope was asked by reporters if Brad King offered to let Heather go free if she testified against Ferrell.

"Absolutely not," he said. "No deal was ever offered, nor did we ask for one. It was more of a meeting of the minds that the grand jury would be the best way to air this out."[2]

It was settled as far as King was concerned. "There were no facts by which one could conclude that Heather Wendorf knew of the murders of her parents."

Circuit Judge Jerry Lockett, who would preside over the trial, said he would review the grand jury transcripts and reserve ruling.

With or without the grand jury testimony, defense attorneys had copies of all the cult members' confessions.

The *Sentinel* wanted the statements, too, especially Heather's, and sued the State Attorney's office for the records.

King said "confessional material" was exempt from the state's public records law.

The paper countered that Heather was no longer a suspect.

"This case is of compelling public interest," said *Lake County Sentinel* Editor Lauren Ritchie.[3]

King wrote a letter to Ritchie saying the release could interfere with the teens' right to a fair trial, and that it was forbidden under the Florida Bar's ethics rules. Also exempt are incriminating statements by the teens against the other defendants, he said.

The latter interpretation was "too broad," *Sentinel* attorney David Bralow argued. The rule should apply only to what the arrested person said, not the statements of other people.

Like a ball in a tennis tournament, the argument bounced from one side of the court to another.

The State Attorney's Office said it was "not unwilling to disclose the requested videotape," but it filed a motion for a protective order because at least one of the defense attorneys objected.

Less than a week later, however, the State Attorney's Office released a redacted version of Heather's transcript statement to police.

The *Sentinel* headline read: "'I want them alive,' Heather warned cultist."[4]

The quote was from her account of a conversation she had with Ferrell and Anderson before she left with Charity and Dana.

King did not release the video. Because all of the lawyers got a whack at the transcript of police interviews with black markers, there were sections that looked like a picture of two black bears fighting in a cave. It was a start, however.

King was probably relieved by the court ruling because it bolstered his claim that there was no evidence showing she was a principal in the murders or car theft.

There were more nuggets in the reams of discovery paperwork made public.

A report by Baton Rouge detectives noted that Ferrell told them he was happy he was caught, but sometimes could be seen "smirking."

The autopsy results were also released, and so was Ferrell's claim that his grandfather, Harrell Gibson, was in a cult that abused him and sacrificed a woman.

Documents included Sondra's admission to a social worker, Debra Mooney, that Rod was "unmanageable."

The worker suggested he re-enroll at Calloway High School, where he had flunked out, and obey a curfew. Ferrell agreed if he could see Keesee.

A juvenile judge ordered him to write a two-page paper on the "detrimental effects of drugs, the occult, and defiant behavior."

He never wrote the paper, and he did not show up on his court date. That was the day he was in Florida beating an unsuspecting couple to death with a crowbar.

CHAPTER 29

"Will end in tragedy"

Neighbors were alarmed when they saw Scott Anderson's 5-year-old brother standing outside the house crying.

Not that the house he was trying to get into was all that great.

Doors were hanging from hinges and windows were left open to bitter blasts of Kentucky winter wind. There was little food in the house and no money.

"Where's your mama?" someone asked.[1]

"She left, and she's never coming back," he sobbed.

If Ferrell's life was a horror show, Scott Anderson's was like a page ripped from *Tobacco Road* or *The Grapes of Wrath*.

"I feel this case will end in tragedy...I feel it won't be long," a social worker reported two years before the murders.[2]

Case worker reports starting in 1993 were filled with accounts of neglect, alcohol abuse, drug addiction, violence, and poverty.

Howard Anderson Sr. admitted that he had used marijuana, cocaine, and LSD. He suffered from major depression, antisocial personality disorder, schizophrenia, and paranoia. Counselors warned social workers that he could become violent for no reason.

Neighbors locked their doors when they heard him arguing and saw him with a gun.

He kept two clubs standing in the corner. "I made them and could kill someone with them," he told a social worker. He assured her that he wasn't talking about her.

Anderson and his wife, Martha, had been abused when they were young, a red flag for social workers who recommended counseling.

In 1994, Anderson Sr. was arrested and charged with felony assault when he reportedly struck his wife in the head with a bottle. She refused to testify against him. When the charge was dropped to a misdemeanor, he was ordered into alcohol rehab for 30 days and told to stay away from her.

It was not long afterward that neighbors saw Scott's little brother locked out of the house.

"The state can take the children," Martha told social workers. "I'm going to be with Howard."

The four boys, ages 5 to 14, were placed into foster care for two years with the deacon of a church, where they were cared for and attended services.

Sometimes the couple battled with child services officials. One time, police had to forcibly remove them from the agency's office.

In May of 1996, social workers allowed the family to reunite and praised the members for learning how to communicate better. Howard Sr. got a pat on the back for learning how to "cool off" and for taking his medication and staying sober. Martha was looking forward to getting a job.[3]

On Thanksgiving Day, *Sentinel* reporter Jerry Fallstrom pulled up in front of Anderson's home in a car he had rented at the airport.

Howard opened the door, then tried to shut it.

"Hold on, hold on, I'm not a cop!" Fallstrom said, sticking his foot in the door. "I'm a reporter. The police are saying your son is a monster. We want to get your side of the story."[4]

"My son would never hurt anyone," Howard said as he let Fallstrom come inside, but he pointed to holes in the wall that Scott had punched in a fit of rage.

"It was a junked-out house," Fallstrom said. "There were dirty dishes in the bathtub. An old TV was turned on to a Thanksgiving Day parade. It was blurry and scratchy," he said.

"They offered me something to eat. I didn't want to be a jerk, so I took a couple of sips of coffee." He stayed for two hours.

In the days leading up to the fateful trip to Florida, Scott asked his family, "How would you feel if I came back from Florida with a wife and a baby?"[5]

Scott had now replaced Goodman in Ferrell's vampire family, and Heather was supposed to be his "dark mate."

Howard traded a 1982 Chevy truck for the little turbocharged Buick. It was to be a family car but mostly Scott's if he could make the insurance payments.

"Tell me that child wasn't trying to be responsible. Scotty had to be under the influence of something," Howard said.

"Rod talked him into it," said Scott's little brother, Nickey.

Scott's 14-year-old brother, Sam, said he went with Scott and Ferrell three weeks earlier to a cemetery where they talked about sacrificing people.

"Rod took a razor and made three cuts on his arm, and a girl named Cindy sucked his blood," Sam said. "They were going to try to get me to cut my arm. I said, 'Uh-uh, that's stupid.'"

Scott's family was devastated.

"Howard began to question himself. He said he wanted to know where he went wrong," a social worker wrote in a Dec. 3, 1996 report. "Howard said that it is hard to think that no matter what has happened that your own child could kill someone. He said that he did not realize that Scott was this bad off."

Six months after Fallstrom interviewed the Andersons in Kentucky, he took me aside and gave me some astonishing news. Martha called to say that she had just flown into Orlando International Airport and needed a ride.

She had come to Florida with Scott's 16-year-old brother, Robert, and only $100 in her pocket for food and shelter.

I found her at the airport surrounded by tourists wearing Mickey Mouse ears, who were either eager to visit "The Most Magical Place on Earth," or were dragging themselves to a gate for the return trip, broke, exhausted, and sunburned.

"I tried to hold off, but I couldn't wait any longer. I had to come see him, to hold him, to see if he's still real," she said.[6]

Fortunately, she had purchased round-trip tickets, but the idea of coming to Florida for what she hoped would be a two-week stay with only $100 was astounding.

"I just came. I just took his Social Security check and cashed it," she said.[7]

No doubt, she thought a large news organization like the *Sentinel* could afford to put her up. Such monetary arrangements were above my pay grade, however, so my mission was to find charitable organizations that could give them a place to stay. I found a one-night free stay with one organization, and then a longer-term arrangement with a homeless shelter. Imagine my surprise when she showed up the next day saying that she and her son were "bored" with the out-of-the-way shelter.

"I'm not begging," she told editor Lauren Ritchie. "I want work. I've worked in fast food restaurants; I can clean. I'm a good housekeeper—a real good housekeeper."

In the meantime, Scott's lawyer, Michael Graves, got wind that she was in town and called me to see how he could corral her. It put me on the spot. Normally, I would have been only too happy to drop her off at his doorstop, but the *Lake County Sentinel* had a cable news show and she was suddenly the guest.

"I'm so sorry, Mike, but I can't tell you until we tape the show." The show was scheduled to be taped the next day.

That must have been a real heartburn moment for a defense attorney. You can never predict what a family member might say to a reporter.

Martha didn't have any blockbuster revelations, but she did say that Scott told her that "Rod went crazy" inside the Wendorf home.

Anderson told a fellow prisoner at the jail that he grabbed Ferrell's arm and shouted, "Are you crazy? Stop! Stop!"[8]

When Anderson first arrived, prisoners gathered at his cell. "He said he can read people's thoughts. He said he can make certain things happen to your family. I think it's all a front," one man said.

One prisoner got into a shoving match with him. Later, prisoners waited until Anderson was asleep, then threw cold water on him.

The talkative prisoner said Anderson claimed to have three personalities, and said he gnawed on the steel bars of his cell and would sit on his haunches for hours like a gargoyle. He said Anderson did not believe he was a vampire, "but Ferrell thinks he's a vampire for real."

Anderson told him he tried drinking blood but "said there wasn't nothing (sic) to it."

He also said the girls had nothing to do with the murders.

Martha never found work, but she did accomplish her goal of seeing her son.

Guards told Scott that he had a visitor, but they did not say who it was. The visitor's area is a no-contact zone, with glass partitions and one-on-one phone connections.

"I could see him screaming, 'Ma! Ma!'" Martha said. "He couldn't get to the phone fast enough."[9]

After two hours, she still wasn't allowed to hold him or touch him, and because Robert was a juvenile, he was not allowed to see his brother.

Ritchie, a hard-nose newspaper woman who cut her teeth on crime reporting, was moved.

"Scott's family can't pay for the kind of fancy footwork defense that O.J. came up with—groceries are going to be a problem this month for Howard Anderson Sr., and the two boys who stayed home in Mayfield, Ky.," she wrote.

"Combine that with the fact that the Andersons aren't the picturesque Appalachian family—they have other troubles that would make Norman Rockwell run the other way. Alcoholism. Mental illness. None of it makes a whit of difference when it comes to a mother and her son."

"I had to see him," Martha said. "I can't leave until I am able to walk away from him without tears in my eyes."

Martha would return several months later, this time in an old Pontiac Trans Am packed with her sons. She thought somehow that she could see Scott, but by this time he had been sentenced and sent to a prison across the state.

"I could tell they didn't have much money and were hungry," Fallstrom said. He happened to have very little cash in his wallet that day, but he pointed to a little soul food restaurant next door to the *Sentinel* bureau.

"You could get a plate of beans and rice for a dollar," he said. "It would fill you up and it was good, but they wanted McDonald's."

Twenty years later, I interviewed Anderson, who was back in the Lake County jail for a resentencing hearing. His parents were now dead, and he said he had had no contact with his brothers.

"People don't know the impact something like this has on your life," he said.[10]

In 2019, he appeared on an Oxygen channel documentary called *Deadly Cults,* that I also appeared in. At the end, Anderson was shown looking at family photos that the producers had obtained.

"I thought my mom got rid of all this stuff," he said. "I've spent 22 years in prison because I let this numbskull

influence me to that level. I mean, if I hadn't driven away..."
And then he wept.[11]

CHAPTER 30

"Feisty"

Defendants have the right to a speedy trial within 120 days of their arrest but hardly anyone pushes for it. In fact, waiving that right is practically automatic, so Dana Cooper raised a lot of eyebrows when she announced in March 1997 that she did not want to wait until February, when the others were tentatively scheduled.

"She's feisty," said Cooper's attorney, Mary Ann Plecas.[1] The same could be said of Plecas.

After graduating from the law school at the University of Georgia and passing the Bar in 1990, she went to work as an assistant state attorney until 1994, before becoming a defense attorney. She later opened her own law firm in Tavares.

"I think anyone that knew her knew that she aggressively pursued what was right," her brother, Franklin, said after she died of cancer in 2002 at age 54. "She was a barracuda."[2]

She sometimes swam with sharks, including F. Lee Bailey, while working on a securities case. Bailey was one of O.J. Simpson's attorneys, not to mention the Boston Strangler and Sam Sheppard.

Unlike Bailey's public persona, at least, Plecas could be sweet, soft-spoken, charming, and thoughtful. Like all defense attorneys, she was also a realist and learned early on to roll with the punches.

She had an assistant who was arrested one day on a Texas warrant. Corrections officers at the jail were surprised and embarrassed when they made "her" take a shower at the jail. She was, in fact, a he.

"I used to get my nails done with her," Plecas said.

***

"She doesn't want to sit around," Plecas said of Cooper. "This doesn't give anyone time to procrastinate. I'll be ready."[3]

The state attorney said he would be ready, too.

Sometimes it is a tactical advantage for a defendant to push for an early trial. Prosecutors need time to prepare, too. However, King didn't need to wait for DNA and other complex evidence from the crime lab, since she never entered the Wendorfs' house.

After the hearing, in which Plecas announced plans for the early trial, I asked her what Cooper was thinking.

Cooper was "dismayed" that Heather was set free, Plecas said. "She thinks it's unfair."

Cooper did let out a visible sigh of relief at the hearing, however, when King said he was not seeking the death penalty for her and Keesee.

The early trial move did put a kink in one of Plecas' initial plans. She hoped all four teens would be tried together. That way, jurors could see just how minor her client's role was compared to Ferrell's.

"Now that won't happen."

Circuit Judge Jerry Lockett set a date of April 18 to hear pretrial motions, and May 5 for the trial.

However, as the trial date approached, Plecas announced that Cooper would waive her right to a speedy trial after all.

Plecas kept doing her research and she filed lots of motions. She had another idea, too, a novelty at the time. She conducted a mock trial using residents from a neighboring county to see how a panel might view her client.

In August 1997, all four defense attorneys announced they wanted separate trials for their clients. King had speculated that Anderson and Ferrell could be tried together.

"No one wants to be tried with Ferrell," one of the lawyers told me privately.[4]

CHAPTER 31

Constitutional clash

There's nothing as ugly as a head-on collision between two Constitutional rights. There's always a lot of ink hemorrhaged onto pages of legal briefs, verbal arguments made by men and women in dark suits, and nervous handwringing by clients and scholars.

As the vampire case moved closer to trial, a battle erupted over journalists' First Amendment rights versus the defendant's Sixth right to a "speedy and public trial by an impartial jury."

It turned into a legal brawl sometimes, especially with defense attorneys trying to limit reporters' access to records and even courtroom hearings, while at the same time trying to force journalists to surrender their information, and to keep all of it out of the view and earshot of prospective jurors.

"Only 70 days has elapsed and the publicity surrounding the case continues like a winter blizzard," Candace Hawthorne wrote in a motion for change of venue.[1]

"This phenomenon has been greatly exacerbated by the fact that at or around the time of the instant offense, juvenile crime has become the story of the '90s with all forms of media reporting the alleged upsurge of violent crimes being committed by youths of our nation.

"Additionally, the twist of alleged "vampire cult" activities, with rumors of blood-letting, and ritualistic voodoo, enhancing the macabre interest in sensationalizing the case. Further, editorials and stories about the pretrial discovery, including statements alleged to have been made by the accused."

She was doing her job, but there was no getting around it. Ferrell was the head of a teen blood-drinking vampire cult, who was charged with murdering a member's parents.

It was a little bit like Leslie Nielsen's zany police detective character in the 1988 comedy film, *The Naked Gun: From the Files of Police Squad,* when he tries to disperse a crowd of onlookers after a fiery car chase. "Alright, move on. Nothing to see here," he says, as a fireworks factory explodes behind him and people run for their lives.

The clash of rights is nothing new, of course. The Warren Commission, which investigated President John F. Kennedy's 1963 assassination, was critical of the news media, saying that if Lee Harvey Oswald had survived the attack by Jack Ruby he likely would not have received a fair trial.

"If the reporters behaved badly in Dallas, so did the Dallas law enforcement officials who displayed 'evidence' in crowded corridors and released statements about other evidence. Conduct of police and other law enforcement officials, however, has by no means been the only source of prejudicial materials which later appeared in the press to the detriment of defendants' rights. All too often, both defense and prosecution attorneys have released statements to reporters which were clearly at odds with the American Bar Association Cannon of Professional Ethics."[2]

It's hard to blame the press for reporting on every development in one of the biggest stories of the 20th Century, and it was a continuous breaking story. TV cameras were rolling when Oswald was gunned down at the Dallas police station. The nation was in shock and would have been angered, frightened, and even more suspicious in a news blackout.

The JFK assassination is a far cry from the vampire case, however. Frankly, we probably would have been satisfied to receive reasonably redacted videotapes of the teens' statements to police in Baton Rouge.

Anderson's attorney, Michael Graves, objected to even that, citing "vampire spin."[3]

"This case ain't got nothing (sic) to do with vampires," he said.

Graves said he was preparing to file a motion asking that King not be allowed to talk about vampires during the trial.

At the same time, Heather's court-appointed guardian, Lou Tally, announced that he had hired an entertainment lawyer to represent Heather for possible book contracts, movie rights, or other deals.

"She hasn't made a deal with anybody," Tally said.

Ferrell's lawyer, Candace Hawthorne, complained about newspaper headlines and said she had gotten a call from a TV show in London.

Sentinel attorney David Bralow argued that she was not an expert on newspaper readers, what they retained, or marketing.

After Heather was freed by the grand jury, Circuit Judge Mark Hill refused to have King edit out references to vampires in the videotapes. "The cat's already out of the bag," he said.

As for Heather, "there's nothing to prevent her from talking to the press now," he said, explaining that she was no longer a suspect.

***

Bralow was brilliant. I was subpoenaed several times while covering the courts for the *Sentinel,* usually after interviewing a prisoner at the jail.

He would get up, make his argument, and turn back and look at me and mouth the words, "We're going to lose." We never did.

Once, I was subpoenaed in a divorce case. The couple had won the Florida lottery and I interviewed them after they claimed the prize money. "We are going to do this," they said. "We are going to do that...." Lawyers wanted me to testify about what they said.

Judge Hill let me off the hook. "If Frank testifies every time he writes a story, he'll never get anything done."

By law, lawyers seeking a subpoena must show there is no other way to get the information and that there is a "heightened need."

The threat of the government or private attorneys probing a reporter's work could have a chilling effect on the First Amendment. This is especially true when an investigative reporter is protecting the identity of a source.

The one argument Bralow would have lost involved a juror who disappeared during a murder trial. When I reached the man by phone, he gave me one excuse. The next day, he gave a bailiff a different reason for failing to return from lunch.

The trial judge cited him for contempt of court, and I was the lone witness.

The man wanted to fight it, but his lawyer talked him out of it. "Who do you think the judge is going to believe, you or Frank Stanfield?"

**

Ferrell's lawyers subpoenaed the *Sentinel* for every record and photograph. They were especially interested in Ferrell's interview with the paper.

There was another source besides the *Sentinel*, however. "Any such information is already in Ferrell's possession, because he himself gave the information to the *Sentinel*,"

Bralow wrote in his motion. Nor was there a compelling need since the notes would be ruled as hearsay and inadmissible.

He also cited "reporters' privilege."

"Compelled production of these materials would constitute an unwarranted invasion of the *Sentinel's* confidential and proprietary newsgathering material." The material was "the fruit of our labor," with commercial value, he said. If released in a subpoena, it would become public record and available to competitors.

Bralow also fought for the paper's right to have the defendants' videotapes and transcripts.

He cited a Florida Supreme Court ruling that requires a three-part test. Restricting public access to discovery material is necessary to prevent a "serious and imminent threat" to justice; there are no alternatives, other than a change of venue; closure would be the most effective protection for the accused.

The state did not meet its burden, he said. "In fact, courts do not consider straight news stories of a factual nature to be hostile or inflammatory."

The *Sentinel* editorialized against the idea of withholding Heather's videotaped statements. It wasn't about the news media vs. government, Lake County Editor Lauren Ritchie wrote. It was about the public's right to see records and keep abreast of things that are of crucial public interest. "...we're glad we won, because—naive or corny as it may sound— we still see ourselves as responsible for the public's right to know. No one else wants the job."[4]

Hawthorne was adamant, however.

"Death is different," she said, referring to King's quest for the death penalty for Ferrell.Later, she made a motion calling for *prospective* jurors to be sequestered in a motel during jury selection.

She said she was thinking about filing a motion to close all pretrial hearings.

The judge denied her motions. He did, however, rule that the lawyers could have a higher-than-usual number of preemptory strikes, and they could question the prospective jurors individually. He also approved a jury questionnaire and a big jury pool.

CHAPTER 32

Vampires don't suck

Vampires don't suck—at the box office, that is.

Anne Rice, whose vampire novels were in the clutches of the vampire cult members right up to the moment they were captured, boasted more than 100 million book sales by 2018. Of the 50 richest writers, she ranked twenty-fourth, at $60 million.[1]

Stephenie Meyers' four-book *Twilight* series were also turned into lucrative movies. She was the highest selling author of 2008 and 2009 in the United States, with 29 million and 26.5 million books sold respectively.[2]

No wonder Ferrell's legal team was worried about publicity.

Ironically, Bram Stoker's *Dracula* novel, which started it all in 1897, did not become a hit for decades.

The gothic classic is set in Transylvania, where the undead monster, Count Dracula, preys on women and children. The character is loosely based on a real Romanian prince, Vlad the Impaler, who reigned in the 15th century.

Pop culture buffs love to sink their teeth into theories about the symbolism and motives of vampires.

"Feminine virtue is at stake in *Dracula*," said writer Melina Druga. One character, Lucy, gives in to the Count's spell, the virtuous Mina does not. It's up to the men in the story to come to the rescue, which is the Victorian ideal. "Victorian men were threatened by fallen women. They believed sexually aggressive women would destroy the very fabric of society and call into question male dominance."[3]

Blood, which is crucial to vampire stories, has a sexual connotation.

"Well, of course it has to do with sex," Thomas C. Foster writes in his popular book, *How to Read Literature Like a Professor.* "Evil has to do with sex since he serpent seduced Eve. What was the upshot there? Body shame and unwholesome lust, seduction, temptation, danger, among other ills."[4]

When I asked Scott Anderson about drinking blood, he remarked, "People do it in communion." The difference is that Christians *symbolically* drink the blood of Christ during the Lord's Supper.

Experts have noted the difference.

"Consuming human blood gives vampires fortification and youthfulness, but in a damning and demonic sense," one writer has noted. "Rather than promoting the Christian ethic of selfless sacrifice and redemption, their consumption symbolizes self-serving greed and corruption. If taking communion promotes human concord with the resurrected deity, being bitten by the count results in a monstrous union with the league of undead demons. Thus, in Stoker's novel, vampires drink human blood partly to mock and subvert Christian theology."[5]

That fits perfectly with Ferrell wearing an upside-down cross and drawing blasphemous pictures of the crucifixion.

"The vampire has lasted...because it can symbolize so many things—conflicted attitudes about sex, conflicted attitudes about race, conflicted attitudes about immortality itself," according to Jerrod E. Hogle, a professor at the University of Arizona.[6]

Buffy the Vampire Slayer, a popular TV show that first aired in 1997, featured vampires and demon characters "as a metaphor for the multiple horrors of high school and later young life."[7]

Fear of death may be the strongest trigger, however. Even young children can grasp the basic premise: When you're dead, you're not coming back. Christians believe in eternal life—in heaven if you're a believer, hell if you're not. But to be undead? Wandering the earth restless and evil for all time? The idea is terrifying.

Margot Adler, the author of *Vampires Are Us,* wrote: "Every age embraces the vampire it needs." She listed six different areas that vampires can help us understand the meaning of life: immortality, spirituality, power, and how to cope with politics, alienation, and persecution.[8]

Apparently, one of the "needs" that contemporary vampires meet is "inclusion," a favorite topic for millennials. "Modern vampires, unlike their ancestors, focus on integrating themselves into human society, offering an exemplary model of human behavior. Instead of projecting fear into the world, these contemporary vampires possess a strong moral code and ethics not previously present in depictions of vampires before the twentieth century. This ability to distinguish right and wrong (or even adapt to a new lifestyle such as "vegetarian") allows the vampire to become more humanized," K. Buckley wrote in her thesis in 2016.[9]

Stephen King, who features vampires in some of his horror stories, thinks writers should drive a stake through the concept of a more moral vampire, and said so in his introduction to *American Vampire.*

"Here's what vampires shouldn't be: pallid detectives who drink Bloody Marys and work only at night; lovelorn Southern gentlemen; anorexic teenage girls; boy-toys with big dewy eyes. What should they be? Killers, honey. Stone killers who never get enough of that tasty Type-A. Bad boys and girls. Hunters. In other words, Midnight America. Red, white and blue, accent on the red. Those vamps got hijacked by a lot of soft-focus romance."[10]

We have a need to be scared, King wrote in an article entitled "Why We Crave Horror Movies. "To show that we can, that we are not afraid, that we can ride this roller coaster."[11]

In Ferrell's case, psychologists lined up for the chance at testifying about all kinds of mental illnesses that might explain his behavior.

In 2017, a blogger asked a question completely unrelated to Ferrell's case: "To you, what do vampires symbolize?"[12]

One person who answered seemed to hit the stake with a hammer: "For me there exists some common traits with Narcissistic Personality Disorder, a serious and quite common mental health problem. More than one author refers to them as Emotional Vampires," Tazio Mirandola wrote.

She listed the following traits: "Preoccupation with fantasies of unlimited success, power, brilliance, beauty or ideal love; believes he is "special" and can only be understood by, or should associate with other special or high-status people or institutions; requires excessive admiration; has a sense of entitlement; selfishly takes advantage of others to achieve his own ends; lacks empathy; is often envious of others or believes that others are envious of him; shows arrogant, haughty, patronizing, or contemptuous behaviors or attitudes. They treat other people like dirt."

She noted: "Vampire stories are always around contests and battles for power or seduction of new prey, that's exactly what the life of NPD looks like."

The vampire hunter character, Jonathan Harker, described the Count in *Dracula* this way: "...as he is criminal he is selfish; and as his intellect is small and his action is based on selfishness, he confines himself to one purpose. That purpose is remorseless."[13]

Ferrell tipped his hand in his not-so-private videotaped rendezvous with Charity in the Baton Rouge interrogation room. "They kept asking me the stupidest questions," he said. "They asked if I felt any remorse for killing them."

CHAPTER 33

"This is not Rod"

A young Rod Ferrell, probably in middle school, stood still—frozen in time—for a studio family portrait. He wasn't smiling but he wasn't sticking his tongue out, either. Nor was his hair long and dyed black in the photo that appeared in the *Sentinel* on Jan. 11, 1998. His left hand is resting on his mother's shoulder. Sondra *is* smiling, and she has her hands on her mother's shoulder. Rosetta had a Mona Lisa smile sneaking across her face. Harrell is to the far left in the picture, looking pained, as usual.

But a "live" *Sentinel* photo of the grandparents in the same edition shows a grief-stricken elderly couple staring into the camera, practically in tears. Ten days later, another photo by *Sentinel* photographer Tom Benitez showed Sondra with bags under her eyes and frizzy hair. She was barely recognizable. The camera lens is pitiless, even if the photographer is not.

"Rod is a good boy," the grandparents said. The described him as sensitive, caring, artistic, and a "scapegoat" for the murders.[1]

"Rod is a good boy and has always been a good boy," Rosetta said.

The family granted the exclusive interview in hopes of convincing the public that Rod was not the remorseless monster described by witnesses.

"He fell in with the wrong crowd," Rosetta said. That crowd, she noted, included Heather Wendorf.

Rosetta said she had no idea how serious his interest was in the undead. Rod started playing vampire fantasy games when they moved back to Kentucky in 1995, she said. "I thought it was a kid's game."

Unlike Rod, who liked to call attention to himself, the couple, who had been married for 50 years, would be practically invisible in a Walmart.

"If there was vampirism, it wasn't going on in our house," she said.

"There hasn't been any drinking, tobacco, or abusive language in our house since 1958," the 68-year-old Harrell said. That was the year the couple joined a Pentecostal church.

They theorized that when Rod confessed to police, he was either on drugs or pretending to be crazy.

Harrell had a unique view of his grandson.

"He has the potential for being a great spiritual leader. I'm a firm believer he will be set free, if not at the trial, soon afterward."

Yet, he was aware that Rod could be executed in Florida's electric chair.

"I've always told him no man knows when a heartbeat will be his last. Be ready to meet the Lord."

Sondra also described Ferrell as a sensitive, caring boy.

"This is not Rod," she told me.[2]

The facts belied her comments, however.

"She told me that he had been involved in drugs in Florida," Janeann Turner, a Kentucky court official noted in her official report. "She's observed her son with marijuana in the house. That he was involved in a satanic cult."[3]

Gibson also told Turner that Rod had threatened to kill her, an occult group threatened her, and that he stayed out all night, cut his arms, and that she could not control him.

"Rod said a lot of things when he wanted to go out and I didn't want to let him go. I'm obviously not dead. It was just talk. Rod has never hurt me."

Matt Goodman, who said he spent many nights at Ferrell's home, had a unique perspective.

"... his mother was real (sic) nice. And in fact, she did not like some of the things that Rod was doing when he first moved back. Different things, like betraying his friends He would use them, he would go out, you know, and do stuff, and he would even threaten her and tell her that she couldn't do this or that."[4]

He said Gibson once told him, "he actually flung a knife at her and stuck it in the wall next to her head because he didn't agree with what she told him; he couldn't go somewhere."

Sondra disagreed with Goodman's claim that Rod had abused the dogs at the shelter.

"Rod would never do that to an animal. He had a little kitten that slept with him. He let that little kitten crawl all over him. He was at home asleep when that happened."[5]

Keesee told police that Ferrell was with her that night.

Sondra did not believe that he committed the murders.

"I believe they were already dead when he went in there. He freaked out and got out of there as soon as he could find the keys."

He confessed, she said, because he thought his friends would go free and that he would "go to a mental hospital for a while."

That statement was probably the most honest thing she ever said. It would explain his claim in Baton Rouge that he was "mentally disturbed," and the multiple personality claim in the *Sentinel* interview. It also fit in with his belief that Charity and the others had not done anything wrong.

If that was her most honest comment, her next statement—about vampirism— sounded like the most sane thing she could have said.

"I look back on it now and see it was stupidness. Hollywood idiocy."

She would later trip herself up on that comment, however.

CHAPTER 34

"Opening the gates to hell"

Whether Sondra Gibson was deluding herself, or trying to fool others, sheriff's investigators were determined in February 1997 to gain insight into Ferrell's mindset. What Detectives Al Gussler and C.J. Thompson found out, was that Ferrell had been preparing to kill for months.

They talked with Goodman, of course, discussed his role-playing games and how he, Ferrell, and Anderson would train with swords, spears and other homemade weapons.

Just before leaving for Florida, Goodman said Ferrell had come to his house to get a decorative sword, but Goodman refused to give it to him.

"Goodman stated that for a couple months before the homicides, Ferrell had become possessed with the idea of opening the gates to hell, which meant he would have to kill a large number of people in order to consume their souls. By doing this, Ferrell believed that he would obtain superpowers," Gussler wrote in a supplemental report.[1]

The detectives also talked to a youth named James Elkins, who used to play a game they invented called Dark Strangers.

"Elkins stated that Rod Ferrell talked a lot about killing, killing anyone, to see what the rush would feel like." It was the very term Ferrell used in his confession.

"It appeared very obvious during the interview that John M. Goodman had a realistic fear of Rodrick Ferrell," Gussler noted.

He wasn't the only one.

Harrell Gibson told a Murray police investigator that Rod was "a good boy," but four days later, Murray Detective Jump noted, "Mr. Gibson was afraid that Rod had tried to 'set' him up to be killed." Gibson felt like Anderson "was in on the plan, too."[2]

Gibson also told the *Sentinel* about the suspicious incident.

Gibson said Rod had asked him for a ride to a friend's house on a Friday or Saturday a few days before the murders. They spotted Anderson's car with the hood up on a narrow bridge. Gibson slowed down, they yelled to Anderson and continued onto Rod's friend's house. No one was home. Anderson pulled in behind Gibson's car. Anderson stayed in the car, then took off. As Gibson approached the bridge, he noticed that Anderson again had his hood up. Gibson said Rod asked him to get out of the car, but he thought better of it, dropped Rod off with Anderson and drove off.

"I just didn't feel safe. I just had a very strong feeling I shouldn't stop."

Months later, he told the *Sentinel:* "I've never been afraid of Rod. Rod's the best boy that ever walked the earth. He's just got himself mixed up in some kind of mess. I don't know what."[3]

He said he just didn't want to hang around in the woods at night.

Jump had information from another Kentucky resident.

Jason Jones, a neighbor of Ferrell's in Murray, "stated that Rod talked to him about killing someone and going to Florida."

Ferrell also told him he was a vampire.

Jones, who talked to Adams by phone, said he last talked to Ferrell about two weeks before the murders. At that time, Rod asked him if he had any bottles he could have.

Detectives also talked to a Eustis High student who said Ferrell was coming back to get money out of a safe, but he did not know any more than that.

They also talked to a former Eustis classmate named Audrey Presson. She said Ferrell was wearing a long, black coat and tried to convince her to run away with his "family." He introduced Charity as his "wife," Anderson as his "brother," and Cooper as his "prodigy."

Brad King later asked Presson: "When you saw Mr. Ferrell on Sunday night, did he specifically give you a reason why he had left the state of Kentucky?"[4]

"Yes."

"What was the reason?"

"He was running from the law because they had found him building bombs."

On Nov. 10, fifteen days before the murders, Sondra called the Murray Police Department.

"When I arrived, Sondra Gibson advised that her son and two other boys had beer bottles, gasoline, and rags in his room, and her son stated that they were making bombs," the officer noted in his report.[5]

"The mother became very upset and told the boys to take the stuff and get out of her house. The boys took the bombs and said they were going to get some guns...."

One of the boys was Scott Anderson.

She had clashed with the other boy a few months earlier.

"Ms. Gibson stated that she had gone to bed and left the boys up. She said that she smelled smoke and got up and the boys were in the living room sitting around a circle. There were candles and a pentagram."

She told Rod's friends to leave and not come back. She later relented, she said, because "her son would threaten to hurt her and tell her to go into her room. She stated that she was scared to do anything."

"There were several letters taken from Rod's room that talked of their clan and of drinking each other's blood. There were several skulls in the room," he noted, adding that another officer found mushrooms.

Police also discovered a vampire clan code book.

"Ms. Gibson stated that Rod put several holes in the walls and the doors. Rod has hit his mother in the past six months and when they lived in Florida. She is scared of him and cannot control him."

Gibson told the officer that Rod later returned for some baseball bats and left again. "I have not seen or heard from him since," she told police.[6]

When he showed up in Eustis that Sunday night, Ferrell told Presson that he had some "unfinished business" to take care of in Lake County.

The next night, the Wendorfs were dead.

Was Ferrell serious when he told Jones he wanted to kill someone in Kentucky? Yes, considering that, as his friends learned the hard way, he wasn't just making idle threats on the way to Florida. The question remains, who did he want to kill? Did a wishful hit list include his grandfather, mother, and Jaden Murphy? Were there others, including people close to his enemies, like Jaden's fiancée?

There was at least one likely victim at one point. The Murray Police bomb-making report said, "Her son also stated that he was going to get the guy that went out with his girlfriend."

CHAPTER 35

Shea: The "half-vampire"

How many nights did Charity Keesee flip open her little kid diary with its cover adorned with the picture of a colorful little horse munching on grass? Inside, there were lined pages with loopy handwriting detailing secret feelings about boyfriends, parties and school—and blood, sex, vampires, and death.

Rod's artwork was on display in notes: skeletons, demons and monsters, and so was his writing.

"She walks through the night under the cold, black sky," Ferrell wrote in a poem entitled *Shea.* "Hell's children dance as flame, throwing their shadows to surround her in drapes of opaque peace."[1]

Early in their relationship he wrote a note saying he had a hard time sleeping.

"I merely watched the ceiling stare back at me all night while thoughts of you and I together danced in my head. Have I fallen into insanity? But mad I am not. I like you, that's no big secret, yet my question still remains. Where do we go from this point of our new-found relationship? Lust, love, love, lust?"

He continues, saying in part, "you are my final light, my last stand."

One note came with a drawing of Christ being crucified upside down and says: "Shea, what do you want me to chill about? The fact I love you or the suicide thing? What's the difference about anything anymore?

I'm sorry, I'm sorry, I'm sorry, I'm sorry that everything is my fault.

I'm sorry everything I do is wrong; from what I've seen everything

would be happier and better if I was just gone. I'm just see-through,

faded, super-jaded OUT OF MY MIND.

And just off-hand while I still have half a thought, why do you care

what happens to me? Know what the shortest verse in the Bible says?

Jesus wept; I wonder why he wept? I will treat you well. My sweet angel.

So help me, Jesus."

Another note from Rod, with drawings of monsters, begins: "My mom is being such a BITCH for some reason. She's saying that I've been going around telling everyone that she's a slut and a whore."

In another portion of the note, he wrote: "I had a dream last night. You came over and we went back to my room, you combed your fingers through my hair. Then we made wild and passionate sex. It seemed like we made love forever. When we finished, I held you in my arms and we cried softly at the beauty of the night. I MISS YOU," he wrote and drew two little hearts.

Keesee's own diary entries are interesting. On May 19, 1996, she wrote: "Diary, a lot has happened since I have last written you. First of all, I met this guy who is a freak just like me, if not more than me. His name is Rod Ferrell."

Nine days later, she wrote that Ferrell asked her to marry him. "Shea loves Rod 4-ever and always," she wrote.

On Aug. 3, 1996, she wrote: "Stayed the night at Cindy's last night. Rod and Steven came over, and they started explaining how they are vampires, and I am supposedly half vampire because I drank Rod's blood, and now they are trying to get me to let Rod drink my blood and me drink his again, so I will be a full vampire.

"It wouldn't bother me except I don't want him biting me, it hurts like hell! I don't even know if I believe in vampires, or that Rod and Steven are vampires. Oh well, I guess I really wouldn't mind being one since I like the taste of blood anyway. Well, better go. C-ya. Shea."

Her reluctance to being "crossed over" by Rod caused a great deal of friction.

Cindy, possibly the same one that Keesee referred to, wrote Rod a note to say how upset she was with Keesee's attitude.

"Rod, I bet when I see Shea next, she will be bitching. I wrote her a two-page note about how she was so stupid, that all this time you wanted to cross her over into our clan and have her as your chosen mate. I told her how now she can't be your chosen mate since she is in a different clan, that she knew this before."[2]

The letter writer ranted and said if she ever did anything so "unloving" again she would "tear her heart out and feed it" to her "father" (the one who crossed her over to become a vampire).

Keesee defended the rival group in one note to Rod.

"They don't just drink animal blood! They rarely do that, and I don't quite understand why you think so harshly of them. They are actually quite fascinating beings."[3]

"Shea, Hello, how's life?" Ferrell wrote in one undated letter.

"While I was walking yesterday, I kinda realized a few things.

1.)I still LOVE YOU.

2.) Now that you've decided to break up with me, I have nothing without you.

3.)Death isn't so bad, even though I'm going to hell, but what is hell compared to being without you? Don't worry, the blood won't be on your hands. Now the question is, is there life after death?"

He said he was not kidding about dying. "I would say that only you could save me from myself, but at this point, I don't think anyone can save me.

"There's (sic) two things I want to tell you.

"1.) I'm sorry for everything I've done to you.

2.) I love you!"

On the back of the letter, he noted that he had made a tape for her. He also drew a heart with daggers stuck in the top. He wrote "Rod" to the side of the heart and penned the words "for a little bit longer" inside the heart.

The page is smeared with dried blood. On the front of the letter is a drawing of Ferrell burning in hell.

On Oct. 20, Keesee wrote that she was "sick" of Ferrell.

"I WANT KEVIN," she wrote on one of the last pages of her diary, referring to a former boyfriend. But on Nov. 22, she was on her way to Florida with Ferrell.

CHAPTER 36

"Mental breakdown"

Heather was practically unrecognizable when she got out of the car on Oct. 14, 1997. Gone was the purple hair, chains, and hanging Barbie doll. Gone, too, was the frightened, nervous girl who looked down at the floor and twisted her hair when facing her first appearance before a judge in Florida.

She looked confident—happy, even—when she appeared at the courthouse for her deposition almost a year after the murders.

She was wearing a light print culotte, sandals, sunglasses, and had her hair pulled back in a ponytail. She even laughed at a group of reporters who gathered outside to watch her.

But if she was having a good day, defense attorneys in the deposition room were eager to ruin it for her.

I asked Brad King what sort of things the defense attorneys were looking for. "I wouldn't even hazard a guess," he said.[1]

"I can't tell you until I see the letters," Hawthorne said, referring to the letters that crime scene technicians found in her room and stuffed into an evidence box. The judge had approved her request to view them, but she had not yet read them.

Heather brought her attorney, James Hope, and a psychiatrist, which bolstered her confidence.

Hawthorne's co-counsel, Bill Lackay, set out immediately to rattle her.

"How many times have you been to your parents' graves?" he asked.[2]

"I think once or twice."

"Do you remember the dates?"

"One was on Easter. I think maybe it was once, it was on Easter."

"Who did you go with?"

"My Aunt Lilly and my boyfriend."

"Did you bring anything there?"

"No, because it was after church and I didn't have anything with me."

"You say you think you've twice maybe?"

"I think it's just once, one, one time, yeah."

He then asked if she drove the Ford Explorer after her parents were killed.

She said, "no," and Hope jumped in. He said he might advise her against answering any question that might incriminate her, especially about events in Louisiana.

Lackay, who was not happy with Heather's "no" answer, asked if she had a driver's license.

Again, the answer was no. She said she was getting her learner's permit after the day's deposition was finished.

He then asked the real question.

"Before the murder of your parents, did you know where the keys to the car were kept?"

"No."

"In your house?"

"No, I don't think there was a specific place. I think just wherever my dad decided to put them."

He also asked about the keys to the other vehicles and if she had any of the keys.

"No, I didn't."

Ferrell would later claim that she told him the keys to the Explorer were in the house, possibly on her parents' dresser. He found them in the ignition. "I wonder why she had told me that," he said.[3]

The implication, of course, was that she had lied to him, possibly to set up the deadly confrontation with her parents.

Detectives had questioned Heather about the vehicle in Baton Rouge.

How long did you and Rod plan on stealing the blue Explorer?" Gussler asked.

"I didn't plan on it," she said.

Defense attorneys gathered for her deposition also questioned her about her current living arrangements. She was staying at the home of an attorney in Tavares. She had no choice, as it turned out.

"I had a mental breakdown," she said.[4]

After being freed by the grand jury, she stayed with mother's sister, Lilian Rapp, but "Aunt Lilly" complained that Heather didn't help enough around the house, and she didn't like Heather's 19-year-old boyfriend.

Heather then moved in with her maternal grandmother, Ethel Gertrude Adams. Like Rapp, Adams also lived in Orange City, which is about 45 minutes from the Wendorf's house.

Heather said she and her 19-year-old boyfriend were "just sitting around looking through the classifieds, maybe to find an apartment or just looking at different things. And my grandmother came out, and I don't know what started it, maybe she was just having a bad day, but she started yelling at him, and so we decided just to go outside, sit on the driveway."

Adams began slamming doors inside the house and she locked the front door.

It wasn't the first time there had been a dust-up.

"One day she got drunk, and she has a gun, and she hid the gun when she was drunk, and when she sobered up, she forgot where she put it," Heather said. She accused Heather and her boyfriend of stealing it, even though they were both out of town that weekend.

She said her aunt and a cousin drove up and talked to her grandmother.

"My grandmother came out and started yelling and crying. I don't know. She started yelling and saying that if I didn't break up with my boyfriend that I would get kicked out, that I would be out on the street. And I didn't know why because my boyfriend had done nothing to provoke this, and she just knew that my boyfriend was the only thing that I had that she could threaten me with."

She said that her aunt and cousin were also yelling at her. After they left, her grandmother went back inside. Heather told her boyfriend to leave.

"I didn't want to go back into the house because I didn't want to get into a fight, so I stayed outside in the yard. And it got real dark, it was night, and I just lost it basically, because I was stuck between a rock and a hard place."

The "rock" was the boyfriend, she explained. The "hard place" was the possibility of being homeless.

"I started to shake, and I started hyperventilating real (sic) bad, and everything sort of like was getting grayish. I couldn't see right. I guess it was because I was hyperventilating."

She said she had had some similar experiences in the past, "but this was really, really bad. This was the worst I've ever had."

She said her grandmother came out and yelled, "I'm not falling for this bullshit!"

"And when I didn't stop, when I didn't stop hyperventilating and having my breakdown, she shot a gun (pistol) up in the air," she said.

"I started screaming to the top of my lungs. It just kept on getting worse and worse and worse, and after a while my hands went numb, and I couldn't feel them. I couldn't move them. They were like paralyzed. And I started screaming and just, I don't know. I couldn't get up and walk. I was just on the ground. I couldn't…it was hard for me to do anything but scream."

Neighbors came over to see what was wrong and her grandmother told someone to call 911.

"All my grandmother kept saying was that Michael, my boyfriend, did this to me, that he gave me something, that it was his fault. And it really wasn't. She was just saying that. I hadn't had anything that day."

Firefighters and police arrived 15 minutes later. Heather was handcuffed and taken to the emergency room, and later hospitalized.

At one point she was prescribed Paxil by a doctor. "He told me that I had like some sort of, it's kind of like bipolarness, but it's not as extreme, and Paxil was supposed to do something chemically in my brain that helps absorb some enzyme or chemical that helps me deal with situations better."

She was not prescribed the drug after leaving the hospital, but said she was taking an herbal supplement.

After that, the only contact she had with her grandmother was a five-minute phone call.

Lackay also asked her what her understanding was of the family estate.

"About half a million, and my sister will get half a million."

When Hawthorne took over the questioning, she asked about her friendship with Rod and Jeanine, how they all met. She also asked about Jeanine's bonfire party on her fifteenth birthday.

"Had you crossed over at that time?"

"No."

"Had you begun drinking blood at that time?"

"Yes."

"When did you start that?"

"I remember I did it in eighth grade."

She said the first time she did it she was alone, but after that she was always with Jeanine.

"I just got really mad one day. I just got so upset, I just cut myself with a razor on my arm, my upper arm, not my wrist or anything, but on the top of my arm...."

She said she had not planned to do it, "it just happened."

Jeanine had tried it before, she said.

It was before she had read any Anne Rice books.

There was not a "process" to drinking blood, she said. "I just licked it off my arm or licked it off the skin, off the cut."

"And did you drink Jeanine's blood?"

"Yes."

"And what was the purpose of this?"

"No real purpose, just the taste."

"Do you like eating rare steak?"

"No, actually, I eat it well done."

"Can you describe to me the taste of your blood?

"No, I can't. I can't describe it to anyone who hasn't tasted it. I don't know how to describe what it tastes like."

"Is it something you would develop a craving for?"

"Yeah, it has a distinct taste. But I don't know how to describe it."

She said she talked about it with Ferrell. "It was no real big discussion; it was just small talk about it."

There is a medical condition called hematomania, which is a blood fetish among people with certain sexual desires and psychological needs. She was never diagnosed with it.[5]

Self-mutilation, including cutting oneself, is another matter.

"Some adolescents may self-mutilate to take risks, rebel, reject their parents' values, state their individuality, or merely to be accepted," the American Academy of Child & Adolescent Psychiatry noted in January 2019.[6]

"Others may injure themselves out of desperation or anger to seek attention, to show their hopelessness and worthlessness, or because they have suicidal thoughts. These children may suffer from serious psychiatric problems such as depression, psychosis, post-traumatic stress disorder (PTSD), and bipolar disorder. Additionally, some adolescents who engage in self-injury may develop borderline personality disorder as adults. Some young children may resort to self-injurious acts from time to time but often grow out of it."

The academy noted that children who have been abused or abandoned may also exhibit this behavior.

Hawthorne asked if she thought vampires were "real."

"At some point in time, I did, but I don't think so anymore."[7]

She became convinced that they were real after she met Ferrell, she said.

"He said he was, and he told me about all the different things he's done and all the different people where he used to live that were just like him."

She said that she found him "intriguing," and she talked to him, because she had few friends. "...the people at school I thought were just too mundane, too ordinary, and just, I don't know. They didn't have a style of their own, they just went by what was in at the time. And I didn't feel like that. I didn't feel like jumping on the band wagon."

She defined her non-band-wagon style.

"I wore black tights with cutoff shorts and knee socks that were black and white striped and black boots, and I dyed my hair red and purple and blue and green and turquoise, all the colors of the rainbow except black, I've never done black. And I liked wearing different hats. But I can't wear hats at school."

She said she also liked wearing flannel, lots of necklaces, earrings, and rings.

Her parents didn't object. "My mom liked it, she thought it was cute sometimes. She liked me being my own person. My dad, he didn't really care. He thought it was funny, cute, you know. He laughed. Maybe he thought it was a phase or something. But they didn't object. They didn't object to anything I wore."

The Barbie doll was the idea of a boy she was dating—the self-proclaimed witch that introduced Ferrell to Jeanine. He put it in her locker. She dangled it from her backpack. The doll was mangled one day by a boy who ran by and snatched it from her pack. "It's not like I mangled it to make it look that way."

Heather had a theory about why the boyfriend came up with the idea of a macabre Barbie. "Barbie doll, I guess, represented all of the stereotypes of band-wagon people, the people that go by fashionistic people...."

Hawthorne also asked Heather if she was familiar with a book called *Necronomicon*.

"It's like the witches' handbook," she said, adding that it was for "casting spells, invoking spirits, things like that."

She said she had looked at the book but had not really read it, nor had she ever tried to do any of those things.

She was also asked about her relationship with her parents and with Jennifer. She admitted that she sometimes got into shouting matches but denied telling any of them that she hated them.

"I don't hate anyone," she said.

"Did you ever tell them you wished they were dead?"

"No."

Nor did she ever tell them she wanted to run away. That idea did begin to take root after Ferrell moved away, however.

"I didn't really feel like going anywhere, but Jeanine, she felt like getting away because she had some problems with her family, and she wanted to get away from them."

Jeanine's parents controlled her "with an iron fist," Heather said. "She's not allowed to dress the way she wants to dress, and she's not allowed to do things that she likes to do. They don't let her draw what she wants to draw. And if they find out she draws something that they don't like, they'll take it and throw it away. They went through her room one day and just threw out all the stuff that they didn't like. They threw out some of the stuff that I had left over there for her to keep while I was away, or anything that she liked of mine, I let her keep, and they threw it away if they didn't like it."

Heather said Jeanine got into trouble a few months after Ferrell left Eustis. People from school told her parents that "she was supposedly in some type of little vampire thing...."

Jeanine's parents moved her to Leesburg High School, where her father was a teacher.

In the meantime, Heather said she would talk to Ferrell on the phone. "It varied. Different times I'd talk to him every other day, but then sometimes I wouldn't talk to him for months at a time."

The trio worked out a system where he could talk to Jeanine.

"He'd call me up and say he wanted to call Jeanine, and I'd say, 'Okay, call her in five minutes and I'll get on the phone with her,' and so when he would call it would just beep in and nobody would know, and she'd just click over and talk to him. So, as far as her parents knew, she was talking to me because I called her."

They talked about his friends, hanging out and having parties at cemeteries. "He'd tell me all about his little vampire buddies and stuff."

Ferrell talked about his "sire," Murphy.

"The person that gets crossed over is subject to whatever the sire wants. Like, the sire is the boss, basically. They have authority over you."

Ferrell gave her "a lot of wild numbers" when she asked how long he had been a vampire, "like 65 years ago, a 100 and some years ago, several hundred and some years ago, a lot of different numbers."

At one point he said he was 500 years old.

"I don't think I could believe him. It was just too large of a number."

Hawthorne eventually got around to asking the burning question: "Did you talk about killing your parents? Did he ever say anything about killing your parents?"

"If he did, it was like insinuation, not like a flat-out question."

Heather said he might say something like it might be easier for her to leave if her parents were not around.

Eventually, Ferrell said the only way they could get together is if he came to Florida and picked them up. "And it just kind of evolved from there."

Hawthorne also asked her to explain the discussion she had with Jennifer about Ferrell potentially attacking an abusive boyfriend of hers.

"Did she know Rod was someone who one might call if they wanted someone taken out?"

"I didn't talk to her about it."

"Do you have an explanation for why she would tell the police something like that?"

"She was probably very upset, and she did not know what was going on. She did not know what happened. I don't know why she would make that statement unless she was trying to fill in gaps in her own mind...."

Hope spoke up and urged her to tell the story about Jennifer's abusive boyfriend.

The boyfriend was furious because Jennifer had dumped him. He showed up drunk in the parking lot where she worked and attacked her.

"And this wasn't the first time that he'd beaten her up. And she was crying, she was in my room and she was crying, and she started telling me how much she hates him, she hates him, she hates him. And I'm like, 'Do you wish he was dead?' And she was like, 'Yes, I wish he was dead.' And I told her, 'I mean, if you really do, I mean, it might could happen. It might could happen.'"

Heather felt Ferrell "could do something about it, maybe not kill him, but maybe like beat him up or something. I don't know. Just make him pay for what he did to my sister."

Heather's credibility and judgment took a hit on that one. Not only had she first denied talking to Jennifer about Ferrell, but if she thought Ferrell was dangerous, why did she have him come to her house to pick her up?

Ferrell's lawyers didn't ask the latter question specifically, but it was hanging out there. That, and Ferrell's claim about the Explorer keys.

CHAPTER 37

"Hideous monster"

Heather picked up a pen in her bedroom, found some paper and wrote: "My soul feels split in two. Like two different people. One, the nonresistant, passive, nonaggressive, whom I usually show to all people. Then two is the essence of vengeance, hate and destruction. Purely chaos molded into a hideous monster writhing and tearing the inside of me to ribbons."[1]

The note was stuffed into an evidence box along with other letters and artwork.

Some of the material was giddy kid stuff. One of the letters she wrote included a cartoon of a rumpled, happy-go-lucky character with wavy hair, a hat and sunglasses, and the words, "Me, basically." Another scribbling revealed that she could not sleep at night without her teddy bear, "Squishy Bear."

Her obsession with the occult was most striking. She wrote to a friend about an art camp that she and Jeanine had attended.

"It was very interesting there. There were a lot of freaks and weirdos just like Jeanine and me. And much to our surprise, there were a few witches and vampires also. There was one vampire there that was so old she would have put

Rod's maker's maker to shame. Good thing she was on our side.

I met witches who helped me cast a few spells of my own on a few people. I should have gotten the recipe for one spell.... The girl who helped me cast it told me vaguely what it did. I think it had something to do with castration. Also, I work a lot more with crystals and energy. So far I can drain some people's energy or give them some."

A few months later, she wrote to warn the friend that Ferrell wanted to kill him. He wrote back to say that he heard it first from Jeanine. He said the rumor was started by Matt Goodman, who had been feuding with Ferrell, so he doubted it was true. "We are in charge of our own lives, and no one can change our destiny whether they want to or not."

Heather and Goodman had been getting acquainted at Ferrell's insistence. Ferrell wanted to form a vampire family, with Heather as Goodman's "dark mate" and Jeanine as his "queen."

She began one of her first letters to Goodman, whose nickname was "Damion," by apologizing for not writing sooner. There had been a lot of things going on, she said, including breaking up with a boyfriend.

The breakup was inevitable. She said she and Jeanine took him to the woods one day to scare him. "We did some phony fire ritual and then cut his hand with a razor to drink. I think he still has the scar and the fear of me!"

There was a lot of talk about running away.

"Jeanine wonders why Valius [Ferrell] has to wait to get his GED to come and get us. As for me, I'd probably need a couple of years here in Eustis before I do anything. I mean, up and leaving is a big thing for me. I'm sure you know that I'd miss all the people I'd be leaving behind. My parents and family and friends haven't caused me enough trouble that I feel I have to run away from them. You know that, don't you? I'm not too sure about Jeanine, though."

Sometimes real concerns popped into her head. "The thing I must wonder about is what are my obligations if I were to go with you and Valius?"

At other times, she seemed eager to leave. In one note, she said she hoped Ferrell would come and pick them up before school started. She said there were so many people she wanted to meet, including "Nos" (Anderson) "and even Rod's sire."

Some of her eagerness was clearly a desire to do whatever she wanted.

"My hair has gone from flat and blonde to curly and blood red. I think it kind of goes good with my three ear piercings and belly-button ring. It's too bad that my parents won't let me get my tongue pierced or get a tattoo. That'll have to wait till I leave home."

She complained about Eustis being "the dullest town to live in," and said she did not even live in town. Her home was 10 miles outside of the city.

"I hardly ever get high. But not that I don't want to. It's just the only person I can get anything from is my cousin, 35 miles away. Getting drunk isn't really my style. I'd hate the hangovers."

She wrote, "what is needed is a family of some sort, (excuse the phrase family, if you wish). I just hope it would contain four of us. What I say is two is company three is a crowd but four is a coven."

In one letter she referred to a phone conversation they had. "P.S. I don't know what you said about love. We shall talk about that in a letter following this one. Alright."

In a note from South Carolina, where she was vacationing with Jeanine's family, she picked up the thread again.

"Some people can toss the love word around as easily as picking roses. But truly, what is the reason for taking up roses only to stand back and look at them for a while? And even if the rose lived for all eternity would you really have the compassion and will to watch it and care for it as long as you are here? Could anyone? As Rod has planned for Jeanine to be his mate, I know that Jeanine can never be completely patient and calm even when she is told beforehand.

"As for me, my feelings are basically the same as Jeanine's. Unsure but waiting. To tell the truth, my way is usually to go with whatever happens. I rarely oppose anything unless I feel something isn't right. Jeanine is to be Rod's mate. Rod tells me you want me to be yours. If that is true, it sounds convenient for all. I don't oppose. However, I can't tell just now what is or isn't right. I need time, Damion. Please give me that. After all, we have all the time in the world."

She wrote about tensions between Goodman and Ferrell, at one point saying she was relieved the two had patched things up and did not want to "murder" each other. Then, however, she wrote that Jeanine thought it would be better for Goodman to be the leader, "considering that all the humanity he has in his whole self is only a fraction compared to what you have."

She then pleaded with Goodman to try to "talk things out" with Ferrell.

She wrote again, probably in the springtime, from her family's condo at Daytona Beach. She wrote that she was high, and her handwriting showed it, tilting slightly to the left and looking almost as if a different person was writing it.

"I don't know if you know but Rod is coming here on Monday. He's not gonna take us anywhere; only just take us out hunting. Both me and Jeanine have been anticipating him coming for a very long time. When he gets here everything will be better. We all will be stronger as a unit."

The next letter detailed her disappointment with Ferrell trying but failing to get to Eustis. Ferrell had hitched a ride with a friend's father, who was a truck driver, because he couldn't get a ride from any "immortals." He was supposed to drive to Florida, but "ditched" him in Louisiana, she said.

She said he called her later, 100 miles from Eustis. "It was funny 'cause he was calling from some house he had just broke into when he heard the police show up and split." He later called from Leesburg, about 20 miles away.

"You can probably figure out that I was pretty excited. It would have been all okay but there was one problem. Rod's sire didn't want Rod to leave in the first place. He got really mad when he called Rod up in Louisiana and told him to come back and Rod's reply was [expletive] you. That's when Rod's sire set out to bring him back home. Well, in Leesburg he finally caught up with Rod while I was on the phone with him."

She said, 'I am so isolated and away from family several states distance."

I really want to cry aloud all the time, but I keep it in or try to kill it with drugs or alcohol. And if I'm not passed out from crying, I want to run and run until I collapse or die. I wonder how far I would get. People often wonder why I scream to the point that my blood runs cold, and why I punch my fist on the wall to leave dents.

I don't know if you understand or even care how close I was to being the happiest I've ever been. I was so close that I could feel Rod's life all around me. I should have told him to drive over and pick me and Jeanine up that very night. It probably would have taken only a few minutes to gather a few of my things I might need.

She said she felt like the "whole situation" was changing her. "Things that I used to feel were important I don't care so much about. Friends, family, school, and even basic humanity."

It was at that point she wrote about the "hideous monster" within, adding: "Should I cry? Should I scream? Or run? Or maybe turn my back and smoke myself away? All are options I could have, and all may just happen. I am already screaming inside. The voice echoes and tremors run through my body. I am crying, inside I am laughing insanely all to nothing is a bit funny."

She quit writing for a few hours and then came back, her handwriting suddenly sloppy, full of typos, and her thoughts disjointed. "It's now about 8:00. I just came back from getting stone (sic) out of my mind. I hope my handwriting doesn't give it away. The funny thing about this is (sic) seems to me it has taken me ten minuets (sic) to write these 4our (sic) sentences. Blood would taste rally (sic) good right about now. Maybe ice cream. Hey! What am I saying? Blood is good all the time!

"Why is everyone so wrapped up in this love thing? It's just some word that's an excuse to get the other person on good terms with you. I know now that its (sic) unsafe for me to say it. I might get hurt too much again.

"Man, I smell like weed. I have to take a shower. Why I am (sic) telling you all this? Oh well (sic) It doesn't matter any way. So, I won't worry myself with it.

"I remember the first verse of a poem I wrote.

This thing called love is my confusion
for some its use as cheap amution [sic}
Another thing for their abution [sic]
Tell me who love has?

"I don't want to be sad again. Before I was happy and laughing.
Now I'll become ill and down.
Not now. Too soon! Help me.

"I'll let go now. Perhaps I'll write you later again."

She also wrote in a letter about a "disturbing dream."

I was in some house, not mine or anyone else's that I know. There were some people close in the other room, and in the room I was in was a small child. It was more of an infant girl. She couldn't have been more than a few days old. She was so small and light I could hold her in one hand. It was like I could hear her thoughts and she could hear mine. I remember I asked her questions, like who she was and if she knew me. She said that yes, she knew me and who I was because she was an old friend. Then I don't know what came over me but I went straight for her little neck. She started to scream and cry. Just like a little baby crying not an old friend. Just a little baby.

I know it was just a dream, but I can still taste the blood and smell her scent.

She smelled like any other infant, sweet and innocent. Usually a dream like this one would seem like a good vision but now this one makes me think about things. It makes me ask questions about myself. Is this what real evil is like?

Did I enjoy it? Does this make me a monster? Do I care anymore?

She also described another dream.

...I was living or working for some rich woman in a large house. Maybe I did something wrong, but in any case, she threw me out. As I walked down the road awhile, I noticed a familiar house. When I went inside, Jeanine, Rod, and you were there. It all seemed so right. After a while of doing the together thing, one of us noticed that two guys had been prowling around outside. Quick as a flash we were there with them....

It was agreed to drain them and to my surprise and delight Rod offered me the first kill. Something inside me started to happen. Something growing. I didn't quite know what it was until the guy I was going to feed from went hysterical. He started shouting, "Oh my God, look at her teeth. Her teeth. Oh my God! Her [expletive] teeth are growing."

When I heard this, that was when I distinctly felt my fangs growing out. And with every second they grew, my hunger grew larger. Right when I was about to drink from him, my mother came in and woke me up. I was very frustrated. I'm sure you can relate.

The thing is, even after this dream was over, I could still faintly feel my teeth with a slight tingle in them. To you, I'm supposing this happening to you is an everyday thing, no big deal, right? But for me, it was a first feel of a new gift, a great (sic) awaited gift. For me, it was a reason to wait patiently for more.

CHAPTER 38

"I always wanted them alive"

The defense teams still had questions about Heather's role and hopes—though slim—that they might unearth something in a second deposition that might help their clients.

For example, did she set up the fatal, deadly confrontation between Ferrell and her parents by not telling him that the keys to the Explorer were in the ignition? That he did not even need to go inside the house? Did she incite the mayhem by telling Ferrell she wanted her parents to be killed? Why didn't she try to escape or call for help? Was she telling the truth, or was she lying?

Plecas wanted to know what Cooper had to say when the three girls were on the way to visit Heather's boyfriend.

There was very little talk, Heather replied, and nothing criminal. Dana, in fact, consoled her after they left Jeremy's house. "I felt pretty bad that it was the last time I was going to see him."[1]

They then went to a gas station where Heather paid for $20 worth of gas and a quart of oil.

Graves made a joke about girls knowing how to service a car, but Plecas was making a point.

"It's actually very helpful, if, for instance, the girls had known that the boys were going to steal the car, do you think you would have put twenty dollars-worth of gas in the car?"

"No way," he admitted.

Plecas also asked Heather about her understanding of why Ferrell and Anderson were left at her house.

"I didn't think they were being left at my house. We discussed that they would go and get Jeanine, while I went to Jeremy's house...."

They were to walk, Heather said, something that she and Jeanine had done many times.

"I want you to think really hard about this. Was there anything that Dana did that you observed that would cause you to think that she thought anything other than the plan was going to happen?"

"No."

The girls went to Jeanine's house, but Jeanine said she needed more time. Heather said they drove all the way back to her house looking for Ferrell and Anderson when "they flew by us in the Explorer.... I was very upset because I knew if they had the car then they must have gotten my keys. My dad doesn't leave the keys in the car. So, they must have went (sic) in my house."

Heather said she kept asking questions until Charity, who was driving the Buick, flashed the headlights, signaling for the Explorer to pull over. Charity got out of the car again and talked to Ferrell.

"That's when Charity told me what Scott and Rod had done."

"She said, 'To put it bluntly, Heather, your parents are dead.'"

Heather said she "started to lose it."

Keesee's attorney, Tommy Carle, jumped in with a question.

"Did she follow that up with the statement, "But he probably just killed some animals, or something like that?"

"When I started to freak out, I think Charity said, 'Well, Zoey, don't worry. Maybe he's just bullshitting. Maybe he's just screwing with us.'"

Heather said Cooper climbed into the backseat to calm her. "She just held me and kept me from flailing around…."

She said she "fell asleep" for a while and when she woke up, the cars were pulled over and the group started piling all belongings into the Explorer.

Carle asked Heather to explain how she felt when Ferrell showed up on that Sunday night. It was "a shock," she said, adding that they had not heard from him in two months.

She asked Jeanine if she still wanted to leave and she said, "Yeah, I guess so."

Carle asked Heather if she wanted to leave.

"Not really," she said. "I just got a new boyfriend, which was working out real (sic) good. And Jeanine, her life was getting together."

Heather said she and Jeanine were upset when he called Monday night and said they had to leave right away. "We had been given a week."

Heather said she spent about 10 minutes each with her parents before she slipped out of the house.

"Well, my dad was looking at a high school yearbook, and he was showing me all the people he knew and pointing out just girls he went out with and people he knew and who his friends were."

She said her mother was watching TV in bed, so she went and laid down with her for a while to watch TV and talk.

She slipped out of the house through the bathroom door by the pool, climbed a fence, and got into the car with the girls.

Anderson and Ferrell were nowhere to be seen, she said.

Carle asked Heather how many times Ferrell made "insinuations," as she put it, about killing her parents.

"I didn't make it a point to count how many times, so I wouldn't know."

"More than five?"

"Maybe. Maybe just five."

"Did you ever take him seriously?

"No."

"Okay. Now, I have two other questions about your behavior," Plecas said, "and I know it's really easy to Monday morning quarterback, so I apologize. I don't mean to offend you, but when you saw your parents' car, for instance, why didn't you insist on going to Jeanine's and call the police at that point?"

"Going to Jeanine's and calling the police?"

"Well, did you think that they were entitled to the car, or that your parents had lent them the car?"

"No, I know they didn't lend the car."

"Okay."

"Because I wasn't really thinking about that right at that second. I was wondering why they had the car and how they got the car. And until I knew that, then I could get thinking straight. Then I could think about what I was going to do next."

Heather said the drivers of the two cars pulled onto a dirt road where they switched license plates. Heather stayed in the back seat of the Buick while Charity and Dana got out and talked to Rod.

"You certainly would have had an opportunity to get out while the four of them were talking and do whatever," Plecas said.

"That was before I knew what happened."

"Well, it was after you knew that they had a car that didn't belong to them, wasn't it?"

"Yeah, but that's not as bad as killing two people."

"So, you could have gone along with them stealing the car."

"I didn't know what was going on."

"Well, you knew that they had a car that didn't belong to them, didn't you, Heather?"

"Right."

"Okay. And that was okay with you?"

"No, that wasn't okay with me."

"Then why didn't you do something about it?"

"I thought things were being done. I thought I was going to know what was going on when they got back in the car. When they got back in the car, they were going to tell me what happened and then I would know what was going on."

"I don't understand. What difference would it have made? You knew the car didn't belong to them, didn't you?"

"Right."

"So, it wasn't okay for them to have it."

"No, it wasn't okay for them to have it."

"Then why didn't you use the two separate opportunities that you had to extract yourself from the situation and do something about it?"

"Because I didn't think of it at the time."

Would Ferrell have permitted Heather to go back to Jeanine's and call the police? Not likely, nor is feasible that she could have escaped on the dirt road where the license plates were switched. However, there did seem to be some other opportunities. The group stopped at a convenience store in Tampa, a Wal-Mart in Tallahassee, and other places.

The lawyers failed to ask why she didn't tell the police officers who stopped them in New Orleans. Ferrell was unarmed except for a small pocketknife.

Another officer talked to the teens when they ran out of gas outside of Baton Rouge.

Plecas did ask Heather about her reaction to finding out her parents had been killed.

"…you were comfortable enough, or your mind was at ease enough, that you were able to, not once, but twice fall asleep?"

"Um, I can be exhausted," she said, then she began stumbling over her words: "I can, I was, can be passed out. I could, I wouldn't say that I passed out…."

"Are you saying that you passed out?"

"I didn't say that I passed out, but you can get hysterical enough to exhaust yourself and that's happened, I was exhausted."

Carle began asking questions again, this time about what happened in New Orleans.

Heather said they were only there a couple of hours.

"Charity started freaking out because she didn't like being in New Orleans. She didn't like being in such a big city and she got scared there."

"Did she say, 'Let's get out of here,'" or something like that, or leave this town, or leave this area?"

"No, I know she wanted to."

Carle asked if anyone stood up to Ferrell.

"Not really, no."

"Anybody afraid of him?"

"Probably most all of us were."

Heather said she saw the crowbar under the seat of the Explorer. Rod told her in detail in New Orleans how he had killed her parents.

Was there a plan going into Baton Rouge? Carle asked.

"Not really. We might have been looking for some pawn shops to pawn stuff for money, but all the pawn shops were closed, it being Thanksgiving and all."

She said they went down by the river, but she didn't watch Ferrell and Anderson dispose of the murder weapon and the other items. At one point, they discussed throwing everything into the river, even their personal belongings.

Carle wondered if Charity and Heather talked about her parents on the long ride back to Florida.

"No, not really. We talked about basically Rod."

She said that when they were still at the detention center in Louisiana, "she still loved him, and she still just wanted to be with him…."

She said that changed when Charity realized "what the real situation was."

Heather said they started calling him names and laughing at him.

Charity never indicated that she was part of a plan to kill her parents, Heather said.

Graves also tried to figure out what Heather was thinking the night her parents were killed.

Heather only had $40 cash, and no credit cards before putting $20 worth of gas in the Buick.

"I knew that I wasn't going to get that far with that much because I have been on trips before, and I know how much gas can cost."

"And you are aware, geographically, because I also understand how smart you are, that Louisiana is a fair poke away, a fair drive away from Eustis."

"Yes, but I didn't anticipate going down to Tampa and back up. I didn't know we were going to waste gas and time doing that."

Someone in the group had also mentioned going down "south," because they knew someone that could "help" by giving them a place to stay. After driving around Tampa for a couple of hours, they headed north to Tallahassee, and then Louisiana.

Graves also asked her about that Monday. She said she met Ferrell and the others at the cemetery, then the group drove to a Wal-Mart where they bought cake snacks and Ferrell bought razor blades so he could cross Heather over to become a vampire.

"Whose suggestion was it for you to cross over?"

"It was everyone's idea, if anything, because Jeanine had already done it and I had half done it...."

"How do you half do it? Do you lick and miss?"

"No, you do it the first time and that just starts you off, and then you have to wait a while to do it again."

He asked what she thought would happen once she crossed over.

"That you see things and hear things and your senses become more acute."

"Other than heightened senses, was there anyone who suggested to you that you might gain longer life or some eternal powers?"

"Yeah, that went along with it."

Heather said she didn't have any heightened senses, but Ferrell told her that it takes a while.

"Did anyone ever suggest to you that by crossing over you had to become part of a group or a cult or a family?"

"Yeah. If someone crosses you over, then it's kind of like they made you, and you're kind of under them."

"Similar to Amway?" Graves joked.

"Kind of."

"I mean, if Rod is an example, crossed you over, participated in your crossing over, that you were underneath him?"

"Yes."

"And anyone I'd cross over would be underneath me, would be underneath Rod?"

"Yes," she said. "He was boss."

People look up to the "boss," she said, seek advice from him, "or just everything, because you made them. They don't know anything. They have to learn from him."

"And that would also have gone for you, too?"

"Yes."

"And you have indicated that if the orders or the direction of the person above you were not followed, that person would get angry?"

"Right."

Graves brought his questions back to that Monday night when Ferrell panicked and said they had to leave right away.

Heather said Ferrell was anxious to leave after a sheriff's deputy questioned them while they changed a flat tire on the Buick. Ferrell told her that the car was stolen.

Could she have said no to leaving?

"Well, I had already told them that I would, and I guess if he told me we had to, I guess we had to, because that's Rod telling us to do it."

She said wasn't concerned about riding in a stolen car. "I didn't know that I could get in legal trouble, because I wasn't informed on what the laws were. It's not my hobby. I don't look at what's after the fact, and what's this and what's that."

Nor was she concerned about leaving with people who might be wanted by the law. "...if we left that night, then I figured maybe we wouldn't get caught."

She said Ferrell asked her how she was going to get out of the house, "and he asked me if I wanted him to come with me to make it look like a kidnapping."

It was an idea he had proposed with Jeanine and her parents.

"But I told them that no, I didn't want that because I didn't want them coming into my house anyway. If I wanted them to come to my house, then I wouldn't have told them to park so far away."

"This was Rod you indicated that wanted to make it look like a kidnapping?"

"Yes, right."

"Did he indicate to you in this kidnapping scenario whether it would be just him that came into the house?"

"I don't think he made it very specific."

Like the other defense attorneys, Graves was both trying to protect his client and check Heather's credibility.

Graves asked her if she questioned Ferrell or Anderson once she was in the Explorer.

"No, I didn't ask anyone anything."

"Why not?"

"Because I wasn't talking. I just wasn't doing anything."

"Well, I'm going to tell you exactly what my concern is. I'm not trying to hide anything from you. By this time

Charity had at least indicated to you that maybe this was just some of Rod's bullshit."

"Yeah."

"Certainly you loved your parents, correct?"

"Correct."

"You would have held out hope against hope that your parents were, in fact, not dead, right?"

"Right."

"And this was, in fact, some of Rod's BS."

"Right."

"Did you want to believe that your parents were in fact still alive?"

"Of course."

"Did you believe that was a possibility?"

"Well, Charity said it was, but I didn't know if she was absolutely correct because she said he may just be bull-shitting, you know.

"Like she didn't know one way or the other."

"Right."

"So, my question is, didn't you at some point want to know whether, in fact, your parents were dead?"

"I kind of put things together."

"What things did you put together?"

"Like, they both didn't have shirts on. And why wouldn't they have shirts on unless there was something on them or they were ruined or something."

Neither Ferrell nor Anderson directly said that her parents were dead. "It was just like insinuations, like just little things. Like I knew that they had been in the house and had ransacked it, had gone through the stuff...."

How did she know that? Graves asked.

"Because Rod had in his hands and was playing with my mother's pearls. And my mother doesn't keep that out in the open."

He asked if she ever attempted to call the police or her sister.

"I could never get to a phone." She said she was either always in the car or someone was always with her. She admitted that no one ever warned her about not calling anyone, nor did she ever hear anyone order that she not be left alone.

Graves asked her about how Ferrell told her in New Orleans that he had killed her parents.

"He told me that Scott froze. That Scott just turned around, just absolutely turned around from the scene, he froze."

She said he also described how he killed her mother, including her scratching his face, and seeing the scratches on his face.

"Did he ever explain to you when he decided to go in?"

"No."

"Did he explain to you or discuss with you whose idea it was to go inside the house?"

"No."

"Based on the knowledge that you have of all of the cast of characters, and the roles that they play, and I know this is an opinion, whose idea do you think it was to go inside of the house?"

"Rod's.

He also asked her if she had heard about the discussion by the teens at Shannon Yohe's house about killing her parents.

She knew what was said because her attorney, James Hope, had read her the transcripts before she testified before the grand jury, but she had not talked to Shannon.

"I told Jeanine and my sister, and we are all real mad at her because I saw her on Monday, and she didn't say anything to me about what they were talking about. I mean, when she easily could have told me."

She did learn from Jeanine before her parents were killed that Ferrell had talked about killing her parents.

"Did you not find that rather odd or scary?"

"No, because I knew Rod didn't like her parents anyway."

She said she didn't think that it was a serious threat anyway. "I mean, the plan was just to leave."

"Have you ever written to anyone or discussed with anyone in any way anything about killing anybody?"

"Not really. I mean, I don't talk about me killing anyone."

"Or having someone killed?"

Graves went so far as to call it an expression, like, "God, I wish they were dead."

"Everyone says that," she said.

"Do you recall that you may have said that to anyone at any time in regard to your parents?"

"No. I don't even say I hate anyone. I don't even like the word hate."

"Would you consider yourself a passive individual?"

"Very much. Passive, nonaggressive."

Yet, in a letter to "Damion," she had written, "My soul feels split in two. Like two different people. One, the nonresistant, passive, nonaggressive, whom I usually show to all people. Then two is the essence of vengeance, hate and destruction. Purely chaos molded into a hideous monster writhing and tearing the inside of me to ribbons."

Was she still feeling split in two? The question wasn't asked.

Graves asked several questions about what happened in Baton Rouge, including at the police station, and whether any of the other teens threatened her.

Then, he asked about vehicle keys.

"Did he ask you in any way, shape or form, or had anyone asked you whether your parents might have any money, or where the car keys were kept?"

"No, nobody asked me anything like that."

"Did you have any reason to believe that anyone was going in there in an attempt to rob your parents?"

"No."

He asked her if she had ever played Vampire the Masquerade or read the book, including the part where a vampire would gain power by killing someone.

Neither one, she said.

Graves asked if Ferrell or Anderson talked about killing anybody else, and she said no.

"Because of the relationship that was developed, in part with crossing over, all of those things you talked about, or where you indicated that when Rod said you've got to go, that you didn't have a choice, I would call that kind of blindly following someone. Was that…true with everyone that was there, with the girls, with Scott, of blindly following Rod? If Rod said take a long walk off a deep pier, then they would take a long walk off the deep pier because Rod told them they had to?"

"Yeah."

"You didn't ask reasons why; you just did as you were told."

"Yeah, basically."

"I think you can certainly see that looking back on all of this some of the steps that you took may not have been the wisest or the most mature steps."

"Yeah, I know."

"And it's my understanding, from talking to folks who know you, that you frankly are too smart to do most of those things if you sat back and thought about them. Would you agree with that?

"Yes."

"So, did you do what you did in part because, in large part, because Rod told you to?"

"Yes."

He asked if she had talked to Jeanine about everything that happened.

"She feels real (sic) bad," she said. "Because we were just so close and she called my parents mom and dad, too, you know."

Jeanine felt bad "about everything," Heather said, introducing Ferrell to her, maintaining a long-distance relationship with him, not taking him seriously, and "that she was just as involved as I was, only that she didn't get out of the house."

Bill Lackay, who started the day with a provocative question about visiting her parents' gravesites, asked another: "Do you want Rod Ferrell to get the death penalty?"

"It's hard to say. Some days I do, some days I don't. It depends on how I feel that day."

A few minutes later he asked: "Before your parents died, did you ever feel that way about them? Some days you maybe wanted them killed, some days you didn't?"

"No, I always wanted them alive. I loved them."

The lawyers had asked pointed questions as respectfully as possible, though they were frequently not satisfied with the answers. They had a problem. Leaning on an orphan in a deposition is one thing; doing it in front of a jury could be tricky, if not disastrous.

CHAPTER 39

Manson vs. Ferrell

When Keesee's attorney in Baton Rouge said, "This is not a Charles Manson case," he was right, of course. The sheer number of Manson's victims (no one knows how many) and the notoriety of having his followers butcher pregnant Hollywood actress, Sharon Tate, in the home of her famous director husband, Roman Polanski, made Charles Manson the nation's "preeminent bogeyman."[1]

But there are some similarities to the Manson Family and other notorious cults.

One of the things Manson did was to change his followers' names. Susan Atkins became Sadie Mae Glutz. She said, "in order for me to be completely free in my mind I had to be able to completely forget the past. The easiest way to do this, to change identity, is by doing so with a name."[2]

Ferrell called himself "Vesago." Anderson became "Nos," and Goodman "Damion."

Manson himself went by different names, including Devil, Satan, and Soul.

A key part of playing Vampire the Masquerade, of course, is changing your identity. That's how Ferrell became so fascinated with vampirism. There is a certain euphoria in diving into fantasy—fun without consequence.

Ferrell's goal was to create a vampire family.

"Among ourselves, we called ourselves the Family," Manson said.[3]

A key characteristic is for the leader to isolate the group, cult expert Dr. J. Gordon Melton told me in an interview for the *Sentinel*.[4]

Manson isolated his "family" by moving them to old ranches or the desert.

Ferrell was willing to go to beyond that easy solution. "...he knows if he kills my parents then I'd probably come to him, I probably wouldn't have anything to stay in Florida for," Heather told detectives in Baton Rouge. "...he wanted to break the ties, we wanted to break the ties to Florida."

Once isolated, cult leaders can begin preaching even the craziest philosophy and the group will buy it in a concept known as "societal construction of reality," said Dr. Jim Lewis, a college instructor and researcher at the Institution for the Study of American Religion.

FBI profiler and *Mind Hunter* author, John Douglas, interviewed Manson. "What he preached made perfect sense," he said. "Pollution is destroying the environment, racial prejudice is ugly and destructive, love is right, and hate is wrong. But once he had those lost souls in his sway, he instituted a highly structured delusional system that left him in complete control. He used sleep deprivation, sex, food control and drugs to gain complete dominance, like a prisoner-of-war situation. Everything was black and white and only Charlie knew the truth."[5]

Author Sean Dolan notes: "The more a person has invested in a cult—in terms of things such as time, money and emotions—the more unlikely it is that he or she will be able to do what it takes to leave. By that point, the typical cult member will have surrendered so much of his or her previous life—friends, family, romantic relationships, education, work and career money, years of a life—that it becomes that much more difficult to admit to having been manipulated or tricked."[6]

Both Ferrell and Manson have been described as charismatic.

"One of the things that really typifies a vampire is this mesmeric personality. We see Rod not merely cultivating it but holding people in thrall, to get them to do things that maybe they would never have considered," according to vampire cult expert Michelle Belanger.[7]

Those "things" included burglary, using a stolen credit card, principal to murder, and accessory after the fact.

It is not clear just who Ferrell's role model was, but one of Manson's idols was Adolph Hitler. "Both had eyes which their followers described as 'hypnotic'; beyond that, however, both had a presence, a charisma, and a tremendous amount of personal persuasive power. Generals went to Hitler intent on convincing him that his military plans were insane; they left true believers. Dean Moorehouse went up to Spahn Ranch to kill Manson for stealing his daughter, Ruth Ann; he ended up on his knees worshipping him," Manson prosecutor, Vincent Bugliosi, wrote in *Helter Skelter*..[8]

Jeanine told her mother that if she saw Ferrell, she should not look at his eyes.

People often called Ferrell "charming," and said his voice was "hypnotic."[9]

"After Rod came back from Florida, he had this charisma about him. People always just kind of gravitated toward him," Anderson said.[10]

One of Manson's tricks was to convince his "family" that he had special powers. Followers would talk about him giving off "vibrations," or say they were afraid that he was reading their minds.[11]

Both cults attracted misfits. Manson attracted hippies and cast-offs, including girls from broken homes and young women who had father-issues.

"Rod, me, Jaden, Charity, and Dana all came from dysfunctional families that were barely making it. I guess, in our minds, it was us against the world," Anderson said.

Dysfunction is not necessarily a requirement for joining a cult.[12]

"Contrary to popular belief, most people who join cults in the United States are not outcasts or marginal members of society. Nor is there a greater incidence of mental or emotional problems among them than in the population at large," Dolan noted.[13]

"Studies have shown that cult members tend to be slightly better educated than average and no poorer than the average. In general, experts do not believe that there is any class or type of person that is more or less vulnerable to indoctrination of cults. Indeed, some experts maintain that under the right circumstances, *anyone* is susceptible to the type of persuasion that cults practice."

Dolan also cited the Cult Awareness Network's estimate that there are 2,000 groups in the U.S. that qualify as a cult. One researcher believes that 4 million Americans have been involved in a cult since the 1960s.[14]

If poverty or dysfunction didn't make Manson's and Ferrell's followers more vulnerable to cult thinking, then at least it was a common thread that helped bind them together.

The defense attorneys initially insisted that there was no evidence to show that vampirism had any role in the Wendorf murders.

"It would be like being on a softball team where the pitcher, shortstop, and second basemen are charged with killing someone," Mike Graves said. "Softball may have brought them together, but it didn't play any role in the murder."[15]

Cults are simply "religion gone bad," Melton said.

It was certainly the case in the Kirtland, Ohio case of self-proclaimed prophet, Jeff Lundgren, who had his splinter Mormon group followers "sacrifice" some cult members in the late 1980s. And it was the case with Jim Jones, David Koresh and others.[16]

There were some other odd similarities between Manson and Ferrell.

Ferrell claimed he was 500 years old.

Manson said he had lived 2,000 years before and implied that he was Jesus Christ.[17]

But the most important—and frightening—similarity may be that both Manson and Ferrell instilled fear in their followers.

"To Charlie, fear was the same thing as awareness…. The more fear you have, the more awareness, hence the more love," one follower said. It was a ruse, of course.[18]

"I would learn, from talking to other Family members, that Manson would seek out each individual's greatest fear—not so the person could confront and eliminate it, but so he could re-emphasize it. It was like a magic button, which he could push at will to control that person," Bugliosi said.

"Fear turns Charlie on," a follower told him.

Goodman quoted Ferrell as saying, "Fear is what drives the world."[19]

People are easy to control if they are in fear, Ferrell maintained, and control was what it was all about.

"He is power-hungry," Steven Murphy told me in a phone interview. "He could control Scott and Shea. He had the power of manipulation."

"He wanted people around him to worship him. He found power in that," Murphy said.[20]

Fear was not the only way Manson controlled his flock. He used sex, sometimes choreographing orgies like a stage director. Everyone had to lose all of their inhibitions, one follower said. "It was like the Devil buying your soul."[21]

Sondra Gibson claimed she was raped during vampire cult rituals in Kentucky. She was also arrested and charged with trying to lure a 14-year-old boy into having sex while crossing over to become a vampire.

Both Manson and Ferrell were engrossed by various aspects of the occult. Ferrell was fascinated by witchcraft, demonology, and then vampirism. Manson was intrigued by, among other things, a satanic cult in California, a weird interpretation of Beatles music and the apocalypse in the Bible.[22]

Manson follower Charles "Tex" Watson told his victim, "I am the Devil and I'm here to do the Devil's business."

There were some significant differences between the cults, however. Susan Atkins tasted Sharon Tate's blood, leading Bugliosi to call her a "vampira." There is no evidence that Ferrell or Anderson drank their victims' blood.[23]

So it was, in the months before Ferrell's trial, that defense lawyers shrugged their shoulders, criticized the news media for covering the vampire cult angle to death—or undeath—and insisted there was nothing to see. But Ferrell's attorneys were plotting a big surprise.

CHAPTER 40

Warming up the spotlight

Circuit Judge Jerry Lockett was a larger-than-life character, and that's saying a lot, because he was a big man—easily over 300 pounds.

The Lake County edition of the *Orlando Sentinel* ran a "Ticked Off" column of one-paragraph pet peeves submitted by readers, and one day a reader was ticked off about his rulings, which in turn, ticked off Lockett.

"I read with interest the recent 'Ticked Off' column in the *Lake Sentinel* wherein one of your readers perceived that I am 'in the pocket' of State Attorney Brad King in the Wendorf case. Let me assure everyone concerned that, because of my rotund stature and my temperament, I would never fit into Mr. King's or anyone else's pocket," he wrote in a letter to the editor.[1]

Once, he jokingly told a jury that a soft drink company was paying him NOT to drink its product in public.

His nickname was "Lock 'em up Lockett," and he liked to see his real name in print. "The most important thing to put in your stories is my name," he joked.

It was no problem, as it turned out. He presided over some of the biggest trials in county history, and he had a knack for attracting controversy.

In January of 1996, just 10 months before the vampire murders, police arrested a 30-year-old woman and charged her with trying to hire a hit man to kill Lockett and two witnesses in a drug case.

Ironically, he had generously given her extra time to report for a three-year prison sentence because she was having some problems with her pregnancy.

"What would she gain if I'm killed? She'd still go to prison. There's no logic to this, no reason," he told me in an interview.[2]

A jury found her guilty of conspiracy, and a judge sentenced her to 50 years in prison.

One of the most sensational trials Lockett presided over was that of James Duckett, a small-town rookie police officer charged with raping and murdering a schoolgirl. Duckett was convicted and sentenced to death in that case.

A former chief assistant public defender and a Navy Vietnam vet, he was used to being around tough guys, so he was amused when one man threatened him in open court.

"I'll see you in your coffin," the man said.[3]

Lockett had just sentenced him to life in prison with no chance of parole and no chance of seeing him in his coffin. Lockett laughed and mentioned his upcoming retirement. "I'll be living down a long straight road and I'll have a rifle with a scope on it," he said.

What he didn't say was that he was armed with a pistol in case the man made it past the bailiffs.

Brad King had been the elected State Attorney for the five-county Fifth Judicial Circuit for 10 years by the time the Ferrell trial was about to begin.

Long active in his Ocala Baptist church and physically fit, he looks as if he hasn't aged a day in 20 years.

An able administrator, he managed hundreds of employees and always managed to retain and recruit highly qualified attorneys.

His arguments are precise, his delivery dry. Mild-mannered to the core, he is the cold- water opposite of a hot grease fire.

King, who recently announced his retirement, has long been a strong believer in the death penalty if the facts of the case justify it.

"To me, if there is no death penalty, the value of that person whose life was taken is less than the defendant's. That's not fair, to me."[4]

When the State Attorney for the Orlando circuit announced she would not seek the death penalty in any of her cases, the governor appointed King to handle them.

King's number two man in the case was Jim McCune, a soft-spoken, scholarly, white-collar crime prosecutor who would later become a judge.

There was Candace Hawthorne for the defense, of course, a bulldog who would wipe out an entire forest worth of paper for motions and do anything she could to save her client's life.

Her co-counsel, Bill Lackay, was a hard-working, longtime assistant public defender, who was an ardent baseball fan, especially for the Atlanta Braves. Sometimes he used examples from the game to illustrate a point for jurors.

The year before, he represented Keith Johnson in one of the nation's first fatal school shootings.

Johnson was a 14-year-old middle school student when he pulled out a handgun and started blazing away under an outdoor covered walkway, sending 300 terrified students running for cover. Johnson fired 13 times at a boy he claimed was a threatening bully. Like the vampires, Johnson confessed without a lawyer or his mother at his side.

Lackay called upon a psychiatrist to help him plead his case.

It didn't help. Johnson was sentenced to life in prison without the possibility of parole.

CHAPTER 41

"Murder is not a private affair"

As the trial calendar kept shrinking, Lockett knew he had to clear his desk of the mountain of motions and make sure there no delays.

One of the biggest hassles had been DNA testing. Genetic evidence was still fairly new and controversial, though prosecutors in Orlando first used it in 1987 to convict a man of rape.

O.J. Simpson's lawyers convinced jurors in his 1995 Los Angeles murder case that samples had been contaminated.

In 1995, an analyst with the Florida Department of Law Enforcement was feeding genetic data from a 1991 Lake County Jane Doe rape and murder case into the new state DNA computer when he suddenly got a match to a convicted rapist. It was a first time a computer identified a suspect.

In the pretrial hearing in that case, the Public Defender's office questioned the way the FBI lab examined semen and the way prosecutors used astronomical statistics to say how unlikely it was that anyone else could have committed the crime. It was 400 billion-to-1 in the case of the Jane Doe killer.

Jurors convicted the man, but they were more impressed with the testimony of a bite-mark expert.

Ferrell's lawyers wanted their own experts to monitor the testing at the FDLE lab. State lab officials objected, citing possible interference and contamination. They said they would provide notes and documentation to the defense.

Lockett was sympathetic to the defense. "The fact that two of the defendants are on trial for their lives provides the most compelling of reasons that a defense expert be present during the testing."[1]

He noted, however: "It would appear preferable if an independent laboratory were funded by the state, which would be charged with the testing of samples such as blood, hair, and fibers."

A private firm was eventually hired, but it would cause Lockett some heartburn.

On Jan. 21, the judge told me he was "sick of being held captive" by private labs.

Lackay accused the state of "dillydallying" with tests of scrapings under Ruth Queen's fingernails and of blood on Ferrell's boots.

King said he had a private lab do the fingernail tests because the samples were so small that they would be destroyed in the testing. "I didn't have to do that. It would have been perfectly legal for me to have gone ahead and done the tests [at the state lab]."[2]

Two days later, Lockett put out the word to the lawyers: "Be ready for trial Feb. 2."[3]

"Everyone's had more than a year to get ready for this trial," Lockett said. "Let's get on with it."

Many of the defense motions were standard objections about the state's death penalty laws.

The law called for juries to make a recommendation, based on aggravating versus mitigating evidence.

Among the defense complaints was the fact that "only a bare majority of jurors is sufficient to recommend a death sentence."[4]

It was up to the judge to make the final determination.

The U.S. Supreme Court has since given juries the power and Florida law has been changed to require a unanimous jury vote for death.

"I've always believed that it is not the appropriate question to ask someone," King told me in a 2018 interview. "That's why we elect judges."[5]

"I hate to sit up here and deny all these motions," Lockett joked. "I wrote half of them," he said, referring to his days as the chief assistant public defender.[6]

He also denied the defense motion to sequester potential jurors. He reserved ruling on whether the trial jury should be sequestered once it started deliberations.

Acceding to Hawthorne's concerns about pretrial publicity, he ruled that each side could reject fifteen prospective jurors instead of ten.

He said he wanted to see if a jury could be selected before ruling on a change of venue motion, or whether a jury should be brought in from outside the area.

King was confident a jury could be selected.

"If we could pick a jury for the Dorothy Lewis case, we can pick a jury for this," he said.

Lewis was a young widow when she took her two young children to a grocery story on a Saturday evening in 1993, where she was carjacked, raped, shot, and her little girls murdered in one of the most heinous crimes in state history.

"There were even more feelings of [public] revulsion" in that case, King said.[7]

Hawthorne remained obsessive about pretrial publicity.

On Dec. 22, 1997, she filed a motion for closure of all pretrial proceedings.

"This case has been the subject of unprecedented and highly prejudicial publicity and media attention in Lake County, adjacent areas of Lake County, a majority of the state of Florida, and even outside the state of Florida," she wrote.[8]

"At every court proceeding, however minor or inconsequential, there has been extensive coverage by the press. It is anticipated that the press will continue to be active and aggressive in the coverage of all events and proceedings in this case."

She said upcoming hearings would deal with sensitive issues, including whether Ferrell's, and the other defendants', confessions should be suppressed.

She even suggested she might file a motion barring the public from the trial itself.

Lockett denied the motion.

The *Sentinel's* editorial writers were aghast.

"Imagine a murder trial being conducted behind closed doors so the public can't see the proceedings. That sort of perversion of justice might be allowed—even expected—in communist Cuba or North Korea. But Lake County, Florida?"[9]

The editorial acknowledged that Hawthorne was expected to be "an aggressive advocate" for her client.

"But to even consider barring the public is a disservice to the justice system. Murder is not a private affair. It is a horrible act. Every time someone is slain, the public's fear of crime is stoked, and the fabric of the community is torn. How justice is reached in a criminal case is the public's business. To try to hide the process of justice would just weaken further the public's trust in the court system, already damaged by the resolution of the cases of O.J. Simpson and the British au pair in Massachusetts." In that case, Louise Woodward was convicted of killing a baby in her care but served less than a year of her minimum 15-year sentence.

"Conducting court proceedings in the open protects the rights of both the accused and the victims. Judges and prosecutors are public officials whose salaries are paid by the taxpayers. Their performance in court should be subject to public scrutiny."

The editorial could have included the fact that the public defender and his assistants are also public officials.

Nor did it point out that Hawthorne was out of line in deciding whether news coverage was warranted for hearings she deemed "inconsequential" or "minor."

The editorial pointed out that there are remedies to ensure fair trials, including gag orders for the participants, keeping secret the names of jurors, carefully selecting jurors who have not made up their minds, and change of venue.

Hawthorne was also concerned about the confessions, and for good reason. A lawyer for one of the other teens told me, "When the jurors see the tape of Ferrell, they're going to want to pull the [electric chair] switch themselves."

Hawthorne also argued that Ferrell's rights were violated by investigators when they didn't follow Louisiana law that prohibits police from questioning juveniles without their parents present.

"Rod Ferrell was not made to contact his family," she argued.[10]

The procedure was handled correctly, King said, because the murders occurred in Florida.

She also brought up a statement Ferrell made when detectives asked him if he had consumed any "controlled dangerous drugs" or alcohol within three or four hours.

"Probably about an hour after I had some," he replied.

Mike Graves said Anderson was not clear about the charges he was facing, and he said detectives made thinly veiled threats, including: "There won't be no mercy when this gets to court, unless someone stands up and says this here is what was behind the whole thing."

Hawthorne's claim that Ferrell may have been intoxicated led to an unusual hearing on Jan. 12, with Rod taking the stand to answer questions strictly limited to the issue.

In a low, clear, controlled voice, he testified that he chugged a bottle of wine in just 10 minutes about an hour before he was arrested.

He said it had a "disorienting effect" and that he did not understand his rights.[11]

"He clearly wasn't intoxicated," said King, who had viewed the tape.

Ferrell also claimed that Baton Rouge Detective Ben Odom threatened "to put me under the jail."

Odom denied it.

On the tape, Ferrell remarked that the Baton Rouge police had not mistreated him. "You didn't beat my ass or anything."

King pointed out that it was Ferrell who offered to tell all if he could just see Keessee.

"Were they abusive?" King asked in cross-examination.

"Physically, no."

Hawthorne claimed that they "hot-boxed" him, chaining him to a chair in a small, windowless room for hours.

The teens were held at the police station for 23 hours before being moved to a detention facility.

Lockett ruled that all of the defendants' tapes could be viewed by jurors, with the exception of some portions that had nothing to do with the murders, like the burglary in Louisiana.

Ferrell's tough-guy vampire veneer was crumbling, and so were his chances of acquittal. He bowed his head at the defense table. His eyes were red-rimmed when they led him out of the courtroom.

CHAPTER 42

"They should all be sent to death row"

The jury questionnaire had to be one of the most thorough—or obtrusive—surveys, depending upon your viewpoint.

Questions ranged from occupation and education to feelings about the death penalty and whether they knew any of the players.

These were the kind of questions that lawyers routinely ask in jury selection. Questions were also designed to find out of the person had any dealings with law enforcement or the court system.

The survey also asked what newspapers they read, how many hours they watched TV, and what they watched.

It asked about the ages of their children and their occupation if they were now adults. Queries included the types and names of organizations and churches. One question asked where they had lived for the past 10 years.

One baffling question, which seemingly did not have anything to do with the case, asked: "Are the people in your neighborhood all white, all black, both black and white?"[1]

A sensitive but necessary question, as it turned out, was: "Have you or any member of your family or any close friend ever sought the help of, or been seen by, any mental health counselor, psychologist and/or psychiatrist? If yes, when?"

Another asked, "Based on the articles you have read and what you have heard have you developed any opinions about people who consider themselves to be vampires? Yes, no, please explain."

Yet another section contained a list and a place to check yes or no. It asked, "Do you have any training or experience in the following areas?" The "areas" were: "psychology, satanism, social work, the occult, cults or other unique spiritual groups, theology, witchcraft, vampirism, paranormal, any other related area (please specify other area)."

The survey included a space for the person to explain.

"Have you, a family member or close friend ever participated in or been a member of any cult, coven, or unusual religious or spiritual type of group?" It, too, asked for specifics.

Other questions included: "Have you ever had any experience with anyone who thought they were a vampire? Have you read any of the Anne Rice novels? Do you ever visit the websites for the Children of the Night or The Dark Gift? Have you, someone you know, or a member of your family ever been a member of the Vampire Lestat Fan Club?"

One overly broad question was, "Has anyone close to you died in the last few years?"

A leading question was: "Do you believe that being raised by a mentally ill parent or a parent who uses drugs can create mental problems in the children raised by that person?" The survey also asked if people had problems with their kids, including running away.

The survey also asked people to list the three "most important problems with law and order today," and how they felt about psychiatry, sociology, "or any related subjects." Those answers could fill libraries.

It also asked if they or anyone in their family had ever seen a counselor, taken Prozac, or LSD.

People were asked if they knew anything about shared personality disorder or schizoaffective disorder.

"The last question was, "Do you have any bumper stickers on your car(s). Please identify what they say and whether or not you agree with what they say."

The lawyers knew that people are reluctant to discuss such personal things in front of other prospective jurors, but they figured a survey might seem more anonymous. In a case without a questionnaire, which is the norm, people can go up to the bench and answer questions in private.

By January, the results were in. More than 2,000 questionnaires had been sent out. More than half the people responded. Not surprisingly, people had strong feelings.

"I am so convinced that Ferrell killed the Wendorfs that I almost feel you could skip the trial part and just go to the death penalty. I can't forget the image of the little jerk sticking his tongue out when arrested."[2]

Another person wrote: "I feel they are all guilty…and I feel they should all be sent to death row!"

Still another wrote: "I don't believe someone who has committed an intentional murder should get LIFE. Example: Charles Manson, he should have been put to death."

"Murderers should suffer the same as the victims," another person wrote.

"I guess I have lived a sheltered life. I'm not sure whether I can handle this or not," one person replied.

"I just think the whole thing is stupid. What's wrong with people these days?" a respondent said.

Not all of the questionnaires were negative.

"I don't believe everything I see on TV or read in the papers. I believe guilt should be proved in a court of law."

The attorneys began picking a jury from a pool of 80 candidates on Monday, Feb. 2.

Ferrell sat at the defense table wearing a blue sweater over a white shirt and tie. With his hair cut dramatically and sporting a pair of large glasses, he was virtually unrecognizable, which was the point.

I said he looked like a "nerd" one night while being interviewed live on a United Kingdom radio show. After signing off, I wondered if the Brits were familiar with the term. They probably said, "What is that crazy American talking about?"

One prospective juror claimed not to know anything about the case.

"You would have had to be blind or deaf to have not seen anything," one woman said.[3]

However, merely knowing something about the case is not the issue, King said. The important thing is whether you can put aside your feelings and base your decision on evidence heard in the courtroom.

It was impossible for some.

One woman wept, saying she knew some members of the Wendorf family. Another said the case had given her nightmares. Still another described it as "gruesome."

A woman said, "If you do the crime, you should pay the penalty, regardless of age."

Life sentences "eat up tax dollars that should go to education and overcrowded prisons," one person said.

As the process unfolded, some of the prospective jurors indicated either an unbending opposition or total support for the death penalty.

Lockett allowed the attorneys to strike those people from the list.

As the process dragged on, Hawthorne and Lackay gave Ferrell paper, pen, and crayons as props.

In the not-so-distant old days, defense attorneys would put a Bible on the table. At one murder trial that I covered, the defendant, recognizing that his case was hopeless, spent his time reading a thriller about buried treasure.

To keep reporters from clogging the courtroom, an adjoining, unfinished courtroom was turned into a makeshift news media center, with a rented photocopy machine, an Associated Press phone line, and tables and chairs. Hundreds of yards of cables ran out the side door to TV trucks, including Court TV. The judge allowed one still camera and one TV camera to be in the courtroom.

I preferred being in the courtroom, but during a break one of the TV reporters spoke to his cameraman. "Zoom in on what he's drawing."

With the lens focused on the table, we could see that he was drawing gargoyles, inverted crosses, and other satanic symbols.

CHAPTER 43

"Disturbed," not insane

Diane Evers of Leesburg was bathing her four-year-old twin girls and her two-year-old daughter in the tub in 1980, while family members were in the next room. When they went to check on her, they witnessed horror so unimaginable no amount of memory scrubbing will ever wipe it away.

Evers, who said she was the Virgin Mary, had drowned the children. She was found not guilty by reason of insanity and was locked up in a mental hospital for decades.

Her attorneys were successful in using the insanity defense, but it is rarely employed.

Florida, like many states, is governed by the McNaughton Rule, which says a person is not legally insane if he or she knows the difference between right and wrong at the time of the crime.

That level of insanity is very unusual.

Secondly, jurors don't like it. They tend to view it as an excuse defense.

Society is frightened of and angry with criminals, Orlando defense attorney David Fussell once told me in an interview. "People want prisoners to be punished harshly." Another problem is that the more horrific the crime, the harder it is for attorneys to overcome it.[1]

In Ferrell's case, not only did he beat two innocent people to death with a crowbar and showed no remorse, but he was a vampire. "The people who suck blood from each other don't seem to be normal people," a would-be juror said.[2]

Add that comment to the woman who said it was "gruesome," another who described Ferrell as a "sick little jerk," and a third who said it gave her "nightmares," and it was clear he wouldn't find much sympathy in the jury box.

***

Dr. Michael H. Stone, M.D., and Gary Brucato, Ph.D., included Ferrell in their comprehensive book on criminal thinking, *The New Evil.*

"By 'evil,' we are not referring to spiritually sinful or societally forbidden acts, per se, since what is deemed abominable by one religion or culture might be fully accepted by another. Rather, we refer to the types of actions that virtually anyone, regardless of faith, time, or place, would find unspeakably horrible and utterly depraved."[3]

The massive study, complete with numerous case histories, sets up a crime classification system of one to twenty-two.

At the lower end of the scale are the more common crimes, like those committed by jealous lovers, or traumatized people who kill relatives and others but have remorse. "At the extreme end are those who subject victims to prolonged, unimaginable torment, without a hint of compassion or regret, sometimes followed by killing and sometimes not. Stated another way, higher rankings reflect more severe levels of *psychopathy*—a constellation of personality traits and tendencies, such as deceit, callousness, lack of remorse, manipulation, grandiosity, glibness, and superficial charm, while the highest levels also involved *sadism,* the derivation of pleasure from the pain and humiliation of others."[4]

Ferrell was mentioned in a section dealing with cannibalism and vampirism—Category 20 out of 22. The authors concluded that he consumed blood as a means of uniting cult members into a cohesive "family."[5]

It is true enough, but one could argue that it also a means of mocking Christianity. Mocking was Ferrell's style, and out-and-out rebellion his calling, especially when he was interested in satanic worship.

***

Despite Ferrell's claim to police that he was "mentally disturbed," he was not insane. Because the state was seeking the death penalty, Hawthorne could use psychologists as mitigation experts, however.

On Feb. 2, Hawthorne filed court papers claiming that Ferrell "was suffering from certain psychological disorders."

They were dysthymic disorder, polysubstance, mathematics disorder, and schizotypal personality disorder. He also had medical conditions caused by "multiple head traumas and childhood encephalitis."

The filing also cited "psychosocial stressors—chaotic family system, frequent geographical moves, cult activity, school failure, childhood abuse, impaired peer relations, developmental delay."

The defense strategy was clear. The lawyers, through their experts, would try to show that his life was out of control, that he was under the influence of drugs and the occult. Even more important, it wasn't his fault.

Sondra Gibson didn't know it, but she was wearing a target on her back.

CHAPTER 44

The shocker

The atmosphere of the courtroom was charged with a wave of nervous excitement on Feb. 5. The bailiffs were extra alert. They didn't say much. They didn't have to. They gave stern warning looks to anyone they thought might deserve it.

Reporters were on their best behavior, but their newshound antennae were up, either looking for color or a detail that might prove crucial for their stories. Some of the out-of-town journalists were whispering to the locals to get the lay of the land.

Certainly, no one was going to trifle with Judge Lockett. He looked stressed, angry even, when the deputy made his "all rise" announcement and he took his seat at the bench.

Ferrell's family and the Wendorfs looked like they might burst into tears. The prosecutors looked cool and calm. Ferrell seemed depressed. His attorneys appeared to be tense.

Soon, the trial was underway. King stood up and began making a stock speech to the jury as part of his opening remarks. The speech, which he has given many times, reminds jurors that people make decisions every day, and that individuals are responsible for their actions.

Lackay interrupted almost immediately. "Mr. Ferrell has indicated...he may want to do something to change things."[1]

Lockett immediately ordered the courtroom cleared. King stepped into the hallway and was instantly surrounded by reporters.

"Have there been any discussions with your office about a plea deal?" I asked.

"None," he said.

King said he did not need a plea from Ferrell. He didn't even want one.

Sondra walked past us on the way to the restroom. She turned and looked at us and said, "We live forever!"

"What did she say?" a reporter asked me.

I was not surprised, even though she had just told me in an interview with her parents that her involvement in vampirism was "Hollywood idiocy."

As soon as I could, I called the office to tell them about the surprising delay. An hour passed, then another and another. Finally, when the doors were opened to the courtroom, Ferrell stood up at the podium flanked by Lackay and Hawthorne.

He cried quietly, took off his glasses, and covered his face with his hands.

Lockett read the litany of required questions, making sure Ferrell knew he was entering a guilty plea of his own free will, that he was not under the influence of drugs and alcohol, and that he realized he was giving up his rights to maintain his innocence before a jury.

"It was my decision," Lackay said in an interview for this book. "I mean, Candance was the lead attorney but she let me do it."

It wasn't much of a risk.

"We were trying to get credibility with the jury," Lackay said. "It was unconventional, but when you looked at the pictures and his two confesssions...."

He knew King was still going ahead with the second phase of the trial.

King said he still had a "burden for the state" to seek the maximum sentence.

"He loves the death penalty," Lackay said.

The day's proceedings left a cloud of uncertainty over the trial.

Sheriff George Knupp was hoping that Heather might be called to testify. He seemed certain that she had some culpability, despite the grand jury's decision not to charge her.

The Wendorfs seemed a bit confused by the surprise move. King huddled with the group at the back of the courtroom to explain what it all meant.

Sondra and Rosetta Gibson were devastated. The defense team had included Rod's family in the plea discussion in the locked down courtroom.

"I don't think reality had really hit," Harrell Gibson said of his grandson as the courtroom was being cleared. "He is a child—more of a fourteen or fifteen-year-old than 17—and to him this may all be like a game."

"I want to touch him," Rosetta said, weeping and reaching out from the spectator section. She never got the chance. Bailiffs hustled him up toward a table by the bench where he was fingerprinted and taken to jail.

At least one person was disappointed that Ferrell had pleaded guilty. Myra Thompson of Umatilla had been in the prospective jury pool.

"I think he should fry," she said. "I don't have any doubt in my mind that he did it."

She did feel sorry for Rod's grandparents, however. "They seem like nice people."

CHAPTER 45

"Transformed"

On Feb. 12, when the jury was reconvened, the judge and King explained to the jurors that they would hear evidence showing aggravating circumstances that could lead them to recommend a death sentence.

"We will not attempt to set forth to you, as I told you early on, that these murders were the result of a vampire or the occult. We intend to show you that these murders were the thoughts and choice of one person, a personal decision of one person, and that person is Rod Ferrell."[1]

He began laying out his case, saying the murders were committed during an armed robbery, that they were committed to avoid arrest, for financial gain and were under the law's definition of "especially heinous, atrocious and cruel."

He said the evidence would show that he beat Richard Wendorf to death with a crowbar.

"And then, after he finished that murder, he turns to be confronted by Naomi Queen."[2]

Referring to his confession, King said, "He will tell you that there was a verbal exchange, that she threw her coffee on him, she scratched him in the face, and he beat her with a crowbar. The evidence will show you that she crossed the kitchen dripping blood, fell in the doorway in between the kitchen and the dining room, and that he beat her until literally he beat her brains out. That is what he is going to tell what happened on that night in that house."

He also explained that the murders were planned, and they were cold, calculated and premeditated, another statutory aggravator for the death penalty.

He talked about the physical evidence they would see and the testimony of witnesses, including that of Shannon Yohe, though he did not mention her by name.

He said they would hear from defense witnesses.

"I expect that they are going to call mental health specialists and have them talk to you about Mr. Ferrell's upbringing and mental disorders, those kinds of things. And what I would caution you in that regard, is to treat them like you treat every other witness. Listen to what they have the ability to know, those facts. And listen to how they used those facts in arriving at a conclusion. Because they are like everybody else. They come to you with some presumption of expertise but listen to what they had to work with and how they worked with it. And I think you will see that it is true, if you put garbage in you...."[3]

"Your Honor, we would object," Lackay said.

"Overruled," Lockett said. "That's a fair comment."

"...can't help but get garbage out," King said.

Lackay, who delivered the defense's opening statement, told jurors that they would see a videotape of Ferrell pleading guilty to the crimes, since the jury was out of the room when he entered the plea.

Ferrell was 16 when he committed the murders.

"Remember, you were told last week that a person under sixteen years of age who commits this type of crime cannot be put to death...."[4]

"We submit to you that the witnesses, records, and everything you will see will show that age will definitely be big, if not the determining factor. We're also going to show you a pattern, show you where Rod came from."

He also promised that they would hear about Rod's fascination with fantasy games.

"What happened to Rod is his world of fantasy mismatched with reality because his life was tainted."[5]

He said they would hear from psychologists who had analyzed lots of evidence from records and other sources.

He said they would hear about how he was "stillborn" because the umbilical cord was wrapped around his neck, that he had a "severe" case of encephalitis and suffered head trauma.

They would also hear about his drug use and mental disorders.

***

Sheriff's Deputy Jeff Taylor was the first witness called to testify.

He described how he entered the home through the garage and then what he saw in the house.

The first thing he saw was Richard Wendorf lying on the couch. "His glasses were bashed up and the thing that stands out is that his face looked like hamburger."[6]

He said he saw Queen in the kitchen. "She had what appeared to be a large hole in the back of her head and a pool of blood underneath her head."[7]

The next witness was sheriff's crime scene technician Farley "Jake" Caudill, who testified, among other things, about collecting skull fragments in the area near Queen's body.

More importantly, he pointed out shoe prints in photos near Queen's body and testified about the clothing Ferrell was wearing when he met him in Baton Rouge, which he photographed, including his boots and the soles of the boots. He later retrieved every item of clothing and brought it back to Florida for further analysis.

Caudill testified that he used a chemical process to enhance the footprints, and even had a tile expert come into the home to remove the tiles with shoe prints.

The next witness was Audrey Presson, who testified that she met Ferrell in the ninth grade at Eustis High.

"Would you tell the ladies and gentlemen what he looked like in the ninth grade, as you were in class with him?" King asked.[8]

"He was just a regular kid. He was kind of tall. He had long, red hair. He dressed in just a regular T-shirt and grubby jeans, kind of dorky, I guess. Just a regular kid, a regular ninth grader."

He moved to Kentucky the next year.

She recalled that he introduced his clan followers. "He said one of the girls was his wife, and she had a child inside of her, and he said the other girl was Naji or something like that. And that Scott was like his son or something or other."

Scott was walking around saying, "We're going to have some fun tomorrow night."[9]

King, remembering his earlier conversation with her, asked her about Ferrell's comment about "unfinished business."

"My understanding is that unfinished business means somebody has done somebody else wrong and they will pay for it. That's unfinished business."[10]

When it was Hawthorne's turn to cross-examine, she got right down to brass tacks and boiling cauldrons.

"During your phone conversations with him, after he had moved, did you ever discuss vampirism?"

"We were both at that time becoming interested in that sort of realm of things and vampirism. And he was telling me how he had started his own clan, and how he was sired and now he is a vampire, and just things like that."[11]

She said they discussed witchcraft, books, and spells.

"Now, was he involved in the witchcraft, or were you?"

"Oh, we were both involved in it."[12]

Hawthorne then produced the book, *Necronomicon,* and asked her if she recognized it. She said it was the book she gave to detectives. "I gave him everything I had of this part of my life. I gave it all to him."

On cross-examination, Hawthorne brought out the fact that Presson had seen him in the summer of 1996.

"He had gotten really pale," Presson said. "His red hair was now dyed jet black. He wore eye makeup. He had dark glasses on. He had on a black T-shirt, black jeans, black coat, black cane, black fingernail polish, funny rings, cuts on his arms. He looked very transformed."[13] Despite the startling transformation, she said he was the same "laid-back" Rod, or maybe even more laid-back.

"Did he at any time talk about killing anyone's parents?"[14]

"No."

"Did he say anything about killing your parents?"

"No."

As for leaving town the next day, all he said was, "I'm leaving on a road trip if you want to come with me."

He never mentioned Heather, but did say that Jeanine was going, Presson said.

Hawthorne asked her if she was still practicing witchcraft.

"No."

"Why not?"

"Because it's a part of my life I don't want anything to do with, it's scary, not warm. It's not something you want to get caught up in."

"When did you stop?"

"Right after Rod had killed, allegedly murdered the Wendorfs."[15]

Twenty years later, I met Presson's father. He recalled how he summoned her back into their home to finish her homework on that Sunday night. He still shuddered at the memory.

King took advantage of a break to talk with the Wendorf family members. He warned them that they might want to leave the courtroom. Next up was Dr. Laura Hair, the associate medical examiner who performed the autopsies, and there would be photos, he said.

They stayed put, but they wept when they heard the testimony.

"On Mr. Wendorf's head I counted 22 wounds, or what I believed to be 22 wounds."[16]

Hawthorne objected, and asked permission for a hushed conference at the bench.

"Your honor, those photographs, the autopsy photographs would inflame the jury unreasonably. They are not necessary for them to see where the doctor found these wounds, she also did diagrams, sketches, which can be used instead."[17]

King again used his argument that the state had the "burden of proof as to the cause of death, manner of death, and as part of which is the proof in this case of cold, calculated and premeditated as the aggravator."[18]

Lockett overruled Hawthorne's objection.

Defense attorneys hate autopsy photos. Not only are they "gruesome" but they show the victim's body being invaded twice—once by the defendant, and again by the pathologist.

Judges are not unsympathetic to the defense lawyers. They routinely make sure the photos are culled to show just the facts, basically. In fact, medical examiners wash away blood so they can examine the external injuries before opening the bodies.

***

For years, I looked at autopsy photos as I wrote stories and prepared for trials. I'm not a ghoul. I took no pleasure in it. Unfortunately, I have seen more bodies than most people do in a couple of lifetimes, but I wanted to be prepared to write about where the bullets struck and exit wounds.

All of that changed, however, when famed NASCAR driver Dale Earnhardt died during the 2001 Daytona 500 when his car crashed into the wall. His widow, concerned that someone would post the photos on the Internet, convinced Gov. Jeb Bush and the Legislature to change the law limiting access.

The *Orlando Sentinel* fought it vigorously in court, sparking outrage among fans, despite stating publicly that it had no intention of publishing the photos.

The paper said its intent was to find out why Earnhardt died. A NASCAR doctor blamed his seatbelt.

A circuit judge hearing the case noted that there were two rights at stake: the right to "distrust the government" and see its records, and the right to privacy.

"We have really found a way to have both of those things collide in this case," he said. He ruled that the new ban was constitutional.[19]

In a court settlement, a judge allowed a doctor who was a crash expert to examine the photos for the *Sentinel.* He concluded that it was not the seat belt but the lack of a head restraint system that caused the fatal injury.

The *Sentinel's* investigation led to several safety changes.

Race fans calmed down once the paper made clear its intent. Now, however, even prosecutors have to file a motion in court to get access to what once was public record.

***

King handed the doctor photocopies of Richard's head and had her mark each injury.

One of the blows penetrated the skull an inch-and-a-half, right into the brain. Some blows landed on his face, knocking out teeth.

She also talked about the mysterious wounds on his chest that some thought might be V-shaped, a mark of the clan.

"There were nine separate wounds, these might be two that are together, there might actually be two that are together, there might actually be ten. And I really didn't know what to make of these wounds when I first saw them. I thought there was a possibility that they could be burns or something. However, there was no evidence that there was nothing wrong with the shirt or singeing of the hair or anything along those lines. And when I did microscopic sections of these, there was dried blood and coagulation on them, so these are wounds that are most likely caused by blunt impact or something gouging causing an abrasion that bled a little bit, and by the time I did the autopsy it dried."[20]

"Dr. Hair, have you ever seen a crowbar that has the hoof at the top and the nail pullers, which are two separate prongs, on the instrument?"[21]

"Yes, I have."

"In your opinion as a pathologist, could that type of weapon cause that wounding that you see in the chest?"

"Sure."

The cause of death, she said, "was chop wounds and blunt impact of the head with skull fractures and brain laceration."[22]

Hawthorne again objected to autopsy photos at the bench, in this case for Queen's examination.

King again argued that they were not only relevant but that they were proof of cold, calculated, and premeditated murder.

"On the wounds, also, especially the wounds to the arms, indicate that she was alive and fought, which is part of heinous, atrocious and cruel, which goes to the victim's apprehension and knowledge of her impending death," King said.

The judge overruled Hawthorne's objection, and ordered a recess for the day.

The next day, Friday the thirteenth, Hair was back on the stand.

King had her define defensive wounds. Wendorf had no such wounds, but Queen did. Like Wendorf, the cause of her death was chop wounds and blunt impact, but there were some differences. Blows to Queen's head were so forceful they severed the brain stem, which controls breathing.

"Would someone with a severed brain stem be able to reach up and scratch another person in the face?" King asked.

"I do not believe so."[23]

On cross examination, Hawthorne asked about Wendorf. "...I believe you told us that he was more than likely unconscious after the first blow?"

"From the condition of the body and where the blows are, he didn't appear to move after the first blow. Whether he was unconscious or not, I can't say."[24]

Hawthorne, of course, was trying to show that his death was not heinous, atrocious, or cruel.

Hair could not remember if his eyes were open. King stipulated that they were closed.

"Did it appear that he had been in a struggle?"

"No."

"Now, on Miss Queen were you able to tell how many people may have been landing blows on her?"[25]

"No."

"Can you tell from a reasonable degree of medical certainty, who actually landed he blows?"

"I have no idea."

Hawthorne also got her to concede that she did not know which blow knocked her out. She further reminded her of a question and answer that she made in her deposition: "'Is it your understanding within your science, the medical science, that once an individual loses consciousness that they no longer feel pain?' And your answer, 'I believe so.'"[26]

"I probably made that statement. I think that it is a very good possibility. I can't say with certainty but it's a possibility, yes."

CHAPTER 46

Schizotypal vs. malingering

Dr. Wade Myers, a psychiatrist and expert on adolescents with the University of Florida, was the first mental health professional to be called to the stand.

Hawthorne presented him as an expert in working with juvenile delinquents and a researcher of children who commit murder.

King did not object.

Myers said he met with Ferrell three times, including some meetings with his mother and grandparents, and he performed three psychological tests.

One of the tests showed he had "a lot of problems with depression. A lot of problems with anxiety or worry. Having the kind of problems that get him into trouble with society and with the law. And he also endorsed a lot of complaints or symptoms where he is maybe hearing voices or seeing things, or not having thoughts that make sense to other people but make sense to him."

Anticipating King's counterattack, Hawthorne asked Myers to define "malingering."

"Malingering would be purposely and consciously faking illness for some sort of gain, be it to get away from a crime you are being charged for, to try to get money in some way, things like that."[1]

He admitted that there was no validity check of the test itself, but said he looked at everything, including clinical interviews.

One of those interviews, of course, was with Sondra Gibson. "…one of the first things she told me was that she had found, when Rod was a baby, just several months old, she found him to be bruised up and his biological father admitted, in so many words to her, that he had beaten Rod."[2]

He said Rod's father had "very little contact" with him as he was growing up. Sondra tried to raise him by herself and didn't want her parents interfering, "but at the same time she was busy with a lot of boyfriends, had a history of drug abuse, and really wasn't there to do much in the way of discipline or guidance as he was growing up."

Two years before the murders Sondra and her parents noticed changes in his personality, he said.

"His appearance changed. He seemed depressed. He seemed apathetic. He wasn't doing well at school. He started getting involved in the occult. For instance, she found him one time at their house cutting himself with this other girl and they were apparently drinking each other's blood."[3]

Sondra told him that Rod had been sexually abused.

"She related a day when Rod was about six or seven when his grandfather took him on a fishing trip and when Rod came home that night, Rod was shaking, nauseated, throwing up, was extremely upset and Rod told her that he had been abused, sexually abused by several men out in the woods on this fishing trip. And from that point on, she said she never felt comfortable having Rod alone with his grandfather again."[4]

Myers said Harrell Gibson told him that Ferrell suffered a bout of encephalitis as a grade-school child, and that doctors told the family that he might die. Encephalitis can have long-lasting effects on a child's emotions and behavior, he said.

The grandparents described Rod as being lost in a fantasy world.

"For instance, the grandfather said Rod would often come home and tell him these sorts of fantastic stories that the grandfather knew were not true, such as Rod describing the hunting trip he had been on, but it was impossible for him to have been on a hunting trip."[5]

They also mentioned him playing Vampire Masquerade, he said.

Myers also testified that there was a history of schizophrenia or bipolar disorder in his paternal grandfather.

He testified that he had seen an evaluation of Sondra Gibson diagnosing her with shared psychotic disorder.

"…it involved her getting involved with a group of folks who are involved in the occult and she began to share their beliefs in the occult that were clearly what most of us would think are not based on reality, these beliefs in special powers and magic and that sort of thing, witchcraft."[6]

Myers testified that he looked at Ferrell's school records, depositions, and other material and noted what he said was a history of paranoia and feelings of persecution.

He was viewed as an outcast and teased. He didn't fit in, didn't participate in sports or any extracurricular events at school or any "positive social activities."

Ferrell abused alcohol, marijuana, Prozac and took LSD about 40 times, he said.

"When I first saw Rod, he had a long ponytail that was dyed black and he had the sides of his head shaved, he had a very unusual appearance. He had a number of cuts up and down both arms that were in various stages of healing, which suggested to me that they had been done over an extended period of time.

"As we were talking, if I asked him a question, he was pretty well able to answer the question in a reasonable way, but if I let him start talking on his own, he would go off into a kind of bizarre fantasy thinking."[7]

Ferrell laughed when he told him about running in front of a semi, "as though he was challenging fate, and he would get sort of high doing this...."

"The other thing that I thought showed a disturbed personality was he would sometimes laugh when he would talk about violent acts that to the normal person would cause them to feel serious and somber, he would smile and even laugh sometimes when we discussed those."

He said Ferrell had above-average intelligence but had a learning disability when it came to mathematics, which can harm a person's self-esteem.

He said Ferrell told him a different story about what happened at the Wendorfs that night than the one he told police.

Ferrell said the plan was to commit a "minor" robbery, tie up Heather's parents, and take their car because Scott's would not make it to New Orleans.

He said when he entered the house, the couple had already been beaten and when he leaned over Heather's mother she reached up and scratched him.

"It was as though it was a game the way he was describing it to me."[8]

Ferrell developed an I-don't-care attitude at age nine, Myers said, "and he calls it a cross between pain and rage inside his head, his emotions."

Ferrell told him that as a young boy he could hear the voices of demons and angels and would smell things that weren't really there, like burning sulphur. The voices were a comfort to him, Myers said, a guiding force.

He reported at one time, however, having a tactile hallucination where a "spell caster" was shoving a knife into his chest.

Myers also said Ferrell made delusional claims, like being able to pick up a 200-pound man with one hand.

"He also said things like he could smell people's blood through building walls." He also claimed that he could radiate a cold wind that would precede him as he walked into a room.[9] Myers said he diagnosed Ferrell as having a schizotypal personality disorder.

Such a person exhibits weird behavior, has an unusual appearance, and bizarre thoughts.[10]

"They often are lost in excessive, strange fantasy life. They tend not to fit in mainstream society very well. They don't relate to other people very well. They have trouble with close relationships. And this is a disorder to have some overlap with schizophrenia in that these people, they may hear voices. They have false, fixed beliefs like they are being executed. This is not uncommon in families with schizophrenia—some of the people have schizotypal personal disorder and vice versa."

The disorder could be treated with psychotherapy and psychotropic drugs, he said, but Ferrell didn't have parents that guided him into treatment. "...he had a mother who herself had a problem with being psychotic, not being in touch with reality."[11]

Myers' second diagnosis was dysthymia, which is a condition where someone is depressed for more than a year. Self-mutilation can be a sign, he said.

A third diagnosis was polysubstance abuse, or abusing multiple drugs and alcohol, and then there was the mathematics disorder.

It was then that Hawthorne asked the big question.

"Would you have an opinion as to whether he was able to appreciate the criminality of his conduct or to conform his conduct to the requirements of the law on that date?"

"I believe that his ability to do so was seriously impaired because of these psychological diagnoses, as well as this mental illness, as well as the other problems he was having in his life, like having been abused, having a chaotic family situation, having failed at school, of being under the influence of substances, regularly."[12]

It was his opinion that Ferrell was under the influence of "extreme mental or emotional disturbance," a legal term that goes right to the heart of death penalty mitigation. It is as close to being legally insane as possible.

King began his cross-examination in his usual calm, methodical way.

"You indicated to Miss Hawthorne that you were hired by the defense to evaluate Mr. Ferrell, is that correct?"

"Yes."

"You were not hired to treat him, is that true?"

"No."

The first thing King did was to produce two reports on tests that Myers had administered on Ferrell.

They were marked with the wrong dates. King had him pencil in the correct dates. A third test didn't even have a date marked.

King then pointed out that one of the assessments, called the Millon Test, was supposed to be done in a clinical setting, while the patient is being treated.

It came back marked "invalid," King noted.

"And the reason indicated was that because the person that took this test was perceived to be not telling the truth about taking the test, correct?"[13]

"It could be that partly he wasn't telling the truth. Apparently, there was a cry for help, partly due to being depressed and being self-depreciating."

"The document that you sent for it to be scored on says it is not valid because he is not telling the truth, doesn't it?"

"I don't see it saying that."

"Well, it is in evidence; I expect the jury can read it for themselves."[14]

"I think partly he has a lot of influence here from fantasy thinking, and also I think he was making a cry for help."

King also pointed out that Ferrell scored higher for paranoia and anti-social behavior than he did for dysthymic or schizotypal disorders.

On another test, he scored highest on delinquency, which is very similar to anti-social behavior, King said.

"Well, it is a sign of anti-social behavior, but it is certainly different from anti-social personality."

"But you would agree that it is a sign of anti-social behavior?"

"Yes."

"Okay. I mean he's talking about lying, setting fires, stealing from homes, swearing, correct?"

"Yes."

"Delinquent behavior?"

"Yes."

"Those are the same kind of behaviors that are anti-social, aren't they?"

"Yes."

King then produced a copy of another test, a test that Myers used to diagnose dysthymia. Yet, King pointed out that the test results showed he could have diagnosed him with conduct disorder.

"But you didn't diagnose him as having conduct disorder, did you?"

"No, I did not."[15]

King asked Myers if he ordered a CAT scan or an MRI.

"No."

"You never did any medical testing to see if he had brain damage?"

"The history from having encephalitis and from being hit in the head and becoming unconscious several times, those sorts of injuries won't show up on a gross examination of the brain, such as an MRI or a CAT scan, most likely."[16]

Myers testified that he asked Harrell Gibson about the sex abuse allegation, and he denied it. The doctor also said he did not do any testing of Sondra Gibson.

"His other grandfather that you indicated to this jury could have, by environment, caused Mr. Ferrell to develop schizophrenia, did you ever talk to that grandfather?"[17]

Myers conceded that he had not, but he had raised Rod's father.

King mentioned Ferrell giving a false name to police in Florida.

Myers said he didn't remember Ferrell telling police in Baton Rouge that he had Charity give police false name.

"Would that be important to take into consideration that he lied to police?"[18]

Myers indicated that it would be important.

"But apparently you didn't take it into consideration because you don't even remember?"

Under questioning, Myers indicated that Ferrell did tell him the following things: that he had taken weapons into the house they burglarized in Louisiana, that if anyone was in the house, "he would [expletive] with them so they couldn't call police," that he would break their knees if they tried to be heroes, that on the way to do a "minor robbery" at the Wendorfs he and Scott would hide in the woods if a car drove by, and that they went to the wrong house but left because he could hear children.[19]

Myers said he couldn't remember what Ferrell told police.

"Actually, what he said was he passed the house by because he didn't kill children, anybody under 16, do you remember that?"[20]

"Vaguely."

Myers did recall Ferrell saying they passed up houses with security devices, and that they walked around the Wendorfs' home before entering.

King also zeroed in on Ferrell's tale of seeing Queen injured and her reaching up to scratch his face.

"You are a medical doctor, right?"[21]

"Yes."

"If Dr. Hair, the medical examiner, had testified that the cause of Ms. Queen's death was that her brain stem was completely severed from her spinal cord, you would know that that story was a lie, wouldn't you? Because she can't move and she can't breathe after her brain stem has been severed, can she?"

"That would be inconsistent."[22]

"But yet, you told Miss Hawthorne that you didn't think it appropriate to confront him with that and say, 'Son, I know you're lying. You need to tell me the truth. You didn't do that, did you?'"

Myers said he didn't want Ferrell to shut down during the interview, so he didn't challenge him.

King also pointed out that Myers also did not challenge Ferrell's claim that he could pick up a 200-pound man with one hand. How did Myers know if Ferrell believed it, or if he was lying?

King wasn't done.

He introduced the Diagnostic and Statistical Manual of Mental Disorders (DSM), the psychology bible, and had the doctor go over the criteria for conduct disorder.

One of the things it mentioned was, "Often bullies, threatens or intimidates others."[23]

Myers had examined Ferrell's school records in Kentucky, including being expelled.

"You read the sworn testimony of the teacher where he threatened to cut a teacher's throat, correct?"

"Would that meet the criteria?"

"Yes, it would."

It would also fit in with the story about Ferrell throwing a knife at his mother, Myers conceded.

Another category was, "Often initiates fights."[24]

King pointed to Ferrell kicking Goodman in the teeth.

Another category was: "Has used a weapon that can cause serious harm."

Yet another was, "has been physically cruel to people." Ferrell self-reported that trait on a test, King pointed out. He was also cruel to animals, which was another category.

"Number ten, 'Broken into somebody else's house, building, or car.' Done that, right?"

"Yes."[25]

"Number eleven, 'Often lies to obtain goods or favors or to avoid obligations.'"

Ferrell admitted that he lies, Myers said.

Has run away from home at least twice, King said, citing another trait.

Truancy was another symptom, which was reflected in his school expulsion records.

King asked if the "next step" from conduct disorder was anti-social personality disorder.

"No. Most conduct disorders do not become anti-social personality disorders."[26]

"But if they get to be adults and keep committing these types of acts, they become anti-social personality disorders don't they?"

"Probably, yes."

King went on to ask Myers about another condition mentioned in the DSM, malingering: "intentionally producing false or fabricated symptoms in order to gain something from it."[27]

King noted that the DSM cautioned that malingering should be suspected when a lawyer refers someone to a mental health expert for legal purposes.

Ferrell told another court-appointed expert that he had multiple personalities.

"That wasn't true, correct?" King asked.[28]

"No, it wasn't."

King also insisted that lying on one of Myers' tests was also malingering.

The prosecutor used the doctor's own words to push home his point that the proper diagnosis for Ferrell should be conduct disorder. King pointed to a 1995 study that Myers had conducted on 25 homicidal youths. The vast majority were conduct disorder cases.

"Dr. Myers, in spite of your conclusions about Mr. Ferrell's mental health status, he knew right from wrong when he went into that house, didn't he?"[29]

"I believe he did."

"He had the ability to say no when given the choice of killing them or not killing them, didn't he?"

"I think his ability was impaired for a number of reasons, including mental illness."

"But he could have said no, couldn't he? I mean, think about what we are saying here, doctor. You already told us that as he is sneaking through the woods and sees a car, he knows he doesn't want to get caught, so he jumps into the woods, right?"

"Yes."

"He is thinking about that, isn't he?"[30]

"Yes, he is."

"He knows he doesn't want to get caught, doesn't he?"

"Yes."

"He goes to a house and there are children there and it violates his personal code about killing people under sixteen, so he goes on. He is thinking, isn't he?"

"Yes."

"He finally goes to three more houses and he sees the high-tech security devices and he doesn't want to get caught so he doesn't go there. He is thinking, isn't he?"

"Yes."

"Was he not thinking when he walked into the Wendorfs' house and beat them in the head twenty times until they were dead? He was thinking, wasn't he?"

"He did not tell me what he was thinking at that time."

"That's right, because he lied to you about that, didn't he?"

"He didn't give me his version of what he was thinking during that time."

"He tried to blame it on somebody else, didn't he?"[31]

"He said that somebody else had done it."

"Didn't want to accept responsibility for what he had done, did he?"

"I think he was trying to preserve himself."

"Just like he lies all the time to get out of trouble."

"He said he often lied to get out of trouble."

King turned and looked at the judge. "Your honor, I don't think I have anything else of the witness."

Hawthorne had more questions for her witness, however.

"Doctor, Mr. King has made a large issue about Mr. Ferrell lying all the time, and can we be sure if he was telling the truth to the Baton Rouge Police Department, or if he was telling the truth to you? I mean, it seems like he was answering some of the questions on these tests correctly. Is that true?"

Myers agreed and said Ferrell could have lied on his self-report about his delinquent behavior.

Under her questioning, Myers said Ferrell could have been diagnosed with other disorders, like obsessive-compulsive disorder. "I believe he exhibited separation and anxiety disorder. Signs of over-anxious disorder. There were a lot of signs of psychotic thinking."[32]

Asked why he didn't diagnose Ferrell with other disorders, Myers said, "I tried to pick out and select and apply to the most clearly applicable diagnoses to Rod, what I felt best described him as a person and best described his mental illness."

On his diagnosis of schizotypal personality disorder, he pointed to paranoia and feelings of being persecuted. Ferrell said during his school expulsion hearing that he had been chased by people with guns and that people were out to get him.

He also mentioned the incident in which he wanted his friends to kill him so he could become a "plane walker," that he could smell people's blood through walls and believed that through the witches' spell book he could have magic powers.

His speech and thinking patterns were "odd," he said.

Hawthorne asked him to describe Ferrell's drawings.

"Well, they are pictures of demons, of skulls, of blood, of eyes free floating in the middle of the page with tears coming down, of weapons, of knives, of clubs, of warriors in very elaborate battle gear, a great deal of aggression, fear, those sorts of themes came out in his drawings."[33]

Myers disagreed with King's assertion that Ferrell was cruel to people. His friends described him as "laid-back," and others said he kept to himself.

Hawthorne asked him to define schizophrenia.

"Schizophrenia is one of the most serious mental illnesses that involves people that hear voices, possibly they may see things. They have a disturbed hypothesis. Their thought may come out broken. Their thoughts may be irrelevant to what they're being talked to about, but they may appear very odd. They may lose their jobs. They sometimes become people who live on the street. It is a very debilitating illness."[34]

"What is the difference between a personality disorder and something like schizophrenia?"

"Well, in this particular case, it's really a matter of degree. If you look at this as a spectrum, it's sort of a minor version of schizophrenia."

Hawthorne also produced a 1994 study that Myers cowrote with three other doctors on the effects of witchcraft and satanism.

The study concluded that kids involved with these practices were more likely to have identity disorder and substance abuse problems.

"They didn't know very well about what their moral beliefs were, or they may have been very confused about their religious beliefs, and in general just being sort of confused about how to deal with life and who they were," Myers said.[35]

King had one more shot at Myers.

He pointed to the conclusion which stated, "the findings in this study do not support a link between adolescent occult participation and delinquent activity."

"That's right."

"So, whatever his involvement with this occult was, your study itself determines that that involvement is not what caused him to go into the house and murder Mr. Wendorf and Miss Queen, is that true?"

"I think that's right."

King also pointed out that none of the youths in the study associated with the occult had been arrested for any violent crimes and it did not seem to be an additional risk factor for violent or nonviolent offenses.

The prosecutor also went back to Myers' observation that Ferrell laughed inappropriately about violence.

"Isn't that saying that his behavior is typical of a sociopath that has no feelings of right and wrong? That is the exact same behavior of a sociopath, isn't it?"[36]

"I wouldn't actually expect them to lie, I would just expect them not to have as much of a reaction to it. Although somebody with a serious disorder like schizophrenia, I might expect them to laugh possibly at something very serious like that, inappropriately."

King also attacked Myers on his theory that Ferrell could not have an intimate relationship.

"Have you watched the videotape of himself and Charity Keesee in the Baton Rouge Police Department for an hour, they're hugging and kissing on each other?"

Myers said that he had seen it, but he said most people he talked to said Ferrell didn't get along well with others.

"Dr. Myers, it's true that you simply chose your diagnosis as you did because you didn't want to stigmatize Mr. Ferrell with a conduct disorder, right?"

"No, I wouldn't say that. I don't think that at this point in his life being stigmatized one way or the other is going to have a lot of meaning to him."

"You said on page 53, 'I don't think it is fair to go ahead and label him with a conduct disorder because of the outside stressors in his life.' Isn't that what you said?"

"Yes, that...."

"That's all I have, your honor."

The judge gave Myers a chance to answer.

"When I say fair, I mean being true to what I think his diagnoses are. It's just like those other diagnoses I didn't decide to diagnose him with either, because of all the information I had and again, my clinical evaluation of him."

CHAPTER 47

Dysfunction junction

Psychologist Harry Krop, Ph.D., didn't just have impressive academic credentials at the University of Florida and the distinction of founding one of the first child sex abuse clinics in Florida. To say that the defense expert spent decades analyzing some of the most bizarre thinking imaginable doesn't even begin to describe the scope of his work. So, when he said Ferrell's family was one of the most dysfunctional units he had ever seen, it was a remarkable moment.

"I have evaluated approximately seven hundred individuals who have been accused of first-degree murder." Out of that group, he testified in court about 80 times.[1]

Krop said he first saw Ferrell at the juvenile lockup in Marion County in December 1996,

"I saw a relatively anxious, scared juvenile who was generally coherent in terms of his ability to communicate with me."

He described Ferrell as "naïve" when discussing mental health issues, including pretending to be more mentally ill than he was. "...during the conversation he did not appear that he was not in touch with reality. I mean, it was clear to me that this was a pretty disturbed juvenile, just from some of the initial conversation with him, but I did not get the impression that he was hallucinating or extremely delusional as part of a multiple personality like he was trying to portray."

Ferrell told him that he had been coerced into making a false confession to police.

"Did he describe to you how the police were able to coerce him?" Hawthorne asked.

"He indicated that he had been awake for a week. That he wasn't able to get any sleep. That he was very tired. He felt very vulnerable when he was talking to the officers."[2]

On his family history, Ferrell told him that he had no contact with his father until he was seven or eight years old, that he had some contact with him after that and that his father taught him how to play Dungeons and Dragons. The contact stopped when he was nine.

Krop said, "I asked him about siblings and his response was, 'They're all dead.' When I asked him what he meant by that, he told me that several, I believe three, were lost during pregnancy, or I believe one child died either stillborn or soon after birth."[3]

"I asked him to tell me about his mother and he described her as a person who 'loses her grip of reality.' He said she tends to become very volatile, have mood swings, and generally is not a stable person. He said when she would start yelling at him that he would simply go into his room and 'crank up the music.'"

"He told me that his grandparents are 'diehard Christians,' and he said he used to be very religious until he was about 13 years old and then he said, 'I started going through little periods.' He didn't elaborate on that."[4]

Ferrell told him that he had been referred to school psychologists several times because of his artwork, but that he was just trying to express himself. He also told Krop that the school thought he was trying to turn the school into an occult setting, and that the people in Murray were discriminating against him.

He said he was expelled for not doing his work.

On the subject of Keesee, he said "he very, very much loved her." He had never been in a serious relationship before, though he had been sexually active. "...Shea showed him that it was possible to have love."[5]

His first "voluntary" sexual experience was when he was nine or ten, and that was with a 16-year-old girl. He described himself as a "nymphomaniac," Krop said.

"...he started talking about an alter ego and multiple personalities, at which time I primarily listened to him, but given my observations of him, did not particularly take these descriptions very seriously."[6]

"It was hard for him, in my opinion, to accept the fact that he had just killed people and was trying to give the impression, or trying somehow to explain, that it was this alter ego, or this other personality."[7]

Krop administered three tests. He concluded that Ferrell was able to communicate and aid his attorneys in his defense and was "very intelligent."

He also concluded that he was malingering.

One day, Krop was called to the Lake County jail. Ferrell had made several drawings and penned statements on the wall, including some professing his love for Keesee.

"There were some statements that certainly could be interpreted as suicidal, relating to 'forgive me, for I have sinned.' There were gestures of a noose around Rod's neck as if he were hanging, professing his love to his grandparents, I believe, were also written on there. And then there were a number of crosses and other types of symbols which are usually associated with some type of cultic type of activity."[8]

Ferrell told him he was just trying to get attention from the medical staff because he had stomach pain.

Krop wrote to Hawthorne saying Ferrell was not a suicide risk or mentally incompetent to aid his legal team.

Ferrell had told Krop the story about the "Black Mask" cult and being sodomized by several of his grandfather's friends when he was six years old. "The focus was basically dark magic and that the goal of the cult was to 'release evil into the world to extinguish the light.'" He said he could not remember if his grandfather was present for the abuse, Krop said.

Ferrell gave him a different account of his struggle with Queen than the version he gave to police. He repeated the story about her dousing him with hot coffee and scratching his face, but said that while he was grappling with her, Scott came up behind her and hit her in the head with a crowbar.

Krop's diagnosis for Ferrell was personality disorder.

"We all have personalities, and we all develop through our living experiences and environment, we develop certain personality traits. Some of us have a stronger desire to be neater than others. Some of us are more compulsive. Some of us are more addictive in terms of cigarettes or eating. We all develop personality traits. That's normal. And these personality traits go a long way in terms of contributing to what our behavior is like at any given time and what our thought processes are like.[9]

"When an individual develops certain personality traits, they become what we refer to as pathological, or they create a problem in terms of an individual's adjustment or adaptation to society and relationships, then it becomes what we call personality disorder."

Some personality disorders have a specific trait. Some have multiple traits and are called personality disorder not otherwise specified. Both Sondra and Ferrell have that disorder, he said.

Among the traits for Ferrell is schizotypal, he said. He has unusual thought processes, views society differently and he is viewed differently, has unusual or delusional beliefs, is depressive, narcissistic, and has magical thinking, believing that he has certain powers.

He also abused various substances, including Prozac.

In addition, he exhibits traits of conduct disorder, he said.

He was not insane on the day of the murders—he knew right from wrong, but he was having a severe emotional disturbance and was "impaired" in his ability to conform to the law, Krop said.

"Can you share with us any opinions that you drew from his family history?"[10]

"This is one of the more dysfunctional family situations that I have experienced, and I indicated that I have evaluated close to 700 individuals charged with first-degree murder."

Ferrell had neither positive male nor female role models, Krop said.

"Sondra Gibson is a very disturbed woman, a very dependent woman who has essentially never lived very much on her own, is not really capable of functioning, other than being in relationships, she has been involved in some very pathological and dysfunctional relationships herself. She has indicated through her interviews that she drank heavily when she was younger and that she prostituted herself. She was gone a lot. That she brought men home that were abusive to her and that Rod experienced some of that, not in terms of being abused himself, but by observing that and basically recognizing that the mother has been an extremely dysfunctional and ineffective parent.[11]

"I think the way she tried to compensate for her inadequate parenting was by being a friend to Rod, and Rod needed more than a friend. Rod has needed a parent, which in my opinion, the mother has not been able to provide."

Moving from place to place has not helped either, he said.

"…he has rebelled, and I think, based on my readings of vampire and vampire cults, and the description of the vampire kind of lifestyle, it is reported to be the ultimate rebellion. I don't believe that Rod is a vampire, and I don't believe that Rod believes he is a vampire, but this is part of his whole personality structure that he has taken both to view himself as being different and to be accepted and also to try and negate to some degree the rejection that he has felt in his life."[12]

Krop said Ferrell would function well in open population in prison if he received a life sentence. "As a matter of fact, he probably might even function better in the kind of structure that is provided in prison than he has in the lack of structure that he has had in this life."[13]

Like he had done with Dr. Myers, King directed a barrage of questions at Krop to demonstrate Ferrell's unlimited capacity for lying.

Krop repeated Ferrell's tale that he was grappling with Queen when Scott came up and hit her from behind.

"Did he tell you at that point what had happened to Mr. Wendorf?"

"No."

"He went on to indicate to you, in essence, that Scott Anderson was the person in charge. That Scott ordered him what to do, told him to get his ass in gear and to do certain things, correct?"

"That's correct."[14]

Krop said Ferrell told him that he saw Wendorf's body on the way out of the house.

Ferrell told Krop he was protecting Scott, his friend of 11 years, and the girls when he confessed to police about being the killer.

Ferrell also told him that he had not used drugs for a week and that he was not a fan of drinking alcohol.

Krop confronted Ferrell about his tale of having multiple personalities. "...he admitted to me that he in fact did not have multiple personalities, and that he was trying to portray himself to be mentally ill."

King then brought up a conversation Krop had with Ferrell in March 1997 about "the code of vampires." It harkened back to April Doeden's comments about how it was "not cool," what Ferrell had done.

"And part of that code was the vampires did not kill and they did not take things forcefully from others, is that not true?"[15]

"Yes."

"Doctor, you don't believe that his ideas about being a vampire have anything to do with these murders, do you?"

"Not directly," he said, though it did relate to the personality disorder he mentioned.

Ferrell told him the whole vampire thing began when he accidentally cut his finger in a biology class and instinctively put it in his mouth. Someone jokingly said he was a vampire. It was when the movie *Interview with a Vampire* was playing in theaters. "...things escalated to the point where he recognized that this was a way of getting attention." Rumors started, fantasy kicked in, some beliefs took over. "But I truly do not think that Rod Ferrell thinks he is a vampire."[16]

Confronted with facts that Krop possessed by December 1997, Ferrell gave more details about the murders. For example, he told Krop that when he and Scott found Wendorf asleep on the couch, they "savored the moment, and danced impishly around."

King said, "He also told you that he swung the crowbar at Mr. Wendorf's head about five times and stopped just short of hitting him, correct?"[17]

"Yes, a few inches from his head."

"And then on the sixth time, according to your notes, he thought, '[expletive] it, who cares?' And he crushed his head with full force."

"That's what he told me, yes."

"And then he went on to say that he hit him repeatedly approximately 25 times."

"Correct."

King showed Krop a letter that Ferrell had written to his mother, repeating the story that he had told Dr. Myers, about the couple being either dead or dying when he walked into the house.

King also confronted Krop about his opinion that Ferrell would do well in general population in prison. He presented discipline reports from the jail, showing fights, setting off the fire alarm and the sprinkler system.

Then, there was the matter of telling a corrections officer how he could escape by taking hostages among innocent bystanders. Krop said he was unaware of that report, but said it reflects his "personality disturbance and extreme immaturity."[18]

* * *

Desiree Nutt was a young, attractive corrections officer assigned to the juvenile "pod" in the Lake County jail.

One can almost imagine Ferrell puffing out his chest and talking macho smack about how he was going to break out of jail. Defense attorneys wanted the story to be kept out of the trial. Judge Lockett was a little skittish, so he had her testify outside of the jury's presence at first. He then allowed King to call her and have her read part of her testimony in front of the panel.

"Inmate Ferrell again approached the CO desk and starts asking questions pertaining to the jail security, such as, 'Are there cameras in the air-conditioning vents? I know there are manned gun ports on the roof.'"[19]

She also quoted him as saying, "But if someone wanted to get out, they could just crawl through the vents, right?"

"What I thought was, I could take out the officer in the shallow room, go through that little window, take out the property person and escape through the vent. When I get on the outside, it would be tough because of the lake in back of us.

"I wouldn't take one of the officers, because the people wouldn't care, that's their job. You can take an innocent person and cops won't do anything to you. They don't want to shoot an innocent person. I would take hostages, innocent ones, so that way if I went, I wouldn't go alone.

"I could take out so many of the dumb deputies; they're not careful at all. Anyway, I'm an amateur assassin. I probably wouldn't try to escape from here because I know too many of you officers.

"But if I don't get out of these charges, I will escape from the transportation people or wherever I'm going. Transportation officers are easy targets...."[20]

The things that were redacted in her report were in some ways even more interesting. For example: "Inmate Ferrell states, 'I don't know why Heather got off, she had it done.'"[21]

He also said, "the other two girls, Shea and Dana went for the ride, Heather was in on it."

Ferrell had approached Nutt, the only corrections officer in the juvenile pod, on Dec. 3, 1997. Even before that day, Ferrell had been talking about his case and asking her questions.

"...I had said that several times, 'I don't want to know anything,'" she said. She even told him that he could get into trouble for talking to her.

"And at one point he had mentioned to me that he could not get in trouble for what he was telling me about breaking into a house in Louisiana, and then I mentioned that, 'yes you can.'"

Ferrell's escape plan was very well thought out, Nutt said. "He apparently put some time into thinking about it."

It could be a fantasy, Krop said of breaking out of jail.

"Doctor, would you want to be the innocent one to find out if he was fantasizing or telling the truth?

"Of course not."

***

When it was Hawthorne's turn for redirect, she took a jab at Heather.

"Dr. Krop, can Rod be manipulated?"

"Rod is both manipulative and can be manipulated," he said, like many sixteen- and seventeen-year-old teenagers.[22]

"Now, you discussed before about Rod engaging in fantasy games with paramilitary type characters. Were these seeds planted, let's say, over the course of the previous year, having to do with the development of these characters, as far as maybe someone who wanted certain people dead?"[23]

Ferrell talked about cultists in Kentucky, Krop said, "but also in terms of Heather making a number of statements implying that she would like her parents dead."

Krop said he saw investigator notes about Heather making statements in phone calls or letters about her either wanting her parents dead or "that she would be better off dead or some kind of inference that her life would be better if her parents were dead."

He said he also reviewed reports that Heather thought she was a vampire.

Hawthorne also asked him about an incident in the school expulsion record. Ferrell was comforting Keesee in the hall when a teacher told him to go to class. A physical education teacher then escorted Ferrell. "...he said something about, 'I was mad enough to slit her throat,' but he did not threaten the teacher."

"He didn't tell the teacher, 'I'm going to slit your throat?'"

"No, not that I can tell from the transcript."

Hawthorne showed him a copy of the transcript. Ferrell was referring to the teacher that ordered him back to class, and the P.E. teacher said, "Rod, you don't mean that."

Krop then quoted Ferrell saying, "No, I probably wouldn't do that."

"But he said, 'I'm mad enough to.'"[24]

Krop said it wasn't unusual for teens to "verbalize emotions."

King had just one question on re-cross examination.

"For Mr. Wendorf and Miss Queen, it wasn't bravado or immaturity or anything else, was it?"

"You mean in terms of the homicide?"

"Yes. He said what he was going to do, and he did what he said he was going to do, correct?"

"If, in fact, when he made that statement that he was thinking about doing that, then yes, that's correct."

CHAPTER 48

"Fantasy world" rage

Elizabeth McMahon, Ph.D., is a wizened, wise, petite psychologist with a pixie haircut. She had testified in court cases for 20 years. "I couldn't even guess how many times."

Her expertise came through in the best way possible—she knew how to explain complicated issues to jurors in an understandable, engaging way.

King had argued that she should be excluded because her testimony would be repetitive, but Hawthorne said she was different. She is a neuropsychologist, a specialist who looks at how the brain and the nervous system effect cognition and behavior. She did a lot of testing, and she spent more time with Ferrell than the rest of the experts.

Ferrell's IQ is "average," McMahon said, but one test had a surprising result. Rod prided himself on his writing and speaking ability, yet his test score on that was lower than his performance IQ.

"He doesn't process information in the same manner in which the rest of us do," she said.[1]

"Consensual reality," is the percentage of people who might see something the same way. She couldn't say what the percentage was for Ferrell, but she said in some people it could be as low as 30 percent.

"Now, does this mean that he is psychotic? No, it doesn't mean that he is psychotic," she said. "It does mean that his ties with reality are very loose and can be disrupted very easily. Very disrupted when he becomes anxious. Disrupted when he becomes emotionally stirred up."[2]

She also described him as paranoid and feeling persecuted. "And the flip side of that, which we often see in people, is a certain grandiosity. That he is immune from some of the physical realm that the rest of us have to abide by; things like mortality, little things like that. That he has powers that other people don't have."

She described it as a defense mechanism. He has "very narrow range" of emotions, and most of the positive ones, like warmth, are missing because of the way he was brought up.[3]

"There is also a great deal of anger and hostility and aggression, rage, in this young man for a lot of reasons. When we don't get our needs met as children, we get pretty angry about that."[4]

Because he lacks empathy, he has poor interpersonal skills, so to get what he wants, he manipulates people. He concentrates more on the intellectual aspect of life to the detriment of the social and emotional, she said. Furthermore, he is immature, and looks at the world in black and white terms with no room for gray areas.

Heather told Ferrell that her parents were hurting her, "that in some way there was either neglect or abuse, or maybe just everyday discipline, but anyway, she felt that she was being hurt," McMahon said.[5]

At the same time, he was living in a fantasy world. "...I don't mean just Vampire Masquerade games; I mean all day. He's not in school, a good part of his time is out wandering around with no structure...taking on this sort of role of the outsider, somebody who is alienated from society and very much living in this fantasy world. And part of that fantasy world then becomes that he is the assassin. And that he is the one who can correct the social ills, evils, if you will, for want of a better word."

For Ferrell, it formed into the notion that he was going to rescue "a damsel in distress," but he never saw the whole picture, she said.

"Heather's parents were not as Heather had portrayed them and these were not bad people. These were people like anybody else. And that he had a very erroneous impression of them when he walked in that house.

"I'm not going to sit here and tell you that he was emotionally torn up about that," McMahon said. He can recognize what happened intellectually but not grasp it emotionally. It's part of his emotional immaturity," she explained.[6]

Ferrell was brought up without a dad, and by a mother who was extremely immature, McMahon said. That kind of situation hinders impulse control, self-discipline, and a strong sense of right and wrong.

"You don't internalize an authority. You don't internalize certain rules and regulations about how to run your life so that you don't hurt other people while you are doing it. And you just sort of run around and do what you feel like doing."[7]

His grandparents couldn't do much to change the situation because his mother was always around and she forbade them from interfering, McMahon said.

Both Ferrell and his mother treated each other as best friends. "You know, a child can have a lot of best friends, a child needs a parent and Rod simply didn't get that," McMahon said.[8]

Ferrell did not have a mature relationship with Charity, certainly not the kind of situation where each person is thinking about the needs of the other person and trying to meet those needs. The vampire clan helped fulfill a lot of Ferrell's emotional needs, she said.

"I think the fact that it was vampire, it could have been called anything. The fact that it was a vampire clan was coincidental."[9]

His "sire" became his father figure, the members his "family" and the hierarchy provided structure. "They have an identity. They now have a support system, as they see it. They have a group of people who accept them unequivocally. Anybody who walks around looking and dressing and acting in the manner in which Ferrell did, he is going to be ostracized by society, and in turn he is turning around sticking his tongue out at society. So, you're not going to have a whole bunch of people in middle or high school who is going to think that this is a neat guy to hang around with. So here, he had the group of people that are ostracized like he is...."[10]

The fact that the cult was goth was convenient because it let him channel his anger, she noted.

Hawthorne asked McMahon if Ferrell had discussed with Heather about getting the keys to the Explorer.

"He said that she had told him that the keys were inside, I believe in the bedroom, and asked him to get two things for her; one was her father's knife and the other was her mother's pearls."[11]

She said she learned from reading Jennifer's deposition that the keys were always kept in the ignition and the house was never locked.

She said she asked Ferrell what was going on in his mind. "He described it as a soldier going into war, or going into battle, you deal with your emotions later. The only problem is, Rod doesn't ever do that. In other words, this was a task, this was a job. He was the assassin. He was to do this, this task that had been assigned to him. And that he was very much into that sort of a fantasy role now, and don't misunderstand me, I'm not saying he didn't know where he was or what he was doing, he most certainly did."[12]

Hawthorne asked if his history of neglect and abuse fueled his rage the night of the murders, or was it simply something Heather had told him?

"I'm not saying that it wouldn't have resulted in a death, but that act is a very, what we call a 'very overdetermined act.' And that comes where you just sort of suddenly unlocked the flood gates of rage, and so it just spills out."[13]

He described Heather's reaction to the slayings as a combination of relief that it was over, depression, and regret.

She said Rod's time in jail was beginning to ground him in reality. Like the other experts, she diagnosed him with schizotypal personality disorder.

He knew what he had done was wrong, but his ability to conform to the law was "impaired," she said.

King, on cross-examination, referred to Ferrell's statement to police about "taking pleasure" in repeatedly striking Wendorf with the crowbar. "That's not rage, is it?"

"Is that rage? Yes."

"Taking pleasure in it?"

"Beating him, and beating him, and beating him, whether he takes pleasure in it or not, that's rage."[14]

Taking a different tack, King reminded her of the rules of the vampire clan, like not taking someone's blood if it was not offered, and his self-imposed rule of not killing children under the age of 16, which he talked about after first going to the wrong house and seeing kids inside. He also brought up her own statement that Ferrell knew right from wrong. "You just think he couldn't help himself; he couldn't stop himself."

"I don't think he could stop himself once he got going." She said she couldn't say where he crossed the line. "Somewhere maybe when he walked in the door...."[15]

She conceded that Ferrell had lied to her a lot, though sometimes it was "more fantasy than lying."[16]

King also noted that Ferrell told her he was aware of the consequences at the time, and that it was like a warning, "kind of like a conscience, if things are too dangerous or wrong you should not do this." Yet, he went ahead and did it anyway.

Ferrell also knew to keep going past the wrong house, to avoid homes with burglar alarm signs, switching license plates and throwing the murder weapon in the Mississippi River, King noted.

Hawthorne had one more shot at her third and final defense expert. "Mr. King has done analogies to try and say that Rod is just like us. Is Rod like us?"

"No. People don't mature equally on all levels—socially, physically, mentally, spiritually, and emotionally. It is only when people are adults that things begin to even out, barring some event like trauma." Then again, she added, "most sixteen-year-olds are not walking around with the stunted emotional development that Rod Ferrell has."

"Is part of that his mental illness? Is the other part the home, the abuse, neglect and abandonment?" Hawthorne asked.

"One gives rise to the other," she said.[17]

CHAPTER 49

"I didn't believe him"

Shannon Yohe raised her right hand, swore to tell the truth, and settled into the chair on the witness stand.

McCune zeroed in on the Monday evening visit. He asked if Ferrell appeared intoxicated. She said no.

On cross-examination, she conceded that she was not an expert on whether anyone was drunk or under the influence, though she said she had seen people who were drunk.

Lackay then showed her a series of photos of what Ferrell looked like before he moved to Kentucky in 1995 and what he looked like when he showed up at her house. Other than wearing a trench coat, he wore normal clothing, and did not dye his hair or wear it long the year before, she said.

"You didn't take too seriously what Rod was saying, did you, that night?"[1]

"No."

"Okay. You didn't call the police or anything, did you?"

"I didn't believe him."

"Because he basically runs his mouth a lot, doesn't he?"

"Yes."

McCune said he had just one more question. "After you found out that the Wendorfs were dead, did you believe him then?"

"Objection!" Lackay said. "Irrelevant."

"Your honor, it is directly in response to Mr. Lackay's question, did she believe him or not."

"Objection sustained," Lockett said. "You don't have to answer."

The next witness was Suzanne Leclaire, who recounted the night of Jeanine's birthday party and discovering that she was planning to run away with Heather and Ferrell.

Hawthorne had no questions for her.

A parade of police officers and evidence technicians also stepped up to the witness stand, including Lake County Sheriff's Detective Al Gussler, who identified Richard Wendorf's credit card records. Baton Rouge detectives Ben Odom and Dennis Moran also recounted their encounters with Ferrell and the other cult members.

"Did you ever make any threats to Mr. Ferrell?" McCune asked Moran.[2]

"Did not, no sir."

"Did you ever observe anyone else make any threats to Mr. Ferrell?"

"No sir."

"Did you do anything to create stress on him, other than what was inherent under the circumstances?"

"No sir, did not."

The teens were fed, allowed to go to the restroom, and Ferrell was brought out into the open squad room sometimes, Moran said.

McCune then took Moran back in time to the banks of the Mississippi with Scott Anderson.

"Your honor, I object to Mr. Anderson being hearsay, and it violates our right to confrontation."[3]

"Overruled. You can go ahead, sir," Lockett said.

"And at that one location he pointed to an area where some evidence had been thrown into the river, pertaining to a double-barrel shotgun and a hunting…."

Lackay jumped up. "May we approach, sir?" he asked the judge.

"You can argue it from there," Lockett replied.

"Sir, we would object to anything about a shotgun. I don't think there is any charges with regards to a shotgun with Mr. Ferrell and we would object to it and move to strike and ask for a curative instruction for a mistrial."

"Your honor, the state would agree to that," McCune said.

"Agree to a mistrial?" Lackay asked.

"Strike the reference to the shotgun," Lockett said. "Folks, disregard it and pretend as though it has not been testified to, and I mean that seriously. As if you have not heard that, put it out of your mind. Thank you."[4]

On cross, Lackay asked about the old, gray, high-ceiling detective office, the fact that there were no holding cells, and that Ferrell was kept for a time locked up in one of the carpeted-wall interrogation rooms.

Lackay also made a point of detectives not talking to juvenile justice officials, but to prosecutor Bill Gross in Lake County.

The next witness was Baton Rouge Detective Thomas Dewey.

"I had spoken with him, of course," Dewey said of Ferrell. "I talked through the interview with him, and he was very nonchalant, very, I call it almost braggadocious that he was the leader of this group."[5]

"We would object, your honor, and move to strike that," Lackay said.

"Why?" Lockett asked.

"The reason is, judge, because it's an opinion as to how Mr. Ferrell was thinking, and we would move to strike it."

"Overruled. Will not strike."

McCune asked if anyone made any promises to Ferrell, and Dewey said no.

Odom testified about his role the night the teens were arrested. He asked Ferrell if he was under the influence of drugs or alcohol.

"There was one part of his response that said he had something to drink about an hour after. It was clarified after the interview that he was talking about an hour after the crime."

Like the others, he said he made no promises, no threats, and did not withhold food or water.

He also talked about the unsuccessful search for the crowbar in the river.

King asked what the river in that area is like.

"Well, it's approximately a mile wide in Baton Rouge. It's, I'd say, from 20 to 30 feet from the bank. It goes down to 45 feet pretty dramatically. The current is extremely swift. In November in Baton Rouge, the water is high and it is pretty dangerous."[6]

On cross-examination, Lackay again brought up the fact that Heather, too, was arrested in the group, and that police found a carving on a tree limb by the river with the initials "ZOE" and "FET."

CHAPTER 50

The dead do tell tales

It was the most bitter kind of irony for a vampire. Ruth pointed out her vampire killer from the grave, and she did it with blood.

McCune teed up the DNA case against Ferrell by calling Timothy Petry, a clinical forensic serologist with the Florida Department of Law Enforcement Crime Lab.

"…I look at items of physical evidence for the possible presence of body fluid stains. Primarily I'm talking about blood, semen, or saliva," he testified.[1]

McCune worked quickly, laying out items for identification: Queen's fingernail clippings, and jeans that Ferrell had been wearing. He had Petry step down from the stand and hold up the jeans, showing five stain areas he had circled with a blue marker. He marked an unstained area that would be the control sample. He pinned square patches marked with letters of the alphabet to mark the spot for jurors where he had cut out samples.

McCune also had Petry identify one of Ferrell's boots and explain how he had taken a swabbing for testing, as well as a kitchen tile and a glove.

He later identified a tube of blood taken from Queen during her autopsy.

"What we do is we take a portion of that liquid blood and basically put it on a piece of cotton gauze or cloth and allow that to air dry and then we have a dried blood sample from the individual that we can preserve for DNA testing," he said.[2]

Petry performed the same procedure from a tube of blood drawn from Ferrell, and he collected a blood sample from Richard Wendorf's T-shirt.

He also prepared a chart that included a boot print from the floor.

The next day McCune called upon Anne Montgomery, the director of operations of Reliagene Technologies, a DNA testing lab in New Orleans.

Again, McCune had the expert explain the process and how they reached their conclusions.

Montgomery talked about the genetic profiles of Richard, Ruth, and Ferrell, using what she called "extremely conservative calculations."

In Ferrell's case, the chance that any other Caucasian would have the same genetic profile would be 1-in-15 million, she said.

McCune had her testify about each fingernail, saying Ferrell either "could not be excluded" or that the DNA was "consistent" with his, including in a mixture of her DNA sample.

Turning to another chart, dealing with DNA found on Ferrell's boots, she said, "What we clearly see on numerous genetic markers, we have to exclude Mr. Ferrell as the donor of these stains on the boots."[3]

She continued with her explanation. "…we cannot exclude Miss Wendorf as the donor of the stains on the left and right boot." In fact, she said, the sample was "completely consistent" with her genetic profile.[4]

As for the stains on Ferrell's jeans, she said she could not exclude Richard Wendorf as the donor.

The prosecutors then called Debra Fisher, a latent print expert from the state crime lab, who identified Ferrell's now infamous boots as the ones that left shoe prints on the kitchen floor. "...there is no doubt in my mind."[5]

CHAPTER 51

The horror movie

Lackay and Hawthorne were not fools. They knew that Ferrell's videotaped confession was a disaster. The best they could hope for was to have some of the damning portions redacted.

"And in particular, judge, what we are trying to keep out are more things like we asked, you know, the questions about remorse," Lackay said in a conference while the jury was out of the room.[1]

He also wanted to exclude information about the home burglary in Louisiana because none of the teens were charged in that crime.

King argued that the jury should be allowed to hear all of it. For one thing, Krop and Myers relied on the tapes to formulate their expert opinions.

Lockett, in his typical take-charge mode, went down the list, saying which items would be scratched, and which would be retained. However, he paused at some items to hear arguments.

In the end, references to the Louisiana break-in were out. So was a reference to the animal shelter abuse.

"I'm definitely not getting into this dog business. That is redacted," Lockett said.[2]

Lockett was also not going to allow jurors to hear Ferrell talk about having the stolen shotgun on his lap, ready to shoot Baton Rouge police officers. The prejudicial effect would far outweigh anything the state would need to prove, he said.

But there were plenty of other damaging things for the jury to see and hear. The lawyers argued about Ferrell's statement, "I don't kill anything that's little. Now adults, that's perfectly fine, 16 and up."[3]

Lackay said it had nothing to do with a specific legal death penalty aggravator; it just shows "bad character."

King said Dr. Myers testified that Ferrell's ability to conform to the law was "impaired," yet this showed he had a code of conduct.

The judge ruled that the jury could hear it.

He also ruled against redacting Ferrell's comment about "taking pleasure in it," referring to beating Wendorf with a crowbar.[4]

King didn't win all his arguments, however.

The judge listened to arguments about the detective's question, "Do you feel any remorse about what you did?" The answer was "Why?"[5]

"We know specifically that lack of remorse is not an aggravating factor," the judge said.

King said it addressed the state's aggravator of cold, calculated, and premeditated. "...it goes to show that he has the ability to preplan and the predisposition to kill a human being without any thought."[6]

King also noted that he talked about killing the Wendorfs at Shannon Yohe's house.

The judge ordered that it be redacted.

There was also an argument over the videotaped "meeting," as King described the one-on-one interaction between Ferrell and Keesee at the police station.

King said the tape basically showed the two kissing and hugging for 45 minutes to an hour.

"I tell the court, my intent is that it be in evidence, not for the purpose of anything that is said in the tape, only to watch their conduct, especially Mr. Ferrell's with Miss Keesee."

"I'm not going to say you have an expectation of privacy in a police office," Lackay said. "I don't think you do. Judge, there is some, I guess you would call it heavy petting, some intimate behavior, there is a lot of kissing going on. There is a couple of positions that they get into where they are kind of close to each other, let's say hips to hips. I think in this case, Judge, in regard to the jury seeing this, they are going to see that this is taken about 74 hours after the incident. The only thing I can see it doing is inflaming the jury. They would be extremely prejudiced by it...."

King didn't fight it. "No response, your honor."

Lockett ruled that the jury would not see it.

Even without the "prejudicial" quotes, when the lights were dimmed and the jury settled in to watch the videotapes, what they saw and heard was a long-haired, cigarette-smoking, foul-mouthed teenager who denied but inadvertently admitted premeditation, which under the law, can occur in seconds.

Odom asked: "Did you all ever discuss these homicides prior to the day you went over there with anybody that you can remember?"[7]

"We never thought about it until 10 minutes before we did it."

"So, it wasn't a planned thing until you went over there?"[8]

"(inaudible)... spontaneous, (inaudible), because if you premeditate something it's easily planned and easily known."

Even allowing for a somewhat fuzzy timeline, Ferrell's 10-minute story didn't ring true.

Yohe said Ferrell and his followers showed up at her house on that Monday between 5:30 and 6 p.m., and he called Heather between 7:45 and 8 p.m. This was after he talked about killing the Wendorfs at Yohe's house.

Hueber said Heather called him between 7:45 and 8 p.m. Thirty minutes later, she called again to say she was coming by to see him. "She said she had to go because Rod might kill her parents."

Jeanine said Heather tapped on her window at about 8:30 p.m.

Gussler asked what he and Heather talked about in the Eustis cemetery.

"About her running away. Asking her if she was sure. Asking her where she wanted to go. Asking her just about her personal life, about her boyfriend, Jeremy."

"Did you discuss with her about her parents at that time?"

"We didn't think anything about her parents at that time. We didn't think about the parent thing until 10 minutes before we did it, so that was kind of spontaneous, it was [not] premeditated."[9]

Gussler said, "I'm asking you again. I'm telling you she's telling us...."

Ferrell also said in the tape that "none of the girls knew" his plan.

That wasn't true either. Cooper and Keesee knew. Heather said she did not.

He also said Queen made him angry when she spilled coffee on him and clawed his face. Unlike what he told Krop, claiming Anderson also struck her, he said on the tape that Scott "froze" while he beat her to death.

Jurors didn't hear the redacted comment about Ferrell not feeling any remorse. They didn't have to. They heard him say how he was "taking pleasure" in beating Richard Wendorf to death, and how he got a "rush" out of it.

Jurors had been wearing their poker-playing expressions, but at this point, some turned and glared at the remorseless killer who used the word "splack" to describe a crowbar smacking flesh and bone.

Ferrell's grandmother had a much stronger reaction. She laid her head on her husband's shoulder, put her hand over her face, cried, and hurried out of the courtroom. Ferrell's strongest supporter could no longer completely convince herself that he was "a good boy."

CHAPTER 52

Broken hearts

Defense attorneys hate victim impact evidence. It has nothing to do with the evidence of the crime, they argue. All it does is make jurors feel sorry for the victims' families. This, while the judge's instructions to the jury warn against rendering a verdict based on sympathy. Legislators, however, were feeling the heat from voters who were calling for victims' rights, so they were willing to bend.

Queen's oldest daughter, Paula Lohse, of Dallas, Texas, was more than willing to testify.

McCune had her identify Ruth in a photo with Richard and his mother, Betsy.

"Now, would you please tell the jury, as best you are able, how your mom, Ruth Queen, was unique as an individual human being?"[1]

"Well, she was a good mother. She raised four daughters and she raised them to be honest and caring. She was just someone to go to for advice. I called her quite often. She liked to talk about her grandkids. She liked to talk about old times. She liked to do a lot of craft things, she would make quilts and she had real good friends, longtime friends that she would do these things with, and she taught us girls each to do things.

"She volunteered at the high school and she gave her crafts away to people after she had made them. I thought that was neat. I really respected and admired her. I didn't realize it so much until I got older and had kids of my own and realized how tough it was."

"Can you tell the jury, please, what loss you and your family, as you understand your mom's involvement in the community, was lost and has suffered as a result of this crime?"

"Well, my kids, her grandkids, looked forward to coming to visit, so they can't do that now. Well, there was a loss to the school, she volunteered but she helped out a lot. Her friends, you know, they would do things together that she just won't be there to do things with anymore."

Hawthorne had just one line of inquiry on cross-examination. She introduced a letter that Heather had sent to her but did not have her read it.

McCune then called Robert Wendorf to the stand.

"I'm Ricky's younger brother," he said.[2]

McCune had him identify everyone in a family photo.

"Ricky was really, really unique. He had a tremendous amount of incredible qualities that made him so unique. One of them was that he is a great brother. I once remember Mother telling me a story about when Billy and Ricky, Billy being Ricky's twin, were just being able to talk. And only Ricky could understand exactly what Billy would say. And whenever Billy would say something, mother would always look over at Ricky and go, 'What did Billy say?' Ricky could always understand everything that Billy said.[3]

"For me, Ricky was an example of what a big brother should be. I remember his patience, the first time when I was learning to ride a bicycle, taking the training wheels off, him running beside me. Me, having the confidence of knowing that if I should falter, Ricky would be right there to catch me. He gave me courage to take that first step.

"When he was older, he said Ricky took him to Interstate 4, which was still under construction. "…of course, there weren't any cars up there and we were riding on his motorcycle, and he got off and he said, 'Okay Bob, do you want to drive?' Did I want to drive? It was great!"

When he had his own family, Richard made sure he saved money, even wearing shoes with holes in them so he and Ruth could build their dream house.

He described him as "an employer's dream," and said when the plant was sold to another company, he was only one of two the bosses kept on the payroll.

"He had all the qualities an employer would want. He was honest and hard-working. He had the attitude of whatever it takes to get the job done, that's what he would do. It didn't matter if he had to work overtime or what."[4]

He also described him as a good provider and father. Recognizing that both girls were gifted, he bought a piano and paid for lessons. Both ended up being able to compose music.

He bought Jennifer a car, but he wanted to make sure it was safe. He didn't want her to break down somewhere. His only rule was that no one but Jennifer was supposed to drive it.

"Well, about a year later, Jennifer had an accident, and she wasn't driving the car. She let someone else do it. And Ricky was so forgiving, that he was so concerned and overjoyed—not that the car was wrecked, but that everybody was okay, and his treasures were safe."[5]

He told Jennifer that he could not afford to replace it with a car just as nice, but he put money he had set aside with the insurance payout and bought her another car.

He was proud when she got a scholarship to Florida State University. He had been worried because she said she wanted to be a doctor, and the scholarship was a relief, Robert said.

At Christmas, Richard decorated the house with Christmas lights. When Jennifer got home from work one night, she walked out to admire the decorations with her dad.

"Jennifer was looking at the lights and Ricky was talking about how balanced the left side of the house was with the right side.... And then he said to Jennifer how she needed to balance her life a little bit."[6]

He didn't say it to belittle her, Robert said, but to encourage her.

Richard also helped his mother take care of his 99-year-old grandfather, Robert said.

"I lost a brother. The children lost a father. My parents lost a son. And the world lost a sensational person. I never met a person that didn't like Rick."

Hawthorne, in her cross-examination, managed to take a dig at Jennifer this time.

"That was a very nice tribute, sir."

"Thank you."

"I noticed that I have not seen Jennifer here in court. Would you happen to know where she is?"

"No, I'm sorry."

***

Rick Ferrell bears a striking resemblance to his son, but if there was any similarity, physically or otherwise, Rick Ferrell wanted no part of it.

He was married to Sondra for a year-and-a-half, but they were only together for about three months because he was stationed in various places in the Air Force, including South Korea.

"Would Sondra work with you on letting you see the child?"

"Very rarely, if at all."[7]

He said he last saw Rod in 1987. He took him flying when he got his private pilot's license.

"Do you feel like you have abandoned Rodrick Ferrell?"

"No sir, I do not."

"Why not?"

"As I have mentioned before, the difficulty in arranging visitation was formidable. Dealing with Sondra was exceptionally difficult. One minute she would be extremely friendly, the next minute she would be extremely, and I want to use a polite term, difficult to work with. Accusative. She would fabricate the most awful lies. It was very difficult to deal with her in any way, shape, or form."[8]

King took up the cross-examination and brought up the fact that Rick Ferrell's father was mentally ill.

"One of the doctors opined the other day that because of that, that that affected you and therefore you being affected, affected Mr. Rodrick Ferrell. Did he ever see Rodrick Ferrell enough to have had any effect on him?"[9]

"I don't think it did, sir."

"Did your father's illness, do you believe have any lasting emotional impact on you?"

"On me?"

"Yes sir."

"Absolutely."

"Do you feel like that was transferred to Rod?"

"I don't believe it could have been, sir. There was no time."

King asked if he made his child support payments, and he said he had.

On redirect, Lackay asked, "Mr. Ferrell, did you send him any Christmas cards after 1987?"

"Not that I recall sir, no."

"Did you send him any birthday cards after 1987?"

"Not that I recall."

Told that he could step down and that he was released from his subpoena, Rick Ferrell walked out of the courtroom.

He never once looked at his son, who was weeping. Rick was an excellent defense witness. Even the most hard-hearted juror would have felt sorry for Rod.

Jurors also saw a videotaped deposition of Betty Jane Ferrell, Rick's mother and Rod's grandmother.

She said she got to see Rod weekly while Rick was in the Air Force, and that she enjoyed a good relationship with him. She said her husband, Bobby, never harmed Rod, and certainly was not the grandfather that Rod claimed raped him when he was five.

Sondra's resistance to Rick seeing Rod forced her to go to court to get visitation rights. When Rick left the service, the visitation agreement went away, too.

"When Roddy saw me last, he put his little arms around me and said, 'I love you Grammy.' And that's the last I saw him." It was 1988.

"So anyway, in March of '89, I got a letter from Roddy and it was just scribbling, and it said, 'I want some money,' or in essence was asking me for money for a Nintendo. He didn't even say 'Love, Roddy.' Didn't even send his love to us.

"I think I kept that in my storage box. I don't know, probably I threw it away because it hurts to read it. So, I thought, I'm not putting this little child between me, my son or myself anymore, so I ceased the relationship. I felt that it was in his best interest. I would have sent him two Nintendos, if anybody wants to know."

"Do you feel that Sondra put him up to the letter?" Lackay asked.

"I think it was under duress and I don't care. I really believe it. Because he was eight by this time sir, and he could write and print well, you know. I won't say that for sure, but that's what it looked like to me. I don't say he wrote it; I don't say Sondra. He wasn't that sort of kid. He was the sweetest little thing."

She said that she and her son did not have the privilege of having had much of an impact on Rod's life.

"I'm sorry about that. When I left him, he was a sweet little boy."[10]

CHAPTER 53

Guts, no glory

Sondra and Rod were not the worst tenants that apartment manager Diana Smith ever had at Southside Manor Apartments in Murray, but they may have been the weirdest.

"I really didn't have that many problems with them," she testified, but they were strange.

"I actually thought they were girlfriend and boyfriend instead of mother and son."

"Why?" Hawthorne asked.

"Because they walked up and down through there holding hands."

"And did they have a unique way of dressing?"

"Yeah, they both dressed in black, black hair, black clothes, black shoes, black nails. Everything was black."[1]

She inspected the apartment when Gibson moved out.

"Well, of course it had a few holes here and there. Most of them do when they move out. It wasn't nothing major. The back bedroom, the master bedroom, had like a pentagram drawed (sic) on the floor...."[2]

"Do you know whose room that was?"

"Sondra's."

Ashley Elkins, a 17-year-old senior at Calloway High School, was supposed to be a good defense witness, but her testimony had some scorching blowback.

Lackay asked if she had ever seen Sondra impose any kind of discipline on Rod.

"No, she would never say anything to him, she didn't even know he was around."

One night, she said, Rod came into his house with a bunch of his male friends.

"She'd flirt with them. She'd, you know, rub them and talk to them and flirt with them, like that."[3]

Heather called Rod several times at her house because Sondra's phone was disconnected because of unpaid long-distance bills, Elkins said.

"I never really talked to her much on the phone, but she wrote us letters and I read those."

Four letters were addressed to her brother. He never wrote her back and he destroyed them after news broke about the murders.

One letter caught her attention because it had a drawing of a teddy bear with a noose around its neck. "…it basically said that she wanted to get rid of her parents because she wanted to be with him, and that's the only way she could be with him, if she got rid of her parents, and she wanted them gone."[4]

McCune brought out the fact that the two of them had never met, but had "crossed paths," at the courthouse in Murray as she was on her way to a meeting with the defense.

She conceded that she had been friends with Ferrell.

"Isn't it true that Mr. Ferrell always tried to intimidate people?"

"That's true. I think he always wanted me to be scared of him."

In fact, she said, he wanted everyone to be frightened.

"And isn't it also true that he wanted people to feel lower than him, inferior to him?"

"Yeah."

"Now, was Mr. Ferrell manipulative?"

"Very much so."

"Is it true that he often would try to play on their emotions?"

"Yes."

"And isn't also true that Mr. Ferrell really only cared about Mr. Ferrell?"

"That's how it seemed to be."

McCune asked if he had threatened her.

She said he called her names and said, "he was going to spread my guts all over the wall so everybody could see them and smell them...."[5]

She said she laughed at him, but she quit having contact with him after that, but he stalked her, and she saw him hiding near her bus stop.

CHAPTER 54

A taste for blood

It was like old home week when I called out Jaden's name in the courthouse lobby. You would have thought we were long lost brothers he was so excited to see me. We had talked on the phone several times, but Murphy has the never-ending energy of a coiled spring. He also likes being the center of attention, and he was about to take center stage.

Hawthorne began by having him tell about meeting Ferrell in high school in December 1995. Interest in vampirism was not the initial draw. "The major thing that attracted me to him was he dressed very similar (sic) to myself [all black] and he didn't really fit in with the redneck or prep genre of the school, so he was more or less an outcast, as I was myself," he said.[1]

"He would wear jeans, faded jeans with holes in the knees, combat boots, and he'd tuck his jeans inside of them. Most of the time he wouldn't tie the combat boots. Just a T-shirt and a trench coat and he would have his hair pulled back in a ponytail or have it just hanging freely." His hair was strawberry blond, Jaden said.

He said he took Ferrell to Vampire Masquerade games, which could last from dusk to dawn. He explained there were other books and games that they also checked out.

Hawthorne moved to have the Masquerade game entered into evidence. King objected, saying it was irrelevant, but the judge overruled him. King was also unsuccessful in trying to stop Hawthorne from entering versions of Dungeons and Dragons.

Murphy described crossing Ferrell over to become a vampire at a cemetery. "We went out there and I had been talking to him about my lifestyle, which I was practicing vampirism. I did not believe that I could fly or that I was immortal or that the sunlight would kill me. I wasn't repelled by crosses or garlic. The strictest definition is I did have a craving for blood, be it human or animal. The first time that I tasted blood I was five, other than my own. We went out there and I basically told him of our own beliefs and our own laws. We don't have a certain idol that we worship or a goddess or anything like that, or a god. I took out a blade that I had brought from my house and I cut my arm with it and he took from me and the same process happened with him. I had him cut his arm and I took from him. And we sat there in meditation for a few hours and then we left."[2]

Murphy said becoming a sire is a big responsibility. "I was the one that embraced him, crossed him over into our way of life, so therefore I was responsible for his actions that he did. If he messed up, then I will pay the price for it from my side."[3]

Murphy said that before he got into the vampire lifestyle he was "into self-mutilation. I had cut myself several times to relieve emotional distress and pain through physical needs."

He said he knew Sondra Gibson, and that she tried to solicit his younger brother for sex during a cross-over ritual.

He also talked about the fight he had with Ferrell. He said when he arrived at Ferrell's house that Rod and Sondra were arguing. Jaden said she then accused him of coming between them. He said he walked downstairs. "...he was getting quite cocky, Rod was, and made a statement of some sort that he felt that I was standing on him, as if he was laying on the ground and I was standing on top of him, you know, sort of like a dominatrix, submissive type of thing, and I grabbed him by his throat and slammed him into the wall."[4]

Hawthorne pulled out a Valentine's Day card that Sondra had given to him and had him read it aloud: "If I could have one wish come true, Jaden, it would be to spend my life with you. Happy Valentine's Day. Star." She signed it, "Eternally, Star, aka Mistress of the Dark."[5]

On cross-examination, McCune noticed that Murphy had been smiling at Rod.

"It's just been quite some time since I have seen him, and I truly missed him."

"So, you and Rod are good friends?"

"We're close, really close."

"In fact, you loved Rod."

"Yes, I do love Rod."[6]

"I'm confused about something," McCune said. "Are you a vampire or are you not a vampire?"

"Yes, I do claim that." He said he took on the lifestyle before he ever participated in the vampire role-playing games. "I don't mean that I have lived eternally for thousands of years. I am 19 years old, and I can die."

He also said he did not have fangs, and to prove it, opened his mouth to show the jurors. It was a moment captured by an Associated Press photographer.

McCune shrewdly brought up the rules that vampires are to live by.

"We are supposed to have the highest admiration for life," Murphy said. The only goal that we have is to coexist, and we don't want any trouble...."[7]

Murphy said that just because vampires live life differently, it doesn't mean that they can "twist things to the way we want them."

"And isn't it true, another law of being a vampire, is thou shall not take any blood without permission of the donor?" McCune asked.

Yes, he said, including crossing someone over. And yes, he taught those rules to Ferrell.

Yet, Ferrell was making threats. "I heard around town anyways…is that he planned to take my life and the life of my fiancée at the time, Ashley Elkins…her head and guts would be strung all over the place."

Jaden told Hawthorne on redirect that he didn't take it seriously.

When Jaden stepped down from the witness stand, he turned and blew a kiss to Ferrell. Ferrell smiled and blew one back.

Outside, Jaden held an impromptu press conference for me and for the reporters from Court TV.

The murders had nothing to do with vampirism, he said, because Ferrell "did not bleed the bodies. There was no bloodletting. He did not take from them."

Ferrell once told him that if he ever did kill someone it would be by "cutting them into little pieces or bludgeoning."[8]

CHAPTER 55

The inner circle

The defense picture of Ferrell's descending metamorphosis continued with the testimony of Matt Goodman.

"When Rod came back to Kentucky in 1996, had he changed?" Hawthorne asked.[1]

He was "more morbid," Goodman said, "he used to be more fun." He wore all black clothing and wore necklaces with pentagrams and images of wizards and began talking in gothic rhymes and riddles.

He also became increasingly serious in the role-playing games they devised, Goodman said. In fact, Ferrell was breaking the rules when he kicked him in the teeth. It was supposed to be a play fight, with soft or no contact, Goodman said. "This wasn't a game. I thought he just wanted to spar or practice, that's what he told me. But this wasn't a game."

Goodman said he followed the rules.

"And did Mr. Ferrell follow the rules when he played the game?" McCune asked.

"Most of the time, yes."

"Mr. Ferrell knows how to follow rules, doesn't he?

"Yes."

McCune also brought out the fact that Ferrell liked to play mind games.

"Now, Matt, when Rod was a young kid, he wasn't playing mind games, was he?" Hawthorne asked.

"No. That wasn't until he came back from Florida."[2]

April Doeden testified about meeting Ferrell for the first time. It was the night before Jaden crossed him over. Rod was upset and couldn't sleep. "...I asked him if that's what he believed and I could help him, and if he was really that scared that he didn't need to be in it."[3]

Hawthorne asked Doeden about Ferrell's relationship with his mother. Sondra told him that she wished he was dead and had never been born, "and said that he killed his brothers and sisters, and that he ruined her life and that he was a demon child, and all this other stuff."[4]

Ferrell ended up living at Doeden's house. She is three years older.

"Did you ever notice him talking in rhymes and riddles or gothic poetry?" Hawthorne asked.[5]

"Yeah. Everybody talks like that for a while, though."

Hawthorne asked her about the book, *Necronomicon*.

"Well, it was originally supposed to be a joke, evil magic spells and stuff, but people took it seriously, perverse and twisted minds, really, people think it can do things because they believe it, and therefore it is."[6]

Rod had a copy, and so did she, she said, but he believed it was real. She also talked about seeing the pentagram on the floor of Sondra's bedroom.

She said she also overheard a phone conversation between Ferrell and Heather.

"I believe I heard her ask him to come get her."[7]

"Okay. And did you hear anything else?"

"He said he would, and she said that they were hurting her. And he said he'd come get her, and she said the only way I can see you, for you to get me out of here, is to kill them."

"April, you said…that you knew Rod because you had gone out with him. In fact, you and he had been engaged, correct?" King asked.[8]

"Yes sir."

"How long had you been engaged?"

"I don't know."

"Okay, but it was for a period of months, correct?"

"Yes."

"And he thought of you as his light and Charity Keesee as his darkness, correct?"

"Yeah."

"In fact, he believed, or pretended like he believed, that the child you had is his child, correct?"

"I don't know that for sure."

"But you've heard that."

"I've heard that."

He also got her to say that she was practicing witchcraft as a "good witch." Even more important, she conceded that she had some memory problems. "…you don't recall today having told me that it was Mr. Ferrell that made the statement about the parents and not Heather."[9]

"I remember very clearly trying to explain to you that it was Heather, and I was very clearly trying to explain to you that she needed to be helped," she replied.

"But when we got into the discussion of that, several times you said, 'I don't remember. I don't remember these things.' Correct?"[10]

"I do not remember telling you that part, no."

Lyzetta Crews, Sondra's sister, also testified.

"How old were you when you moved out of the house?" Hawthorne asked.[11]

"Fourteen," she said, and Sondra was about a year-and-a-half to two years of age. "I moved out because I was very unhappy. It wasn't a good atmosphere, I didn't feel. And I ran away and got married at fourteen. Was married to the man for twenty-one years, by the way."

She said she moved out because there were three incidents before she was 12 where her father was "sexually inappropriate with me."[12]

"Now, would that be fondling?"

"One of the incidents, he had picked me up from my cousin's house and was bringing me home and he pulled off the side of the road and pulled me over to him and started to kiss me. I don't remember anything from there," she said.

"There was one time when he made me lay down on the bed by him and rubbed himself against me, and he rubbed his hands up and down my body. And the third time, I was twelve, and I told him to get his hands off me."

"And did you ever go to your mother with this information?"

"No, I didn't. The time I confronted my father, he said to me, 'What are you going to do, tell your mother? It'll only hurt her, and she won't believe you anyway. And I still think he was right, so there was no reason."[13]

Hawthorne next called Crews' daughter, Sandy Crisp, of Daytona Beach, and asked if she had ever seen Sondra discipline Rod.

"She was like his friend; she didn't discipline him at all."

Hawthorne also asked about Sondra's relationship with men. "She's told me and showed me pictures of several men over the years, I'd say over the past fifteen years."[14]

Hawthorne asked if she had "normal" relationships with me.

"No. They were usually pictures of men dressed as women, makeup on, you couldn't even tell it was a man. I remember on several occasions, you know, I was a lot younger, this was probably ten years ago. It was quite a shock to see such things."

After the slayings, Sondra came to live with Lyzetta for a time. "And she was always telling me about this great music and these movies that I just had to see...and it was all glamorizing the vampire life. She thought it was wonderful, she was really into it."[15]

She wore all-black leather clothing. "I go to college at night, and on my way home I have to drive down a road called Ridgewood, and I would see her walking down the street at night, and this is an area that is well-known for illegal activity, and it's definitely not a place you typically would see someone walking down the street, so I definitely noticed if she was there."[16]

She said Sondra also walked down Main Street in areas where bikers frequent, and she also hung out in a cemetery.

Rachel Cox, who was a student at Eustis High in 1995, testified about overhearing a conversation Heather was having with friends near her locker. "She was mad at something that her parents would or wouldn't let her do, and she said that she wanted her parents dead."[17]

Next on the list was Alice Bennett of Orlando, who testified that she had been friends with Rick and Ruth for 28 years. She said that she and Ruth would often go out together to eat or see a movie.

The last time she saw her friend was on Friday, Nov. 22, at the Fashion Square mall in Orlando, and Ruth talked about Heather and Jennifer. "She was in a very stressful state because she was having trouble with them. You know how teenagers get sometimes, they disobey and get disrespectful, and that's not the way they were raised."[18]

Jennifer was doing better, and had been accepted into FSU, but Ruth was still worried about Heather.

"She proceeded to talk to me about Ferrell, that is the first time I heard his name. She was talking to me about him, and she told me that he was in town and she was like, she had a concerned look on her face. She proceeded to tell me about the kind of person that he was, that he was in some kind of cult, and she did not like him. That's not the kind of person she wants for her daughter. She didn't like him. And she proceeded to tell me that his mother was in some kind of cult, too, and she didn't like it either. Neither one of them, Rick or her, liked this person."[19]

She said Ruth told her that he was "in town."

Hawthorne asked if she and Ruth had ever gone on trips to Cassadaga, a tiny town in Volusia County filled with psychics and mediums. Bennett said they went out of "curiosity." Ruth said, "Maybe we should go and see what they tell me. But I don't want to know the bad things, I want to know the good things."[20]

King was subtle on cross-examination and hoped the jury picked up on a big discrepancy in the testimony. "Miss Bennett, you said this conversation you had was on a Friday, Nov. 22?"[21]

"Yes, three days before they were murdered."

"And your understanding was from Miss Naomi Queen that Mr. Ferrell was already here?"

"Yes."

Hawthorne also called Jennifer Wendorf as a defense witness and had her testify about the "have you ever plotted mom and dad's death" conversation. "I was appalled, I said, 'no,' and that was the end of the conversation." Jennifer also testified about the talk she had with Heather when Heather asked if she wanted an abusive boyfriend killed, and the time she pointed her fingers like a gun in the direction of her half-sister in the next room.

CHAPTER 56

No 'goody two-shoes'

Sondra Gibson seemed nervous when she took the stand. Her voice went up about a half an octave, and she fidgeted a bit. It wasn't long before she was grabbing for the tissues to soak up some tears.

Hawthorne asked her about giving birth to Rod when she was sixteen.

"When he was born, he had the umbilical cord wrapped around his neck and he was blue, and they had to work with him to get him to breathe."[1]

Rod was her only child, she said. Other pregnancies ended in miscarriages. She did not say how many.

Hawthorne led her through a litany of questions, including how long she lived with Rick.

"Approximately, I would say actually living together about a month. Nine days to a month, something like that, a week or two, whatever."[2]

She said they both decided they were too young to get married.

Hawthorne asked how many times she and Rod moved (nine), and about the time, when Rod was one, that she went alone to St. Louis to work in a nightclub for about a month-and-a-half.

"And were you a waitress?"[3]

"No, I was a dancer."

"What kind of a dancer? A topless dancer?"

"I don't know what they…no, it wasn't topless.

"Okay. Did you ever work as a prostitute?

"Yes, I did at that time."

"Did you bring men home?"

"Yes."

"And was your son around during those times?"

"Not in St. Louis, he was living with my parents at that time."

"Did you use drugs during this time?"

"Yes."

"And were you abusing alcohol?"

"Yes, I was."

"What kind of drugs were you using?"

"Ecstasy, I did some speed, I did some…anything I could get, pretty much." She moved back to Murray to be with Rod and her parents.[4]

She talked about Rod having "convulsions" one day when he was two.

"I was in the bathroom taking a bath and I had the door open, and he came in and he said that he was like choking, he was pointing to his throat…and I thought maybe he got a toy, or something lodged in his throat."[5]

She said they rushed him to the hospital, "and he had to stay, and they said they didn't expect him to live overnight. That they thought he had some type of disease, or I don't know exactly what it was."

The family moved to Eustis and shortly afterward she met and married a man named Darren, a man she said smoked pot every day.

"Do you know if he ever supplied your son with drugs?"[6]

"I was under the impression that he did."

She said he would take Rod out in the car. "I thought they were just doing like the bonding thing, stepfather/son thing…" She said she found out later they were smoking pot.

The happy couple, Rod, and his grandparents all lived under one roof for a time. Darren and his friends were involved in occult activities, but her parents didn't know it, she said.[7]

Hawthorne also had Sondra recount a clash she had with Jeanine Leclaire.

Jeanine had come to the house on a Sunday with a boy named Matt, undoubtedly the witch that introduced Rod to Jeanine as a vampire. The teens stayed for only about thirty minutes, then left and came back and went into Rod's room.

Sondra said she went to check on them later and found that the lights were off, they were cutting themselves and dabbing the blood with tissues.

"He (Rod) said they were doing a soul exchange thing, or something like that, something to that effect. Something like soul mates or something."[8]

"And whose idea was this?"

"He said it was Jeanine's."

"I started screaming. I went out of my frigging mind. And I said to get out of my house, and don't ever come back again, and she didn't."

The family moved back to Murray around Christmas 1995.

The plan was for Darren and Sondra to move to Michigan and to send for Rod after the school year was over.

She said she didn't discover until she was in Michigan that Darren had a different idea. He had taken Rod aside and told him that his mother was not coming back. "That it was for the best and for him not to tell me."[9]

She said she hopped on a Greyhound bus and headed back to Murray. Rod was waiting at the bus station when she arrived.

She said she was "pretty much sure" that Rod was using drugs during this period. He was also smoking cigarettes, even at school. "I let him smoke in the house, but he wasn't supposed to smoke at school."[10]

His grades plunged at school and didn't improve, "because they wouldn't give him the kind of classes that he wanted to take and that he liked. They were like deliberately giving him classes that he didn't like, and he said forget it. He goes, 'I'm not even going to do the work.'"

She said Ferrell had received some counseling from a mental health center in Kentucky and at school, and at a center that did some testing.

She also admitted writing the letter to try and solicit Murphy's younger brother for sex. "I was having problems, I guess you could say, with his older brother, who is Jaden Steven Murphy."[11]

Hawthorne wanted to know what kind of problems she was having with him. "He was going around town telling everybody that I was his woman. I was his whatever, and he was saying that he was the prince of the city, the vampire prince of the city, and that I was going to be his vampire bride and all this." She said he would park his car outside her room and stare at her bedroom window all night. "I was scared of him at that time."

"Did you ever tell anyone that Steve Murphy drugged you?" Hawthorne asked, referring to the psychologist who examined her in a court-ordered exam after her arrest for solicitation.

"I don't think I did. I don't believe so."[12]

"Did you ever tell anybody about your son and others drugging you and having sex with you?"[13]

"I never told anyone that my son had sex with me. That's ridiculous!" Nor, she said, did she recall ever accusing Murphy of raping her.

"Did you ever tell anybody that the reason you wrote the letter to the fourteen-year-old was because you were trying to get into the cult so you could get your son out of the cult?"

"I may have said that to someone, but I don't really recall saying that, no."

"You knew your son was using drugs during this time?"

"At that time, I knew he was using heroin and LSD, yes.

"Okay. And you didn't place him in a hospital for treatment?"

"No, I did not."

She said she went to the Kentucky family and children's services agency and signed a form saying he was uncontrollable, in hopes that someone would treat him for drug abuse.[14]

"Did they try to put him in the hospital?"

"No, they did not. Nobody did anything. Nobody has ever done a thing for my son." She conceded, however, that officials had him go to group counseling once a week and for her to attend parenting classes. She said she quit going to the classes because it was "a joke."

She said she approved of him staying up all night and sleeping all day, and during a visit to Daytona took him to a "freak" nightclub. She said she dated an ex-felon handyman at the apartment complex who put tattoos on Rod's arm. "And you knew he was doing that?" Hawthorne asked.[15]

"I was sitting right across the table when he did it."

She also recalled overhearing Ferrell's end of the conversation that he was having with Heather over the phone.

"I heard him responding to what she was saying, and he goes, 'Chill out.' He goes, 'Like I'll be down there, or I can come and pick you up.' Stuff like that. And I told him, 'What are you talking about?'"[16]

She told him to tell Heather that she could stay with them for a while.

She also heard him say, "I won't do it, but there is a guy over in Orlando, you can go over there and hire somebody for five hundred dollars to do it."

The phone was a problem, she said. At one point, she had her phone disconnected because the long-distance charges went up to $1,000.

After getting Sondra to admit she was on probation for the sex solicitation charge involving Steven Murphy's little brother, Hawthorne asked her why she sent a Valentine's Day card to Steven.

"I'm in love with Steven, that's why."[17]

"Okay. How old are you again?"

"I'm thirty-five."

"And how old is Steven?"

"I don't know for sure. I know he's an adult. I made really sure before I ever wrote anything like that."

King began his cross examination by showing her hospital records indicating that there no complications with Rod's birth. "This paper says this, but there was a number of people that will say differently that I could have as witnesses," she replied. He also showed her an infant assessment sheet that showed no problems, and she insisted that it, too, was incorrect. Nor were there any notations in his baby book about any significant illnesses or accidents, including her claim that he had encephalitis when he was two years old. School records also showed no past health problems.[18]

King took a shot at the defense idea that Sondra had not been doing anything to help her son. He asked her why she went to juvenile court to report him as being out of control and on drugs. "And that was done, so that under your opinion, somebody could help him, right?" [19]

"So that someone actually could help me and him both, but especially him, yes, because I wanted him off the drugs, yes."

King also had her look at a letter that she had written to someone about him, guessing what he would ask and how he would present her story to the jury. "Part of this letter indicates that you are not going to let me make you look like a goody two-shoes, correct?"

"That I'm not a liar. I said in that letter that my opinion was that you were going to present me as that, and everyone knows that I am not."[20]

She claimed that the juvenile judge in Kentucky let Rod off with no punishment. As part of his punishment, he was ordered to write a paper about the dangers of the occult. "I know he was supposed to write the paper," she said. "It says he was supposed to come back on Nov. 4. I know he didn't write the paper and he went to court. I know this for a fact," she said.

King produced the record. "Doesn't it say at the bottom that he is ordered to appear back in court on Nov. 25?"

"Yes, it says that."[21]

"1996?"

"Yes, uh-huh."

"That's the same Monday that these murders were committed, correct?"

"I have no idea, actually. I'd have to see the documents."

King could have sneered, thrown the papers down on the desk or changed his tone in a theatrical manner. He didn't. Nor did he produce records showing that she suddenly got "amnesia," as a detective put it, when asked under oath if she overheard Heather making death threats. A few days after the murders, she told the *Sentinel* that Heather "was saying she was going to kill her parents for a long time."[22]

"I don't have anything else, your honor," he said.

Hawthorne, on redirect, showed Sondra a series of pictures of Rod's room, and asked her if she approved of the décor. The photos showed the upside-down cross, candles and the skull, which she claimed was ceramic, and *Necronomicon.*

"Yes, uh-huh. I still do."[23]

CHAPTER 57

The last hope

Sheriff's Capt. Kevin Drinan always looked as if he was about to burst out of his perfectly pressed shirt. A longtime body builder, he always made sure his carefully-trimmed mustache didn't look as if it was bursting out of his upper lip. It was all part of his meticulous professionalism as the superintendent of the jail.

Like she did with Krop, Hawthorne asked him about the ominous drawings that Ferrell made on his cell wall, and how he had been placed on suicide watch.

"Now, there have been a couple of other instances where Mr. Ferrell got in trouble in jail."[1]

"That's correct."

"Overall, has Mr. Ferrell been a real management problem?"

"We wouldn't consider him a real management problem, no."

King got right to the point in his cross-examination.

"Captain, are you familiar with the disciplinary report where Mr. Ferrell was found with a shank in his cell?"[2]

"Yes."

"What's a shank?"

"A shank is a general term used to describe any object that may be fashioned into a knife."

"Something that you can stab somebody with?"

"Yes."

Hawthorne jumped back on redirect.

"Now, there were other people who had access to that cell, prior to that shank being found, isn't that correct?"

"Yes."

Hawthorne also called Carmine Walters, a neighbor of the Wendorfs. She testified that that she and her husband were returning from the mall "late" on the night of the murders when they saw Heather standing with other teens on the road near the Ford Explorer.

"My husband thinks it's 7:30 and I think its seven o'clock. I don't know what time it was."[3]

She verified for King that she had testified before the grand jury. It was the only question he asked of her.

Lackay also called a 19-year-old Eustis High senior, who said he knew Ferrell only from school.

"Going to try to graduate in May?"[4]

"Maybe."

"Did he ever discuss with you that he did not like the fact that he did not have a father?"

"No."

The teen said Ferrell did seem depressed.

"Would that be because he didn't have a dad?"[5]

"I don't know."

"Do you know if he used drugs?"

"Not for sure."

"Did he talk about using drugs?"

"I don't remember, really."

"Did you play games with him? Like vampire games or anything?"

"Huh-uh."

"What about poetry? Did you write poetry with him?"

"Yeah."

"Did he write a lot of poetry?"

"Yes."

By this time, Lackay must have wanted to tear out his thick black hair.

"Did you ever see him with any cuts on his arms or anything?"

"I don't know. I'm sorry."

Hawthorne then called Jennifer Wendorf to the stand.

She asked if she remembered "a very odd conversation" with Heather about two months before the murders.

"I don't quite recall exactly what was said, but I know it was something along the lines of, 'Jen, have you ever plotted mom and dad's death?'"[6]

"And what was your reaction to that?"

"I was appalled, I said, 'no,' and that was the end of the conversation."

In a flurry of questions, Jennifer acknowledged that yes, Heather said if she wanted a boyfriend killed, she knew someone who could do it: Ferrell. Yes, she knew Heather read vampire novels. Yes, she knew she cut herself, and yes, she had "mentioned" that she was a vampire.

Hawthorne next called a classmate of Heather's, Brandy Gonzi, who testified that she overheard Heather talking to other students.

"And did you overhear what Heather Wendorf was saying?"

"That she wanted her parents dead."[7]

Next up was a Florida juvenile justice official who testified that a minor can be held in a police station no longer than six hours.

On cross-examination, the official admitted that Florida rules do not apply if a juvenile is arrested in another state.

***

Prosecutors called three rebuttal witnesses to deflect Sondra's claim that nobody had ever done anything for her son.

"I cared about Rodrick Ferrell," said Debra Mooney, the social worker. "I was concerned about him."[8]

After attending an initial counseling session in May of 1996, he skipped the next three without canceling the appointments. When he came back for a fifth in October, she had to cut it short because an emergency had cropped up with a suicidal patient. His appointment was rescheduled for December.

Ferrell was referred by social services to juvenile court worker Jane Ann Turner on July 22.

Sondra was concerned about Rod, Turner said. Not only had she smelled marijuana in the house, but she said she was worried about his occult involvement. Rod and some of his cult friends had threatened to kill her.

Rod entered into a behavior contract on Aug. 1. Four days later, Sondra called police to say he had left home because he was upset with his girlfriend.

On Aug. 9, Turner spoke to Sondra and she said things were working out okay, but there were some incidents later, including on Aug. 26. "She stated that his girlfriend had broken up with him and that he was breaking the curfew and that he had come in wild and on two occasions he had broken curfews. That he was verbally abusive to Sondra."[9]

The agreement was terminated, in part, because he failed to keep his appointment with the social services counselor. He was given notice that he was to appear in court on Nov. 25, but that was the day he was in Florida, killing Heather's parents.

Lackay went on offense in in his cross-examination.

"In regards to the allegations, she said something about the occult, that Rod was into the vampire things, stuff like that, but did she tell you she, herself, was involved with the occult?"[10]

Turner said she did not.

"And in order usually for these plans to be successful to work, usually the kid is going to have to have a pretty good support system to help them, won't they? Like mom and dad to help them?"[11]

Dennis Fisher, the high school's assistant principal, said he also tried to help.

"I thought Rod was very intelligent, and I told him so. I just told him that he needed to use that intelligence in a better way, as far as not getting into trouble. You know, I tried to counsel him and tell him that he had, I thought, a great knowledge of art and he could channel that into that area."[12]

His response was "nonchalant," he said.[13]

He said he thought Sondra was trying to do the right thing, including encouraging Rod to get a job.

The day before the expulsion hearing, Sondra called Fisher to say that she had removed a lot of things from his bedroom and that he was enraged.

"I said, 'Listen lady, call the cops, stay with your mom and dad. If you're afraid of your own son, I can't help you, I'm sorry.'"

Ferrell was given several chances at school. The "final straw," Fisher said, was the incident where a teacher told him to go to class when she saw him comforting a weeping Charity in the hallway. He "blatantly cussed her out and she felt threatened."[14]

"I could just slit her throat," Ferrell told him.[15]

"Now, Rod, you don't mean that, do you?"

"No, probably not."

CHAPTER 58

It's unanimous: Death

Members of the Wendorf family held hands, held their breath, and used every ounce of strength they had to keep quiet when the jury was about to announce its advisory sentence. There was a good reason for jangled nerves.

The psychologists had done a good job pointing out that if Ferrell wasn't insane, he was certainly damaged by his dysfunctional upbringing. Added to that was the testimony of Sondra's sister, who left home, she said, when her father—Rod's grandfather—molested her.

Then, there were the witnesses who testified about their involvement in vampirism. Jurors seemed amused sometimes at Jaden's testimony, including opening his mouth to show he did not have fangs, but they also tilted their heads and squinted at Goodman's detailed explanation of role-playing games.

It was impossible to gauge their reaction to Jennifer's testimony about her sister's strange comments. They were listening, that much was clear.

It was not clear what effect King's painstaking cross-examination had on the psychologists.

After they began their deliberations, the jurors came back with a request. They wanted to again see Ferrell's videotaped statements to Baton Rouge Sgt. Ben Odom.

Lockett warned against any outburst in the courtroom when the verdict was about to be read. Unlike TV shows, where the jury foreman reads the verdict, the verdict form was passed to the bailiff, then the judge, who handed it to Deputy Clerk Debbie Cummings.

"In the Circuit Court of the Fifth Judicial Circuit of the state of Florida, in and for Lake County, the state of Florida vs. Rodrick Justin Ferrell, case number 96-1913-CF-A-JL. Advisory sentence: As to count three, Richard Wendorf. A majority of the jury, by a vote of twelve to zero, advise and recommend to the court that it impose the death penalty upon Rodrick Ferrell. Dated this twenty-third day of February, 1998. Joseph E. Crumpton, foreperson. Advisory sentence: As to Naomi Queen, a majority of the jury, by a vote of twelve to zero, advise and recommend to the court that it impose the death penalty upon Rodrick Ferrell. Dated this twenty-third day of February 1998, Joseph E. Crumpton, foreperson."[1]

Ferrell's family made a collective sound like a hiss, but it was exhaling, and then they cried softly.

Ferrell got red-eyed, too, but his first reaction was a raised eyebrow.

Lockett thanked the jurors for their service, then dismissed them and the courtroom was cleared.

"Richard and Ruth's honor were restored," said his twin brother, Bill. He had chafed at the defense strategy of trying to show that they had somehow mistreated Heather.[2]

Lackay said "gruesome" photos may have swayed the twelve-member jury, but it was clearly the videotaped confessions.

It was never clear what the jury wanted to see in the second viewing of the videotape. Usually, in such cases, it is the result of a juror who has a different memory than the rest of the group.

The state had "insurmountable" evidence, including Ferrell's DNA under Queen's fingernails. Another juror cited the bloody boot print, Crumpton said.

Crumpton said McMahon's testimony was impressive, but "psychology is such an inexact science; you have to be able to make a judgment call."

"A life recommendation would have brought closure to this case today," Hawthorne told me, fighting tears.

CHAPTER 59

Ferrell blames Heather

By now, Hawthorne had few options. The only thing that wedged itself between the jury's recommendation and sentencing was what Florida calls a Spencer Hearing. Basically, attorneys can throw anything up against the wall in hopes that something sticks.

She had no luck in persuading the jury that Ferrell was unduly influenced by his poor upbringing, the occult, or by Heather. But would the judge buy into the legal argument of proportionality?

Hawthorne began by submitting a transcript of remarks made by Heather's boyfriend, Jeremy Hueber, to a prosecutor and a detective in the early hours after the murders.

"...she knew Mr. Ferrell was threatening to kill her parents," Hawthorne said. "Mr. Ferrell was at her house, according to her, yet she does not apparently alert her parents, she does not alert law enforcement, she decides to go with Miss Keesee and Miss Cooper to go to Jeremy Hueber's and basically decides to go with them. And our position is, we would argue that she was involved in it."[1]

Hawthorne also submitted phone records to bolster Sondra's claim that she overheard Heather saying she wanted her parents to be dead because they were hurting her.

Then, things got interesting. Keesee decided she wanted to testify on Ferrell's behalf, even though something she might say could be used against her.

Keesee's attorney, Tommy Carle, stood beside the witness box ready to signal her if he thought she should not answer a question.

"During the months that you first met Rod and the end of October 1996, did you see changes in him?" Hawthorne asked.

"A few."

"Would you please tell the court some of the changes you observed?"

"Like, at the beginning he'd act like normal, he didn't have his mood swings and stuff as much. And he...didn't sound like he really believed it, but then later on...like he really believed it."

"Okay. What kind of stuff would he say?"

Carle tapped the edge of the witness box and she asserted her Fifth Amendment right to not incriminate herself.

"Were those statements bizarre?" Hawthorne asked."

"Yes."

"Did they begin to come with more frequency?"

"Yes."

"Was Sondra Gibson able to control Rod?"

"No."

"Were you able to control Rod?"

"No."

"Were you able to reason with Rod?"

"Sometimes, depending on what we were talking about."

Keesee said Rod was using marijuana and LSD. Asked if she was taking drugs, too, she again asserted her rights.

She said Rod did not threaten the teacher when he was trying to comfort her at school.

"Now, did you tell Rod that you were pregnant?"

She pleaded the Fifth, and again when Hawthorne asked her if he thought she was pregnant.

"Have you lost a child in 1996?"

She refused to answer again. She would not even answer the question about whether she had been held at the Baton Rouge Police Department.

There were a few more questions but no more answers.

Sometimes love is the most powerful form of amnesia. Rod's staunchest supporter, Rosetta Gibson, took the stand to champion her grandson just days after she watched the videotape of her grandson bragging about what a "rush" it was to bludgeon his victims to death.

"He was like our only son. We never had a son. Rod was a very gentle person. I mean, they've made him out to look like he's some kind of monster, but he wasn't. He's always been a very gentle person. He has big feelings. Even as a small child, he would never hurt anything or anybody. We never had a problem with Rod in the house."[2]

She said she and her husband took him to church all the time. "He knew the right way, he knew how we lived, and he knew what our standards were."

Hawthorne noted that in his later years he lived with his mother.

"And of course, I can't really testify for a whole lot that went on there because I wasn't there...."

She also addressed the animal abuse allegations. "Rod loved animals. He had a little cat one time, and he would just lay down and let it crawl all over him and play with it, I mean, he's never harmed anything. I've never seen him harm anything. Even when he went fishing, when he caught a little old fish about this long and Harrell said we can't cook it. And they said, 'Well, we can't keep it. So, they took it out in the back yard and buried it, and he would go into where the little thing was buried, and he would dig it up to see if it was all right. He couldn't stand it because he was a gentle person. He'd never hurt nobody."[3]

Hawthorne had her describe the time, when Ferrell was three years old, and he had to be hospitalized overnight with some type of illness. She said a doctor or nurse told them, "If this is what we think it is, then he may not live until morning."

She said she and her husband stayed at the hospital all night, prayed, and the next day he was better.

King had few questions, but he asked her if her husband was a member of a satanic cult.

"No, my husband is not a member of any kind of cult."

"Has he ever been?"

"No, he has not."

Finally, there was nothing left for Hawthorne but to let her client take the stand.

Hawthorne tried to pry out of him his claim that he had been raped by his grandfather's friends as a child.

"I truthfully would rather not discuss that."[4]

Hawthorne asked if his remarks to Sgt. Ben Odom were "fantasy."

"I really couldn't tell you. There's a point in my life that I've blacked out completely because it was too much. It was immense pain, and a very young child couldn't handle that, no matter who it was. So, I've blocked most of that out of my memory."[5]

"Were you raped as a young child?" she asked.

"Yes."

"Were you raped more than once?"

"No."

He testified that he started using marijuana and LSD in 1994 and became interested in demonology with a friend who was a classmate in Eustis in the eighth and ninth grade.

"Demonology is a subtext to satanism. You take a demon, there are many demons, and you pick a certain one and you basically worship that one fully and wholly, and you ask that demon for powers instead of Lucifer."[6]

"Now, we heard from your grandmother that you were raised in the Pentecostal church."

"If you could say that, yes."

"Well, did you attend church?"

"I attended it and slept through most of it."

Hawthorne steered the questions back to Heather and Jeanine.

"They had thirst for an actual and true vampire. And evidently, they believed I was a true vampire at that time," he said.

"At that time, I took it as a joke. There was an incident in my biology class where someone had seen me sucking on my finger when I had cut it, and that was just when *Interview with the Vampire* had been released, so everyone...it went around that I was a vampire."[7]

She also asked him about the time Sondra caught him and Jeanine and their friend Matt cutting themselves and drinking blood in his bedroom in Eustis.

Jeanine called it a "soul exchange," he said, a cross between witchcraft and vampirism.

He talked about Sondra's husband, Darren, who described himself as a Druid. "They're basically sorcerers who are set out to protect the earth."[8]

Ferrell also testified about crossing over with Murphy at the old Salem Cemetery in Murray.

He said he told his mother about his lifestyle but not his grandparents. "I knew because of them being Pentecostal, a very strict religion of Christianity, that it would be unacceptable."[9]

He described it as "freedom of dress, freedom of speech. If you want to stay up all night, which is actually normal for vampires, you can...who wouldn't want that?"

How did he feel about his mother telling him that he was responsible for the children she lost?

"Not good. It's just, again, by this time my emotions were getting numb. It was too strenuous for anyone my age at that time. So, I was trying to distance myself from feeling."[10]

As for people trying to help, he said, "I thought Mr. Fisher himself actually cared, as an individual, but I felt as if what he was trying to do wouldn't help."

He said he didn't feel like he could live up to the assistant principal's expectations. "And I didn't feel that my mother could help either."[11]

By the summer of 1996 he had dyed his hair black, but that wasn't all. "I was using marijuana, LSD, speed, and miscellaneous pills, such as Darvocet, codeine, Lithium, Prozac, whatever I could get hold of."[12]

It was the early part of summer in 1996 that he ended up talking to Heather more than Jeanine, he said, and the talk was driven by her "lust for that lifestyle."

He said she also told him that "her problems with her family were increasing."[13]

She didn't say what kind of problems, even during four-hour phone calls. "...she said that her father was okay, but that her mother was...she didn't like her."

"Did she ever tell you that her family was hurting her?"

"Yes."

"Did she ever tell you that she wanted to run away?"

"There were times when she would actually, like, she would cry and get hysterical over the phone, and me coming from an abusive life and being around people that have had abuse, like Scott Anderson, my best friend, the symptoms from her crying and her hysteria as being real, it seemed like she really was being abused."

"Did you ever ask her specifically what kind of abuse she was talking about?"

"No, just from her demeanor I took her at face value."[14]

"Did she ever say anything about the fact that her parents would never let her go and she would like to actually get rid of them in order to leave?"

"Yes."

Hawthorne eventually led Ferrell up to the day that he and the other cult members met Heather after school, and he crossed her over.

"Did she say anything to you about her parents?"

"No, just the fact that her mother was going to pick her up that day."

However, he said there was a life-changing conversation that night outside her house.

"I told her that the Buick we were driving at that time was not really adequate enough to keep going in. That it was having engine problems and the tire had just blown out and I asked her if it was cool to basically go and steal her parents' car."[15]

"She didn't have a problem with that," he said.

He said he asked who was in the house, and where he could find the keys. She said the keys were in a dresser drawer in her parents' bedroom. "And she also asked me to grab her father's knife and her mother's pearls."[16]

"Why did she ask you to do that, do you know?"

"To this day, I still couldn't tell you."

"Did she ever tell you that there was a set of keys in the Explorer itself?"

"No."

"Did you say anything to her about taking her parents out?"

"I asked her, I said, 'Since you have spoken so much about killing your parents over the past year, do you still want me to?'"

"And what did she say?"

"She said yes."

Scott was out of earshot, he said, so he took him aside and told him what Heather had said.

"I don't know why I asked her because all I intended to do was steal the car," he said. He then claimed he just wanted to hear what she would say.

"I asked Scott how he felt about taking out the parents."

"Why did you ask him that?"

"Because at that point in time I was still under the impression that Heather's parents were actually hurting her."

Scott indicated he didn't care one way or the other. "In fact, it kind of excited him," Ferrell said.

"How did you feel?"

"I didn't."

After killing the couple, they ransacked the house looking for the Explorer keys. They found a set in the ignition.

"I wondered why Heather basically told Scott and I to go into the house to get another set of keys when there were already keys there."

Heather never attempted to escape or tip the police officers they encountered on the way to Baton Rouge, he said.

"There is a lot about life in general that I am still confused about," he said.

"But the fact is, I myself, was still under the assumption of what Heather had kind of ingrained in my head at that time...." He knew about the house, where Richard worked and other things, he said, "but nothing about the fact that they had value as people, or that they were really human. In fact, most people referred to them as the victims, not as anything that would be described as even human. But once the trial and all that started, they started producing things about it. Also, William Wendorf, I kind of looked at him and the expression that was on his face."[17]

He said he had changed, that he had a "better concept on reality," and that his "value systems have changed."

CHAPTER 60

"Disturbed" is no excuse

Judge Lockett was grim when he took his seat at the bench and looked across the crowded courtroom. It was Feb. 27, 1998, the day of reckoning, and it was "excruciating," the former public defender said.

"When I first agreed to accept appointment to this case, I always knew that today might arrive, and this day has arrived. "I want to start by telling you just because one has done this in the past, doesn't make it any easier to do...."[1]

Then, he abruptly shifted gears.

"It is the opinion of this court, after having heard the testimony of numerous witnesses throughout the course of this trial, that significant questions remain regarding the involvement of Heather Wendorf in the murder of her parents."[2]

He acknowledged the statement of Heather's grandfather during the impact statement, that the trial was about Ferrell, not Heather, "and I agree." However, the judge continued, several witnesses testified at trial that did not appear before the grand jury, and several exhibits and pieces of evidence were also presented.

"It is the strong suggestion of this court to Mr. King, our elected state attorney, that the grand jury be reconvened, these witnesses be presented to the grand jury in efforts that

Lake Countians can understand once and for all whether or not Heather Wendorf is, in fact, involved in these brutal killings."

There was stunned silence in the courtroom. No one saw this coming. Lockett did not have the authority to order a new grand jury, but he was playing to the court of public opinion. The jurist ,who sometimes liked pushing the boundaries to make case law, had been listening to the sheriff, lawyers, and everyday folks during happy hour, where tongues are loosened.

"Now I will turn to the issue before us," he said quickly.

"We can know a few things, I think. There is a genuine evil in this world. There is a dark side and a light side to each and every one of our lives and those sides compete for human domination. I'm not talking about any particular religious denomination or affiliation; I'm talking about basic fundamental truths as I see them. And it's not so hard for some of us to understand how a person like Ferrell, with one of the most dysfunctional family environments anyone could ever be cursed to be raised in, would have turned out in such a manner.[3]

"In some respects, I think Mr. Ferrell's mother, Mrs. Gibson, should be on trial for some of this. At every stage of the way, she thwarted every attempt to find Mr. Ferrell the psychological help that he needed. Purposely, advertently, she kept him from receiving the help that he so desperately required.

"How can a parent not realize when a child resorts to self-mutilation and bloodletting and vampirism that there isn't a serious, serious problem with that particular child?

"And when we have these kinds of dysfunctional families, where do they lead us? In this case, as Dr. McMahon so eloquently explained, I thought, to a search for another family in a different way, a cult, a satanism, a witchcraft, a vampirism, some place where there is structure and order of its own kind. Some place where there are people that feel as alienated as you do, so that you can at least have your own society, in your own group, in your own way.[4]

"And then what happens when we have lost total touch with reality, we begin to play the fantasy games, the Dungeons and Dragons, the vampire games. And suddenly, the fantasy becomes reality. The games that involve violence, the games that involve sword play and rescuing maidens who are in distress because of people who hold them in positions of authority, and suddenly we wake up one day and we have what we have before us now.

"And I say to Rod, I say to you, I think you are a disturbed young man. I think your family failed you. I think society failed you. But I am also here to tell you, in the considered judgment of this court, a troubled and disturbed youth cannot serve as an excuse for cold-blooded, premeditated murder such as you perpetuated upon the Wendorfs in this case.[5]

"If we have to learn a lesson, and I am told, Rod, that you said this on television, I don't watch much of that stuff, there has to be a lesson to the young people of this country and to their children and to the youth of America, these seemingly harmless games can turn into something very evil. I think they are not intended to do that, but it doesn't require a lot of thought to understand how that happens. And I can see how that did happen, and I believe that did happen. I believe much of what Dr. McMahon said to be true," he said.

He paused for a moment so the bailiffs could bring Ferrell closer to the bench.

"You stated it best to Baton Rouge Sgt. Ben Odom a long time ago when you said, and I paraphrase, 'When I kill these people, I felt a rush. I felt like I was a god. But I guess if I was a god, I wouldn't be here today now, would I?' And that is just as true today as it was in Baton Rouge in the interrogation station."[6]

The aggravating circumstances far outweighed the mitigators, he said. "It's no wonder the jury unanimously decided to recommend to this court that Rodrick Justin Ferrell should die for each of his crimes."

After explaining that Ferrell had thirty days to appeal, and clearing up some loose ends, he ended by saying, "Folks, we could all attempt to reconcile our wounds now and hope for the healing process to go on. Hopefully, Mr. Ferrell will spend his time, before his time comes, like all of ours surely will, searching for the light side and begging for forgiveness."[7]

King was angry about the judge suggesting he call another grand jury to examine Heather's role. "There was no evidence she was involved in the murders." He said would not call up another grand jury.

"I wouldn't want to go to court based on what Mr. Ferrell says." He even lied to the psychologists who were trying to help him, he noted.

Sondra Gibson was angry, too.

"I'm a better mother than a lot of other people. The judge doesn't know me."[8]

James Wendorf said he never asked Heather if she was involved. "I told her, 'If you're guilty, you'll pay the price.'

CHAPTER 61

Dominoes

Anderson pleaded guilty on April Fool's Day, 1998. He made the decision because he was worried that he, too, would be sentenced to death.

"It was my choice to come with them. It falls on my shoulders," he told me. But he also blamed Ferrell. "Because of his actions, my life was ruined."[1]

In July, Cooper, who had been charged as a principal to first-degree murder and was facing a life sentence, pleaded guilty to principal to third-degree murder, armed robbery, and armed burglary. She was sentenced to seventeen and one-half years in prison. It went down hard, but it was better than life.

Just two months earlier, in May, she told interviewers on *America's Most Wanted* TV show, "I didn't do anything. I'm still paying for a crime I didn't commit. I'm guilty by association."[2]

She also disclosed some of the things Ferrell had said.

"He said things like he could fly, he was five hundred years old, he could be invisible if he wanted to. It was baloney."

She said the cult gave her "a sense of belonging, friendship, unity. I had people coming to my apartment, people coming to see me."

It was a different story by the time they reached Baton Rouge.

"Detectives informed me Rod planned to kill me. They found my bags floating in the river. I don't know if it's true or not, but it put the scare in me."

One remarkable thing that did occur, she said, was that she became a Christian in the Lake County jail. Keesee was saved, too, she said.

Like Cooper did at her sentencing, Keesee cried and took a plea deal, but hers was for ten-and-one-half years.

"I didn't really think he would do it," she said, and she didn't believe it, even when she saw him in the Wendorfs' Ford Explorer with scratches on his face. "My first thought was, 'He's trying to scare us.'"[3]

She said she still loved Rod.

She also said the earlier reports of her becoming a Christian were not true, that she didn't believe in God. Nor did she believe she was immortal. Rod did, however.

Asked what she wanted people to know about her, she said, "I'm not evil, that's all I can say."

CHAPTER 62

Wrong, not criminal

Heather waited patiently for me on a bench outside a Mount Dora restaurant on August 13, 1998. She was with true-crime author Aphrodite Jones, who was writing the book *Embrace* about the case with her cooperation. Heather wanted to tell her story to me, and I was ready to hear it.

Surprisingly, she was opposed to Cooper and Keesee being sent to prison.

"Just like me, they didn't know what was going to happen. They were oblivious," she said. Speaking of her parents, she said: "I never wanted him to go near them."[1]

She insisted that she did not have any serious problems with her parents, but just wanted to go on a "road trip."

"They never hurt me," she said.

Nor did she ever tell any classmates that she wished her parents were dead. "I don't know why they did it," she said. She pointed out that one teen recanted her story. The girl admitted she didn't even know Heather.

"Some people just wanted to stick their face in the limelight," she said.

She also denied asking Jennifer if she ever thought about plotting their parents' deaths.

"I never said that. I was sitting next to her watching the news when I saw her say that in court. I just looked at her and she said, 'Well, maybe you didn't say that. I don't know.' If she really thought I said that we wouldn't be as close now."

As for Ferrell, he is not to be believed.

"This is the same guy who once said a rival clan did it,' she said.

I asked her about the conversation where he supposedly said, "You spoke so much about me killing your parents. You still want me to?"

"It never happened," she said.

She didn't try to escape, she said, "because I was terrified of him." For one thing, he kept a razor-sharp knife near his belt buckle."

Ferrell had a hold on her because he had indoctrinated her, she said. "He was your maker. Charity was the dark mate."

Cult members were "siblings."

"We were one blood, like kin. He was always talking about how he was the father," she said. "It was like reconstructing your whole family."

On the other hand, she tuned out his talk about killing. "He talked about it so much it just became invisible in a conversation."

He also talked about being an immortal hundreds of years old, about killing a police officer, It being a monster, and how a rival clan had killed his children. "He claimed he died and came back to life again."

It was unbelievable, but the fantasy was appealing, she admitted. "It was like a fairy tale. So much more interesting than getting up, going to school, going home and going to bed."

The fun ended the day her parents were killed.

"I feel so guilty for even knowing Rod. I feel so bad. I was so naïve. Everyone tells you, 'It's not your fault.' But he came to Florida. He left Kentucky to pick me up," she said.

"I know a lot of people don't think much of me. I know people who think I'm cold because I'm not bawling all the time and not ranting and raving. What they don't know is that I had such a good relationship with my parents. I can rest easy."

She had one concern, however. She said she hoped authorities would never again consider her a suspect.

Her worst fears would be realized four months later. The State Attorney's Office, bowing to pressure from Sheriff Knupp and Judge Lockett, called up another grand jury. "There is outrage for this in the whole community. She wasn't even tried," Knupp fumed.

Heather would not testify this time. She had moved to North Carolina to attend an art school.

Knupp was confident, saying his detectives had amassed new evidence.

The panel would be dealing with her case and that of a young father who had beaten his six-year-old daughter to death and pretended she was missing for three days.

Among the evidence carried into the grand jury room was Heather's teddy bear with her mother's pearls draped around its neck. Jennifer testified, emerging from the room after an hour-and-a-half with tears in her eyes. And in an unusual move, King took the stand to explain how the first grand jury reached its conclusion.

"We find that the evidence identified as new is not credible and will not act upon it," the grand jury said in its report.[2]

"We share the opinion of the first grand jury that the actions of Heather Wendorf were inappropriate and wrong. We also share its conclusion that while wrong, her actions did not rise to the level of criminal activity."

"It's a great day for I-told-you-sos," said her lawyer, James Hope. "It's a day for the sheriff to listen."

"He was just making stuff up," King would later say of Knupp.

CHAPTER 63

Life, not death, or maybe...

They don't leave prison gates open, but guards unlock them on a regular basis so prisoners can go back to court to appeal their sentences.

Ferrell's first appeal came almost immediately, with Hawthorne and Lackay claiming the jury did not give enough weight to alleged statements made by Heather. They also failed to weigh the evidence property, the petition said.

Motion denied.

The following year, he claimed his attorneys were not given enough time for closing arguments.

Again, motion denied.

The Florida Supreme Court, however, opened Ferrell's death row cell door in 2000 and sent him into general population with a life sentence. The ruling was based on one the court had made the year before, saying that no one younger than 17 can face the death penalty. Ferrell was sixteen when he committed the crime.

A conservative group, The Rutherford Institute, filed a brief on Ferrell's behalf stating: "Execution of juveniles is inconsistent with Florida's standard of decency and its commitment to rehabilitation of children."

It was a sign of more lenient rulings to come, and it would make a mockery of Gloria Wendorf's statement two years earlier after the trial when she said, "At least it's over."

In 2003, a circuit judge rejected his new claim that he received bad advice from Hawthorne and Lackay at trial.

He would get another potential break, however.

Juveniles are different from adults, the U.S. Supreme Court noted in *Miller v. Alabama* in 2012. "A child's lack of maturity leads to needless risk-taking and impulsivity, yet it also allows for a better chance of rehabilitation...." Therefore, the justices said, juveniles should not be subjected to mandatory life sentences.[1]

In 2018, Anderson was able to ride the wave of the Court's ruling that included a demand that a judge or jury must consider unique mitigating circumstances. The ruling affected twenty-nine cases in the five-county circuit that includes Lake. Twelve of the cases were Lake County's.

Prosecutors agreed in 2018 to a forty-year sentence for Anderson. He had written a letter to the judge asking for thirty. "...if I have to accept a forty-year sentence I will be fifty-one years-old and will have to depend on disability and family members to get by. Because I don't know anyone who would hire a fifty-one-year-old ex-con to work for them."[2]

The Queen family was okay with the reduced sentence for Anderson. "We just want Ferrell, said Paula Lohse said.[3]

"That's the one we're waiting for," said Ruth's sister, Lillian Rapp.

CHAPTER 64

Still a vampire?

Ferrell sends shivers up the spine of people who watch true-crime documentaries.

In 2003, he described vampirism as "seductive," and said that it gives practitioners a sense of power. "Your deepest fantasies, not hidden, your heart's desires. That's what the world consists of for a vampire," he said. "Vampirism plays as big a part in my life as it ever has.[1]

In 2016, a different psychologist-interviewer for Discovery ID deduced that his "grandiosity had turned into a full-fledged superiority complex." He exhibited traits of narcissism, if not psychopathy, she said, and probably has a personality disorder. He had tried to charm her during the interview.[2]

Ferrell has enjoyed the attention of a host of love-struck groupies, and he was married to one woman for a time, according to his mother.

One Texas woman who wanted to visit had been arrested in 1970 for public intoxication, shoplifting, public nudity, and criminal mischief.

Another wanted to save his soul.

"I am 69 years old, and it is heart-breaking to see so many young people going the wrong way. I'd like to tell them that with God they can find peace and forgiveness, no matter where they are. I've written to David Berkowitz also. I know lives can be changed."[3]

Berkowitz was the notorious "Son of Sam" who murdered six people in New York in the 1970s.

Ferrell got into trouble in 2005 when one woman sent him a photo of the two of them kissing inside the prison walls. Officials suspended her visitation rights for two years.

As his resentencing hearing drew near in November 2019, a woman who described herself as his fiancée said she would give him a home and make him get a job.

The resentencing hearing was shaping up to become an interesting legal battle between two very good lawyers.

Rich Buxman, who took over homicide prosecutions from the very capable Bill Gross when he retired, is smart, his defense attorney foes say. You have to be if you are handling capital cases. You almost have to be a doctor, a psychologist, and a scientist all rolled into one. Certainly, you must know which questions to ask, and Buxman presents himself well before jurors.

Defense attorneys hire mitigation specialists to interview family members and examine school, sports, and military records to see if the defendant has ever suffered head injuries.

Neuropsychologists perform tests for reasoning skills and impulse control. The test results can lead doctors to order a brain scan.

"If you get a neuropsychologist who recommends a PET scan, and if you don't do it, number one you're a boob. Number two, you're going to be reversed [on appeal]," said John Spivey, the executive assistant public defender for the Fifth Circuit.[4]

A PET scan, or positron emission tomography, uses radioactive materials to present color pictures. Doctors also order an MRI scan, or magnetic resonance imaging, which has images in black and white.

A radiologist physician must examine the scans to see if part of the brain has shrunk or shows signs of injury.

A psychiatrist, who is also a medical doctor, is brought in to decide if the scans indicate why the person acted the way he did.

A child-abuse expert is hired to see if the defendant was abused, lived in poverty, was a victim of fetal alcohol syndrome, or subject to other trauma.

"Now, I've got two psychologists, a psychiatrist, a neurologist, and a radiologist. I've just spent $150,000," Spivey said in a 2017 interview.

There is a reason for stacking experts, however. "The jury presumes we're lying," Spivey said. "It's not an excuse for the crime but rather an explanation for how that person got into the position that he did."

Buxman was going up against Terence Lenamon, a big man physically and big man on campus among Florida criminal defense lawyers.

Lenamon, who has been a lawyer for more than 20 years, is a former assistant public defender in Miami-Dade County. He says on his website that he has "successfully litigated against the death penalty in over ninety-five cases and has tried seventeen first-degree murder death penalty cases against the State of Florida."

He founded the non-profit Florida Capital Resource Center in 2009 to help defense lawyers in death penalty cases.

"Every person has a story," he says on the web site. "There is always some underlying common humanity in even those convicted of the most brutal crimes. It is my job to bring these mitigating factors to the jury, to shed light on the darkest heart and most disturbed mind."[5]

Prior to the resentencing hearing, Lenamon filed a motion seeking to bar any state psychologist witnesses.

Buxman countered, noting that Lenamon had included a psychologist, a psychiatrist, and a neuropsychologist on his witness list. Circuit Judge G. Richard Singeltary rejected the defense motion.

Buxman and Lenamon were familiar with each other. They had been battling in a first-degree murder trial of a man in Orlando who had killed his pregnant girlfriend and later allegedly killed a police officer.

CHAPTER 65

From a perfect life to "nothing"

Jennifer Wendorf bent her head downward, inhaled, and sobbed.

"The pain will never go away," she said.[1]

"When you lose someone, who loves you so deeply, you drown in a sea of emptiness and confusion without them," she said, reading from a prepared statement.

"Life was perfect before the murders. I had a scholarship to FSU, great friends, I was co-captain of the cheerleaders, I had been promoted at my part-time job at Publix, I was able to save money and even pay some of my bills. My life was so full. I had love, I had it all—until I had nothing.

"Until a Monday night, 8,393 days ago, it was all taken from me. I was reduced to nothing. No home, no school, no family, no normalcy. No mom to tell me about lady things, no dad to take me on our daddy-daughter dates to the oyster place, no mom to help me pick out my graduation dress, no dad to tell me he was proud of me…All the ways a child depends on their parents to help them and be with them through life. I didn't have that.

"I had morbid images that stuck with me every time I closed my eyes. I had the realization that you just saw your mom's brains splattered all over the kitchen. I had the recollection that the body I saw on the couch that looked like slaughtered beef was my dad, and where did his face go? I was riddled with guilt and anxiety. I'll never be able to erase what I went through; it will haunt me forever.

"I will never have my parents back. But may I please have safety and security? May I have a place that is not traumatized by looking over your shoulder? If he ever gets out, I will be destroyed. I will be brought down to that scared and lonely little girl of nearly twenty-three years ago. I will be fearful for my life and the lives of my children. I pray that this is never a world in which I have to live in."

Ferrell bowed his head and refused to look at the gruesome crime scene photos, and he tightened his jaw muscles as she testified.

Judge Singeltary leaned forward in his chair from his perch on the bench, getting as close as he could, maintaining eye contact and listening to every word.

Singeltary is a former assistant state attorney who has been on the bench for decades. Like his father before him, and his son, who is an assistant public defender, he loves the law and the profession. A history buff, especially local history, he is conservative, cautious, and painstakingly thorough in his research.

Jennifer testified that after her parents were killed, she lived with her father's twin brother, Bill, and saw him cry every night. "It broke the hearts of everyone in the family, including "my tender little sister, Heather. She didn't get a chance to say goodbye."

Also testifying was Shannon Yohe, Ferrell's friend and former classmate.

At one point, Ferrell was in the kitchen, noticed a gap in the cabinets, lifted himself up with his arms, and said he wished the Wendorfs had such a setup so he could use it as a springboard to "break their necks," she said.

Lenamon, on cross-examination, pointed out that the other cult members also chimed in. Anderson said his favorite way to kill was "decapitation."

"Isn't it true that Scott wanted to tell you how he wanted to kill somebody, and you said you didn't want to hear it? Do you remember that?"

"That sounds accurate."

"So, at least two of the four people who were there were having this conversation. There is bloodletting going on at your house. And now, in retrospect, and even after this happened, you looked back and said to yourself, 'I wonder if these people were trying to recruit me, trying to impress me, trying to embrace me.' Do you remember that?"

Yohe said she "put a lot of thought" into why Ferrell told her the things he did.

"...I have no idea why he would ever think that I would ever participate in something like that. I was not, I didn't drink, I didn't do drugs. I wasn't a vampire. I had nothing to do with that lifestyle."

Audrey Presson, the former Eustis classmate who once dabbled in witchcraft, also testified.

She said she was doing math homework when he showed up at her door with his "coven" the night before the murders.

He was wearing a top hat, she said, and had cuts on his arms in various stages of healing. He introduced the cult members, including Scott, who he said was his "son" or partner.

There was no talk of murder, but he indicated that he had come to get the girls. "He asked me to go with him."

"What did you say?"

"I said, 'no.'"

Buxman asked about his demeanor and if he appeared to be intoxicated.

"He was stone-cold sober. He was extremely calm."

She asked why he was in town. "Unfinished business," he replied.

"He got strange enough that I didn't want him in my house."

When her father stepped out the door to ask her to come back inside, she was relieved. It had only been 30 minutes, but it seemed much longer.

Outside the courtroom, she said she did not know what he meant by "unfinished business."

"I didn't ask. I didn't want to know." She said she just knew that it was going to be "unpleasant."

It was a different time, Presson said. "Teenagers didn't kill people." By contrast, her sixteen-year-old daughter was afraid one day because there was a rumor that someone was on school grounds with a gun.

CHAPTER 66

"He's a different person"

Lezlie Bullard is, by all appearances, a normal, intelligent person who is dedicated to her profession. An English teacher for twenty years in Texas, she was nominated for the National LifeChanger of the Year Award for the 2019-2020 school year.

"As a survivor of domestic abuse, Bullard is committed to helping students overcome adversity and find constructive ways to balance their mental health," a press release from her school district said.[1]

"During her first couple of years of teaching, after sharing her experience, one of Bullard's students came to her and revealed that the student was experiencing abuse at home. She was able to help the student get the help that was needed. 'From that day forward, I have always been completely honest with my students regarding my sobriety, recovery, and history with abuse. If I can help one student, I can help more. I will never apologize for being honest with my students, especially if it saves someone.'"

She is obviously a good teacher who cares about her students. She is also undoubtedly smart. Then again, no one ever said love has anything to do with smarts.

How deep was their love? "Beyond romantic," she testified. "I will do anything for him." "Anything" includes providing him with a home, helping him get an education, and making him get a job, she explained.[2]

Bullard sent money over the years to people and organizations interested in juvenile justice reform. "I've been in education for 20 years and I've seen kiddos lost in the trenches. Had one person followed through I honestly don't think we would be here today."

She read about Ferrell's case, got interested, and offered to do leg work for his mitigation specialist. She said she was "surprised" when her interest turned into a romantic relationship.

She even moved to Florida to be near Ferrell in 2015 but had to move back to Texas. "Unfortunately, Florida doesn't pay its teachers very much."

She reached other conclusions, too.

Sondra is "flighty" and "weird," does not act her age, and never had a nine-to-five job. "She would get very jealous if attention was not focused on her," Bullard said.

Ferrell asked her how to pray. She agreed and taught him about "the lighter side" of worship. He was brought up with "fire and brimstone," she said.

It all sounded good to defense psychologist Heather Holmes. Having a strong support system is key to rehabilitation, she testified.

Psychologist James Garbarino brought up an obvious but crucial issue for the defense. Teens are impulsive, subject to peer pressure, and cannot always appreciate consequences, he explained, echoing the Supreme Court's majority opinion in *Miller v. Alabama*.

He took a shot at Ferrell's dysfunctional family: No father present and a mother who exhibited "overt sexual behavior in his presence." He did not elaborate.

Ferrell took a self-administered test that showed he had eight out of ten possible risk factors for juveniles, which affected his thinking at the time of the crime.

"His escape plan was very dumb," Garbarino said. Leaving in the Wendorfs' Ford Explorer "guaranteed apprehension. The crime itself was stupid," he added.

Buxman disagreed with the notion that Ferrell was incapable of planning. He pointed to several examples, including switching license plates and escaping to another state, talking about killing several times before committing murder, and passing up going to the wrong house when he saw small children inside.

Ferrell was the acknowledged leader of the three other Kentucky teens, and he executed a plan to get Heather and others to form a vampire "family," Buxman noted.

If anything, that put more pressure on Ferrell to be the "baddest," Garbarino said.

Heather reportedly told him that her parents were hurting her. "He was trying to save or protect or be a savior to Heather Wendorf," Garbarino said.

That was not the only reason he left Kentucky, Buxman pointed out. He was caught making firebombs and was supposed to appear in juvenile court the day he murdered the Wendorfs in Florida.

Ferrell has changed, the psychologist said. "He feels tremendous guilt. He's a different person."

The crime was horrific, Garbarino acknowledged, but "the severity of the crime is not a good predictor of rehabilitation."

Unmoved, Buxman introduced a video clip from an HBO documentary, *The Vampire Murders,* that quoted Ferrell.

"In a childish manner, Scott [Anderson] and I impishly danced around his body before he was dead. Just strangely enough, it was a rush, a teenager's rush to know that he was asleep and not know that we held his fate in our hands. And after we finished our foolish dance, I stood over him and began to strike his head repeatedly with the crowbar, until his life was taken. I don't know if it was my conscience or not, but by doing this you could utterly destroy your life and the life of others. And then, after all of the consequences and thoughts about not doing it came through my head, one single voice came forth and said ['expletive] it,' simple as that, and that's whenever I brought the crowbar down."[3]

Buxman also included a portion of another documentary where Ferrell talked about throwing the kitten against the tree.

Among the friendly faces Ferrell found in court that day was the man who runs the Horizons Communities prisoner rehabilitation company.

Nathan Schaidt described Ferrell as "very wise, very helpful" as a facilitator in his program at Tomoka Correctional Institute.

Leah Elliot testified that she met Ferrell four years ago while visiting her husband in prison. "Rod was always a gentleman," she said, and he seemed much happier once he joined the Horizons program.

Elliot also provided a negative view of Sondra.

"I have a 13-year-old daughter. In all respect, that is his mother. They could stand next to each other and relate to each other. She would be bouncing around like she was visiting her boyfriend, not her son."

Defense attorney Melissa Ortiz also called upon ex-warden and prison consultant Ron MacAndrew.

MacAndrew downplayed disciplinary reports, which included having tobacco contraband, failure to report to work, refusing to comply with a urine sample drug test, and other infractions.

He also brushed off Ferrell's escape comments to jailer McNutt. "My opinion is that he was just joking around."

She clearly thought otherwise when she testified that he named five transport guards, listed their personalities, and said he could "take them out."

Buxman pointed out that jail officials found homemade knives in his cell two different times.

"Someone else could have put them there," MacAndrew said.

MacAndrew also downplayed a jail report of Ferrell hitting another inmate. "A fight," MacAndrew said. In jail, that could be as insignificant as a punch in the shoulder.

He also dismissed a 2010 incident in which a girlfriend sent him a photo of the two of them kissing during a prison visit and him touching her breast. Was it fondling? It was a still photograph, MacAndrew said. "I try to be fair."

MacAndrew said he would not have written a report of inappropriate touching by another inmate. It was initiated by the other inmate, MacAndrew said.

Ferrell was downright "heroic," when he reported an alleged murder-suicide plot by an inmate on a female guard girlfriend, the ex-warden said.

However, there is a lot of confusion about an incident report dated Feb. 2, 2010.

According to the report, a guard said Ferrell approached him to say that a prisoner boasted to him that he had had sex with a female guard and had even inked a tattoo on her neck. Now, she was breaking off their relationship and the man was talking about either murder or suicide. "There is supposed to be a knife at the inside grounds pavilion and/or the short wall across from the staff canteen," the guard wrote in his report.[4]

Ferrell claimed the man also talked about jumping a fence near a storage shed on the recreation yard and starting a fire.

The guard reportedly searched and found a six-and-one-half inch piece of plexiglass fashioned into a knife blade that had been buried in the pavilion area.

The prisoner was locked up in confinement. "Inmate Ferrell was also placed in confinement pending investigation."

Interesting story. The problem is, the female guard, or at least another prison employee with the same, unusual last name and identical first initial, was fired the next day from a different prison for associating with the wife of a death row inmate at a birthday party she hosted in July, according to DOC records sent to me on June 24, 2019.

When I tried to verify the story about Ferrell performing his "heroic" deed of saving a guard at Tomoka, a DOC spokesman sent me an email on Aug. 14, 2019 with the details of the guard's dismissal from Florida State Prison near Starke.

"No discipline records for the incident as alleged by Mr. Ferrell exists," he said.[5]

Was the record of the "heroic" deed a fake, or some type of error? Was the spokesman in error? The State Attorney's Office was not able to verify or disprove the account.

Not surprisingly, Robert Wendorf and other family were not impressed by the defense witnesses.

"If my brother could speak, maybe he would want to ask Rod, 'Why did you kill me?' When Rod was asked that question by the investigators, his answer was, 'just wanted to see what it was like to kill someone.' Maybe it is best that he will never know that he died for Rod's thrill."

"Judge, please keep this man in jail forever so that he never hurts anyone else again."

CHAPTER 67

Sexual damage

Ferrell was enraged when Heather told him her father was sexually abusing her, and he was "mortified" to learn she had lied, psychologist Heather Holmes testified.

He was enraged because he had been gang-raped by his grandfather's friends when he was five years old. When he told his mother about the abuse, she loaded him in the car and confronted the homeowner.

"She saw it as sticking up for her son, but I see it as retraumatizing the child," Holmes said.[1]

Ferrell was not raped any more, but was molested and subjected to his grandfather's exhibitionism, she said. When your own mother doesn't think enough about you to protect you, it causes serious self-worth issues.

Gibson told Holmes that, like her older sister, she had also been sexually abused by her father.

Ferrell had a love-hate relationship with his family, said psychiatrist Dr. Michael Maher.

Sondra "failed terribly" as his parent, Maher said. "She failed to create an environment that was safe and consistent and reasonable to him, provide guidance, particularly moral issues, that she failed to protect him from sexual harm from other family members...because of her 'blindness,' and neglect."

He would grow up, Maher said, but without a parent.

"There was a sexual component with his mother. It is a devastating psychological factor in the development of a child and adolescent," he said.

Sondra suffers from bipolar disorder, as evidenced by her failure to keep parental boundaries, Maher said.

Ferrell wanted to be "fair" when talking about her, "because she is his mother," Maher said. However, she failed because she did not protect him from sexual abuse and was neglectful because she did not get him psychological help. "He was a child who desperately needed to be heard," Maher said.

As for drugs, "this was a child who wanted to escape his environment in any way."

Ferrell was reluctant to discuss the sexual abuse he endured. As for his involvement in crime, Ferrell told him, "I don't want to blame other people for things I'm responsible for."

Maher, who specializes in treating victims of abuse and dependency issues, said the lack of abuse protection, insufficient rules, and moral guidance leads to a lack of a development of humanity, how other people feel and bond, especially physically, and having sexual boundaries.

"In the old days, we talked about nature versus nurture. What we know now is that without the proper interaction the brain can't develop without a proper nurturing environment," he said.

"People are not perceived as real, with hurt and sorrow. Teens without the proper environment lack humanity."

Ferrell has changed, Maher said. He no longer has the impulsivity issues he did before. The key is structure.

"Death row, which is by no means a rehabilitative environment, was in some ways better. The rules are rigid, unambiguous, and someone is not sexually abusing you."

"People, especially teenagers, have a tremendous need to achieve a sense of identity. 'I am…an athlete, I am

Tom, Sally…." Ferrell took the path of psychological self-destruction, including self-mutilation as a vampire. "He wanted to be seen as "somebody who was important in that realm."

Lenamon asked if it was a coping mechanism for being sexually abused as a child.

"It's preferable to be bad than to have no existence. He was desperately seeking to have some control over his life."

He had attached his identity to a cult because "he had no other family."

He wanted to be idolized. He had an elevated view of himself as Heather's protector. "It is consistent with a very disturbed relationship with his mother and with women in general."

Maher said Ferrell was suffering from post-traumatic stress disorder in 1996.

"He does not have PTSD now. We tend to think of it as a lifetime disorder because it can be persistent and reoccurring."

Maher said Ferrell's relationship with Bullard was different than it was with his previous girlfriends. "They have a very substantive relationship. Honesty, psychologically meaningful to one another, realistic with understanding that both can get something real and valuable, but it is limited in some respects."

Some inmates develop relationships to gain status or benefits, Maher said.

"He acknowledged to me that he had seen himself as a 'womanizer,' and had pen pals, people putting money in his canteen. "He realized that was not the path he wanted to be on. He wanted something new."

As for interviews, the only thing people were interested in was that he was a vampire killer, Maher said.

"Being taken off death row made sense to him. He knew he had to be punished but didn't deserve to be killed. That was a key element in making different choices."

He is a different person, a different personality, Maher said. His emotional IQ was "zero," and he manipulated people in his peer group. He has put himself in real relationships, mutual, non-exploitive.

Not surprisingly, the state's expert, forensic psychologist Gregory Prichard, testified that Ferrell does not suffer from mental illness but does have some personality issues.

To begin with, he strongly disagreed with Dr. Myers' diagnosis of schizotypal disorder.

"That's really rare, Pritchard said. "A person having that is so odd that he has trouble connecting to people." Ferrell, on the other hand, had friends and attracted people to him. Yes, he had odd beliefs that were somewhat magical, he said, but he did not fit the rest of the profile.

Buxman had Pritchard talk about his three-hour interview with Ferrell, including a statement he made to Rod up front. "Honesty is important to me," Pritchard recalled telling him. "I wanted to fairly portray Mr. Ferrell then and now."

He then laid out a series of inconsistencies between what Ferrell told him in his interview, and what he had told authorities over the years.

Pritchard, for example, noted that Ferrell once claimed to have taken LSD right before the murders, but he told him that he "popped a few pills and drank some Wild Turkey." He told Baton Rouge detectives that he took drugs after the murders, and he told prison officials that he had not taken drugs during the crime.

Also "inconsistent," he said, was Ferrell's claim that he did not plan to murder the couple. It did not jibe with what he said at Shannon Yohe's house.

Ferrell also offered a different account of the murders.

"He said he went into a blind rage, that he had a kind of flashback of his grandfather's sexual abuse of him, and that Heather was reporting to him that her father was abusing her. That was the first time I had heard that."

Pritchard described it as "blacking out," and said such a claim was "inconsistent" with Ferrell's detailed recollection of events inside the house.

Ferrell was not in the grip of a mental disturbance, he opined.

He was not leaving Kentucky because he was abused. "He was pursuing his interests." Those interests included his "vampire freedom," Pritchard said.

Nor was the crime "impulsive," Pritchard said, and gave a hypothetical example of a teen who was robbing a store and pulling the trigger on a gun if a clerk made a sudden move.

Ferrell was not a victim of disorganized thinking. He planned to come to Florida to get Heather and go to New Orleans. He switched license plates on the vehicles, and he chose a crowbar over a machete and a chainsaw as his weapon.

Did he appreciate the consequences of his actions? Buxman asked.

He was not insane, Pritchard said, nor was he under pressure by anyone else.

The psychologist was also asked to describe the vampire cult. "Fringe," Pritchard said. The others probably had dysfunctional lives of their own. It was their preferred peer group, but it was not a healthy influence, not a healthy outlet. It was dangerous, a little antisocial and asocial, he said. "They did not fit in the mainstream."

On cross-examination, Lenamon got the psychologist to mention other things that Ferrell had said, including quoting Ferrell as saying, "I saw red." during the attack.

Toxicologist and pharmacist Daniel Buffington, Ph.D., testified that Ferrell was such a chronic drug abuser that he considered him to be impaired during the crime.

Neuropsychologist Robert Ouaou, Ph.D., hit on the Supreme Court's reason for giving juveniles a chance for resentencing. A person's brain is not fully developed until they reach age 25, he said.

Lenamon also brought up the abuse and neglect of Ferrell's childhood.

"He told you that he really believed he was Vesago, a 500-year-old vampire," he said, adding that his drug use made the situation even worse.

CHAPTER 68

"Truly sorry"

Not only did Rod Ferrell look much different than he did 23 years earlier, but he certainly acted differently.

"My name is Rodrick Ferrell. I've been incarcerated since 1996," he said, becoming emotional right away while reading from a written statement.[1]

"I'm thankful for the opportunity to address the family of my victims, as well as the community," he said, pausing to exhale nervously.

"The first thing I need to explain to all of you is that I shamefully admit to the fact that I am guilty of these crimes…. To you, the members of the Wendorf and Queen families, I know that no matter what I say or do, I cannot bring your family members back, or erase the pain I have caused you," he said sniffling.

"Still, I want to apologize with every fiber of my being for what I've done to you. I'm hoping it might offer some solace. I have had years to reflect and better understand the ramification of what I did. I have actually allowed myself to see how terribly I have wronged you. Having witnessed the video clips of my much younger self, which Mr. Buxman played, was much harder to view than I had envisioned.

"As the disturbed child that I was, I could hide behind the mask of vain arrogance and sadistic sarcasm, both of which were frail defense mechanisms. However, after having seen all of this as a grown man, it has offered me a slight insight as to what you might have experienced. I can never know the full depth of your pain, and please, don't think that I presume to grasp all that you have endured. I'm merely saying that I am likewise appalled and disgusted by myself of twenty-three years ago.

"Back then, I could not fathom the lasting impact that my actions would have on your family. I was blinded by my own pain and stupidity caused by the abuse that I had suffered at an early age. However, this is merely an explanation, not an excuse for my actions.

"When Heather had alluded to me that she was in some way being abused, my vastly distorted mind clung to that concept. Regardless of this fact, it was still my own actions which took the lives of your loved ones. I cannot tell you how many nights over the decades that I have wished with all my soul that I could take that night back to prevent any of this from happening, to save you the grief and suffering I have caused your family...[and] the damage done to my friends and their families as well.

"I hope that you will be able to find it within your hearts to know just how truly sorry that I am to each of you. I hope that you will be able to consider on some level this very sincere apology. I also want to apologize for all the chaos and damage I did to the community....

"It was years before I understood the ripple effect.... When I first came to prison, I was a child whose both emotional and mental state had yet to mature. It was years before I was able to understand what I had done. In fact, for the first ten years in prison, I clung to my morbid mindset because I was afraid to accept the reality that was threatening the fragile fantasy world that I had built to protect myself. It still took another ten years, after I decided to stop hating so much and fearing so much in the world, that I decided to stop lying to myself before I got my feet under me and my head on straight. The gradual change took me from being an extremely messed up minor to a man who is both mature and capable of remorse. Honestly, I'm still growing as an individual.

"You've heard testimony about all the various courses and classes I have taken. However, it was the victim impact class that affected me the most.

"It actually defined what a victim was and just what it meant to be one. It allowed me to see all who I had hurt and how I had done so. Victim impact taught me how to have empathy. It was extremely difficult to face many things which this class brought to the surface. I experienced severe loathing and depression when confronted with what I had done. After coming to terms with what I had done, I was able to strengthen my resolve to become the best man that I can be, regardless of my situation or circumstances. This was perhaps one of the most humbling moments of my entire life.

"Another meaningful moment was when Lezlie came into my life. Initially, she came in as an advocate. Our correspondence quickly became a close friendship, which blossomed into a bond of love and trust. Through her love and encouragement, I was finally able to confront my few remaining doubts. She showed me how to have the strength to be vulnerable. She also showed me the benefit of having a humble heart. Lezlie introduced me to wholesome values she had growing up, as well as the Christianity she had been raised in. Her helping hand and gentle guidance has been a godsend.

'I cannot express enough the fact that, yes, in the '90s, I was a child who had become a monster. But I've since left that disgraceful part of me behind and become the man who stands before you today. As I said earlier, I cannot change or take back what happened, but I can assure you of my change. In closing, Robert, I swear to you, as one man to another, that your brother did not die for a thrill or a rush," he said, crying.

"I said those things back then to hide my own fears and confusion. His passing was a terrible mistake and a very sad tragedy.... Just please know how deeply sorry I am and for all the hurt that I have caused. I'm sorry for your pain and your loss. I'm sorry for everything. Thank you," he said.

"I'm getting a little bit worried," said Sandi Queen, one of Ruth's daughters, after three days of sympathetic testimony by defense experts.

It's not that she was moved by Ferrell's statements. "I didn't even want to hear his voice or what he had to say," she said, nor did she believe it. "It's the Rod show. I know Robert didn't want to hear it."

She was worried about what impact it all might have on the judge.

CHAPTER 69

Sondra claims change

Sondra Gibson was never happy being described as the worst mother possible.

"At first, I was really upset by it," she said of the depiction by defense attorneys and their mental health experts. "I know their job is to help Rod."[1]

She did not like the characterization of her as a 13-year-old by a woman who befriended her son while visiting her husband in prison. "She barely knows me!"

She wasn't all that crazy about Bullard, either.

"There have been a lot of girls," she said.

She said she is no longer the kind of person described at trial as a mentally ill parent and cult member who tried to solicit sex with a 14-year-old boy.

She has moved to a city in an adjoining county, has a jewelry business, and is taking care of her 90-year-old mother. Her father now has dementia, she said, and is confined to a memory care facility. "It's like he's in jail."

After Ferrell's arrest, Sondra and her parents moved into a mobile home in the small town of Umatilla, in Lake County, so they could be close to Rod. In May of 1998, residents were surveyed by Kentucky probation officials, and it touched off a firestorm.

"I strongly object to allowing this person, with her background and connection and cults...in this area. I have grandchildren and great-grandchildren," wrote a woman who lived in an adjoining town.[2]

Soon, a petition was circulated, garnering 44 names.

Sondra couldn't see what the fuss was all about.

"I've lived here for half a year. That ought to tell you something," she told me in an interview.

The family eventually moved again.

That was then.

"He's changed so much," she told me in 2019. "Of course, he's thirty-nine. He was sixteen at the time."

He now has a wastewater treatment license, his GED, and he had enrolled in re-entry classes, including a course on empathy.

"There's a lot of positives to look at," she said. "I know he wants to do really well, to be in the right location, to get on with his life. He doesn't want to hang around with the victims. I'm a lot like that. As I've gotten older, I've learned that it's very important to live a decent life. You can really make a difference."

CHAPTER 70

"Irreparably corrupt"

Judge Singeltary had leaned forward from his seat on the bench to absorb every word Jennifer Wendorf said during the resentencing hearing.

"May I have a place that's not traumatized by looking over my shoulder? If he ever gets out, I'll be destroyed. I'll be back to that lonely little girl nearly 23 years ago," she cried.[1]

Five months later, it was easy to picture the judge leaning into his fifty-five-page ruling, and it was as if Jennifer's words were still hanging in the air.

"It is the court's responsibility to evaluate whether the defendant was 'the juvenile offender whose crimes reflect unfortunate yet transient immaturity, or the rare juvenile offender whose crime reflect irreparable corruption,'" he wrote, quoting the case law.[2]

But after looking at Ferrell's history, "and based on the evidence presented, (the court) finds that he is irreparably corrupt," he wrote.

"In this case, the facts of the double homicide of Richard and Naomi Ruth Queen, as well as the armed burglary and armed robbery, are among the most appalling.

"These two victims were peacefully going about their daily lives when the defendant violated the sanctity of their home. Rather than restraining them or tying them up as he had contemplated, he entered their home and beat them to death with a crowbar. After his arrest, he described these events to law enforcement (and later journalists) without any remorse and without any indication that he was psychologically impacted by having beaten two human beings to death."

Ferrell told police the killings were "a rush" and that he felt like "a god."

The judge specifically mentioned Jennifer's impact statement.

"Her plea to the court was based not only on the fact that the defendant had murdered both of her parents but was also founded upon her sincere fear for her own safety and that of her children. Her fear is justified, not only because of the murder of her parents, but also considering the following statement Rod Ferrell made to the Baton Rouge Police Department: 'Thought about waiting for Zoey's sister, but decided, nah, why bother? Let her come home, have a mental breakdown, call the police, which I was correct, she did.'"

Singeltary also noted that Ferrell has a long history of lying, which shows he is not a reliable candidate for rehabilitation.

There is no evidence he consumed drugs and alcohol in the afternoon of the murders, Singeltary said.

Ferrell told one defense expert that he drank half a bottle of alcohol in the late afternoon before the murders, smoked a lot of pot, consumed eight to ten strips of LSD, and took about 15 Prozac pills within an hour of the murders.

He lied to his own psychologists, including saying that Anderson attacked Queen, and alternately that Queen was dying and Wendorf was dead when he entered the house.

He admitted pretending to be more mentally ill than he was to one psychologist before his trial.

The judge also said that Ferrell's new claim that he came to Eustis to save Heather from being sexually abused by her father "is not credible."

"We're very, very pleased," Queen's daughter, Paula Lohse, said of the ruling. "It's been tough. It's like there's been a weight on us."

CHAPTER 71

Heather

Heather is now a grown woman, married with children and an accomplished artist.

She left Lake County as soon as she could to go to an art school in North Carolina. It was there that she met her husband. She has lived in North Carolina and Georgia over the years.

"It's a very complex story. I am in the center of it. The people looking at it from the outside can't understand it," she told me in a 1998 interview. She did not respond to a request for a new interview, and Jennifer also declined the offer.[1]

"I regret that I was paralyzed with fear," Heather told a *Sentinel* reporter in 2006. It was her explanation for not trying to escape once she realized her parents were dead. "You can't really anticipate what you're going to do to deal with the situation if you've never been in anything like that before," she added.[2]

"Part of it was just a game to me," she said.

"He was charming," she said. Even more appealing to her were his flights of fancy, as dark as they were. "It was like a fairy tale. So much more interesting than getting up and going to school, going home, and going to bed," she told me, and that is the key. She let her flights of fancy and desire for total freedom drift into the unthinkable area of imagining her parents being dead.[3]

Jennifer testified to that when she quoted Heather as saying, 'Jen, have you ever plotted mom and dad's death?'"[4]

There was also the testimony of classmate Rachel Cox, who said she overheard Heather talking to friends. "She was mad at something that her parents would or wouldn't let her do, and she said that she wanted her parents dead."

April Doeden, said she overheard Heather in a phone conversation say her parents were "hurting her," and that the only way Ferrell could get her "is to kill them."[5]

These witnesses did not have anything to gain by testifying to these things. Certainly not Jennifer.

Sondra Gibson was trying to protect her son when she told the *Sentinel* that Heather "was saying she was going to kill her parents for a long time." She changed her story under questioning by investigators.[6]

Ferrell, of course, delighted in trying to heap blame on her at his presentencing hearing in 1998. "I asked her if it was cool if she stole her parents' car. She said she didn't have a problem with that." He then claimed to have said, "You spoke so much about killing your parents. You still want me to?" She said, "yes," according to Ferrell.[7]

Heather denied it in her depositions, and no one witnessed the alleged conversation outside her house the night of the murders.

Keesee's statement to police seems to back Heather's account of her not wanting her parents to be killed.

She said when the group arrived at the Wendorf house, Scott and Rod got out of the car to talk to Heather. "And then Zoey started screaming, so Dana and I got out of the car to see what was the matter with her. And she sat there screaming, 'No, you're not going to do it! You're not going to do it!' And Rod was like, 'Fine, we won't. Just go get your stuff. Go get your clothes, we will be back.'"[8]

Ferrell's problem is that he told so many different, contradictory, wild stories that he ended up with zero credibility. One wonders if he was even sincere during his tearful apology speech at the resentencing hearing.

Was Heather "okay" with Ferrell stealing her parents' car, as he claimed? Did she tell him he could find the keys in her parents' dresser drawer? She denied it in her depositions.

"She knew her parents were home. She had to know there would be some kind of confrontation," said Mike Graves, Anderson's attorney, in an interview for this book. "Common sense will tell you she had some kind of liability."[9]

"I thought he was just going to take me away," Heather told detectives in Baton Rouge.[10]

She told authorities that she thought Ferrell and Anderson were going to walk from her house to Jeanine's. Even though the houses were some distance apart, she said she herself had done it many times.

She did concede, however, that Ferrell had expressed an interest in killing her parents.

"Did you think you really did get through to him? He's the leader, is he not? You're the follower, are you not? Do you really think you are going to tell him what to do and he's gonna listen?" a detective asked her in Baton Rouge.[11]

"I thought he cared what I thought."

Two grand juries believed her. Yet, because she did not testify at trial or at his resentencing hearing, her role is still a head-scratcher for many, but not for Brad King.

"There was no evidence that she knew of or participated in killing her parents," he told me in an interview for this book.

King is a lawyer, of course, a prosecutor sworn to uphold the law, so evidence is key. But what was his gut-feeling? Did she say it was okay for Ferrell to kill her parents?

"I don't believe she ever said that," he said.

Ferrell is the only one who made that claim, King said. "I wouldn't rely on his word."

Heather expressed regret for even knowing Ferrell in my interview with her.

"It's hard not to feel guilty when every news station in America is telling you you're guilty," she told the *Sentinel* in 2006.

She denied hating her parents. "Most of my childhood was just perfect. I'll always have that to build upon."

There was trouble, however.

Among the artwork and writings seized by investigators from her bedroom was an undated, untitled poem.

Do I try to be different? Do I try to be the same?
What does life come to? Am I to blame?
These are the questions that go through my mind.
The answers to them, someday I may find.

I walk the street. This is how it goes.
No one comes with me. I cry as the wind blows.
I hold myself to keep myself warm.
The full moon is soon covered by a storm.

As the rain falls, it hides away my tears,
but the cold wet drops open up my fears.
I drop to my knees filled up with pain,
and I hope it will be washed by the oncoming rain.

So, I lay and plea, in a pool I lay,
to the unseen God, I beg and pray.
Then I stop and get up to go,
I'll have to explain something I don't even know.

My parents ask questions throughout the night.
They think to themselves, is she all right?
We all know the answer, but they don't give aid.
"It's her problem," they say, "the problem she made."

It would be incredibly unfair to blame the victims, especially since they are not around to defend themselves, but Suzanne Leclaire's attempt to warn Queen is haunting. "…she agreed that it beared (sic) watching. But in the end, I guess she didn't do anything about it."

One wonders what would have happened if the Wendorfs tried to follow the Leclaires' example of talking about their belief system, or at the very least making her get rid of the "dark and dreary" things in her room. Of course, the Leclaires were almost victims themselves.

Perhaps the most stunning aspect of all is that no one—not Jeanine, Heather, Shannon, Jeremy, or any cult member—warned the Wendorfs or police that a sixteen-year-old vampire cult leader was talking about murder.

Certainly, he was a "liar type person," as Yohe said. Times are different now, too. Numerous school shootings have created the catch phrase, "If you see something, say something."

Unfortunately, it's too late for Richard Wendorf and Ruth Queen.

EPILOGUE

Much has happened since 1996 when Lake County residents woke up to find out their quiet little county had become the eye of a bloody news hurricane. About 209,000 souls called the county home in those days. Now, more than 367,000 live in the area about 50 miles north of Disney World, "the happiest place on earth."

The county used to get one or two newsworthy murders per year in those days, and everybody in the courthouse knew the details. Now, not even the judges cannot keep up with the who's who. There were a record nineteen homicides in 2018.

Unlike some elected state attorneys, who practically forget what a courtroom looks like, Brad King has always liked trying cases and he has put some of the nation's most evil murderers on death row, including Aileen Wuornos, the notorious female serial killer.

Asked how the vampire case stacks up, he said he does not try to rate them. "I just try them."

He had served the five-county Fifth Judicial Circuit since 1988 when he announced his retirement in April 2020.

Lockett retired from the bench in 2001.

"I just can't do it anymore," he told me. He had become ensnared in a dispute with the sheriff in a messy case, had battled the state's child welfare system in the horrific murder of a child by her father, and he was tired.[1]

He died in 2013 at the age of seventy-one.

Sheriff Knupp was forced out of office in 2004 when he was charged with lying to a grand jury that was looking into his department's use of surplus vehicles. He died in 2010 at age 70.

Candace Hawthorne and Bill Lackay went into separate private practices. Lackay, who was "second-chair" for the vampire case, had nothing but praise for Hawthorne's trial strategy. "She made something out of nothing," he said in an interview for this book. The odds were stacked against them. "Two confessions, gruesome crime...."

Tommy Carle still has his own practice, and so does James Hope.

Mike Graves was elected public defender in 2016 and is now serving his second term.

In August of 1998, Cooper asked Lockett to reduce her seventeen-and-a-half-year sentence to eight years with five years' probation. She said she had a heart condition known as Wolff-Parkinson-White Syndrome. "With WPW, the defendant's heart has an extra valve that pumps blood through her septum," she wrote in a handwritten pleading. She said the condition causes dizziness and blackouts.[2]

A Mayo Clinic online post describes it as "an extra electrical pathway between your heart's upper and lower chambers [that] causes a rapid heartbeat."[3]

The site said the fast heartbeats are not usually life-threatening and a catheter-based procedure known as ablation can permanently correct the problem.

She said she was scheduled for surgery before the murders.

"The defendant acted under extreme duress under the domination of another person," she added. "The defendant was intimidated by the codefendant, and [was] in fear of him."

Lockett denied her request.

In February of that year, Keesee was reportedly caught drinking the blood of another prisoner.

"She was seen kissing or touching another inmate's arm after they had cut themselves," a prison spokesman said. The spokesman would not identify the other prisoner. Everyone wondered if it was Cooper.[4]

On Feb. 18, 1999, Cooper was disciplined for fighting with another inmate.

"Based on inmate witness statement testimony…both stated that the subject did hit inmate [redacted] because she didn't want the subject to talk to inmate Keesee."[5]

Keesee was released from prison in 2006, and Cooper in 2011. Both returned to Murray, Ky.

Heather reached out to her family, including her grandmother in 2002, through a Christmas card and a note, according to the 2006 *Sentinel* interview.

"She called up, and we didn't talk about it; we just said, I'm sorry."[6]

She attended her funeral in 2003.

"It was weird because it's a funeral," she said. "But it was weird because it was a family reunion."

She said she remains close to Jennifer.

The Queen family told me in 2019 that she is doing well.

She changed the spelling of her nickname from Zoey to Xoey. Besides proudly showing photos of her family on social media, she also displays her artwork and lists some of her favorite movies, including *Dracula*.

"I don't have anything against goth," she said in 2006. "I still wear black sometimes. It's not like I'm happy sunshine girl."

The Wendorf and Queen families are still grieving. It has been more than twenty years, but Paula Lohse's family still thinks about her mother all the time.

"We just get sad. Someone will say, Ruth, or mother, would have loved this," she said. "She would have been so happy to see that her kids and grandkids are doing so well."[7]

*"Thank you for your interest in our titles. Contact us at **promos@wildbluepress.com** to learn how to receive a FREE audiobook or ebook of your choice."*

For More News About Frank Stanfield,
Signup For Our Newsletter:
http://wbp.bz/newsletter

Word-of-mouth is critical to an author's long-term success. If you appreciated this book please leave a review on the Amazon sales page:
http://wbp.bz/coldbloodeda

WORKS CITED

Academia

Buckley, Kate, "The Evolution of the Vampire Other: Symbols of Difference from Folklore to Millennial Literature" (2016). *Honors Theses.* 504.https://egrove.olemiss.edu/hon_thesis/504.

https://study.com/academy/lesson/blood-in-dracula-symbolism-imagery-significance.html.

faculty.um.edu/bmarshall/Lowell/whywecravehorrormovies.pdf.

Books

Bugliosi, Vincent; Gentry, Curt, *Helter Skelter, The True Story of the Manson Murders,* New York: W.W. Norton & Co., 1974.

Clark, Lynn Schofield, *From Angels to Aliens,* Oxford: Oxford University Press, 2003.

Dolan, Sean, *Everything You Need to Know About Cults,* New York: The Rosen Publishing Group, Inc., 2000.

Douglas, John, *Mind Hunter,* Pocket Books, 1996.

Foster, Thomas C., *How to Read Literature Like a Professor,* New York, HarperCollins Publishers, 2014.

Life Application Study Bible, Wheaton: Tyndale House Publishers, 1991.

Melton, J. Gordon, Ph.D., *The Vampire Book, The Encyclopedia of the Undead,* Third edition, Canton, Michigan: Visible Ink Press, 2011.

Nelson, Harold L.; Teeter, Dwight Jr., *Law of Mass Communications, Freedom and Control of Print and Broadcast Media,* Mineola, N.Y., 1978, The Foundation Press.

Stanfield, Frank. *Vampires, Gators and Wackos, A Newspaperman's Life,* Create Space, 2014.

Stoker, Bram, *Dracula,* (London: Arturus Publishing Ltd., 1956,

Stone, Dr. Michael H., M.D.; Brucato, Gary, Ph.D., *The New Evil,* Amherst, N.Y., Prometheus Books, 2019.

Court documents

Adams, Ken, deposition, July 7, 1997.

Anderson, Howard, Scott, confession to Lake County detectives, Nov. 29, 1996.

Anderson, Howard, Scott, letter to Circuit Judge Don Briggs.

Clarida III, William, deposition, Nov. 3, 1997.

Calloway County Sheriff's Department Incident Report, Nov. 5, 1996.

Cooper, Dana, confession, Nov. 29, 1996.

Defense motion to declare Section 921.141 Florida statutes unconstitutional, Sept. 30, 1997.

Dewey, Tommy, deposition, Nov. 3, 1997.

Discovery materials, 1996-cf-1913.

Doeden, April, interview by David Norris.

Ferrell, Rod, confession to Baton Rouge Police, Nov. 28, 1996.

Ferrell, Rod, confession to Lake County investigators, Nov. 29, 1996.

Ferrell, Rod, videotaped conversation with Charity Keesee, Nov. 28, 1996.

Florida Department of Corrections Incident Report, Feb. 2, 2010.

Fla. Dept. Corrections Disciplinary Report, Log # 314-990280.

Galloway, S., Murray Police Uniform Offense Supplementary Report, Nov. 11, 1996.

Goodman, Matt, interview by David Norris, Feb. 15, 1997.

Grand jury presentment, Jan. 28, 1997.

Gussler, Al, investigative report, Feb. 2, 1997.

Gussler, Al, supplemental report, Feb. 5, 1997.

Hawthorne, Candace, Motion for Change of Venue, Feb. 7, 1997.

Hueber, Jeremy, interview by Bill Gross, Nov. 26, 1996.

Hueber, Jeremy, deposition, March 20, 1997.

Jury questionnaires, court documents.

Keesee, Charity, confession to Lake County detectives, Nov. 29, 1996.

Leclaire, Suzanne, deposition, March 21, 1997

Leclaire, Jeanine, interview with Ken Adams, Dec. 4, 1996

Leclaire, Jeanine, deposition, Oct. 14, 1997.

Miller v. Alabama, 2012.

Moran, Dennis, deposition, Nov. 3, 1997.

Motion for change of venue, Feb. 7, 1997.

Motion for closure of pretrial proceedings, Dec. 22, 1997.

Murphy, Penny, sworn affidavit, Sept. 17, 1996.

Murphy, Penny, interview with David Norris, Sept. 17, 1996.

Murphy, Steven, interview with David Norris, Dec. 15, 1997.

Nutt, Desiree, testimony at hearing, Jan. 21, 1998.

Post-conviction [capital resentencing] supplemental discovery exhibit # 15.

Presson, Audrey, proferred testimony, Feb. 12, 1998.

Shirley, Ron, deposition, Aug. 20, 1997.

Singeletary, G. Richard, Sentencing Memo, Jan. 31, 2020.

Sively, Robert B., Ph.D., Psychiatric Report, Sept. 9, 1997.

Taylor, Jeffrey, death investigation report, Nov. 25, 1996.

Taylor, Jeffrey, deposition, July 2, 1997.

Trial transcripts, Florida v. Ferrell, Fifth Circuit, 35-1996-cf-0001913.

Turner, Janeann, deposition, Jan. 6, 1996.

Welborn, James, deposition, Nov. 3, 1997.

Wendorf, Jennifer interview by Detective Ken Adams, Dec. 9, 1996

Wendorf, Heather, interview with Lake County detectives, Nov. 29, 1996.

Wendorf, Heather, letter to Jennifer Wendorf, discovery.

Wendorf, Heather, letters to Jeanine Leclaire, discovery.

Wendorf, Heather, deposition, Oct. 14, 1997.

Wendorf, Heather, deposition, Jan. 4, 1997.

Wendorf, Jennifer, recording of 911 call, Nov. 26, 1996.

Wendorf, Jennifer, interview by Ken Adams, Dec. 9, 1996.

Yohe, Shannon, interview by Bill Gross, Ron Patton, Nov. 27, 1996.

Yohe, Shannon, deposition, March 25, 1997.

Internet

The Society of Professional Journalists, spj.org/ethicscode.asp

Thecelebworth.com, May 30, 2018

https://stepheniemeyer.com/bio

https://www.melindadruga.com/hidden-means-in-dracula

https://www.quora.com/To-you-what-do-vampires-symbolize.

(https://www.aacap.org/AACAP/Families_and_Youth/Facts_for_Families/FFF-Guide/Self-Injury-In-Adolescents-073.aspx.

https://lenamonortiz.com/terence-m-lenamon-esq/

https://www.crandall-isd.net/apps/news/article/1119684.

(https://www.mayoclinic.org/diseases-conditions/wolff-parkinson-white-syndrome/symptoms-causes/syc-20354626#:~:text=In%20Wolff%2DParkinson%2DWhite%20(WPW)%20syndrome%2C%20an,serious%20heart%20problems%20can%20occur.

Interviews for book

Fallstrom, Jerry, March 16, 2020.
Graves, Michael, April, 2020.
Gross, Bill, 2019.
Hope, James, 2019.
King, Brad, May, 2020.
Klepper, Rob, email, Aug. 14, 2019.

Magazines

Dorwart, Laura, "The Trauma of Coercion: Disabled Elementary School Students and Isolation Boxes," *Pacific Standard*, March 1, 2018.

Newspapers

Daily Commercial
Flood, Alison, "Stephen King explains how to make vampires 'scary again,'" *The Guardian*, Sept. 30, 2010.

Hoover, Angela, "Immortality lecture: Vampires symbolic of society's fears, anxieties" *Arizona Daily Star*, Oct. 29, 2015

Orlando Sentinel

The Guardian, "Use of isolation booths in schools criticized as 'barbaric' punishment," Sept. 2, 2018.

Television documentaries

"The Mind of a Murderer," Discovery ID, Season 2, Episode 6, 2003

Ward, Michelle, Dr., *"The Mind of a Murderer,"* Discovery ID, 2016.

Vampire Clan, Deadly Cults, Oxygen, Episode 1, Season 1, Feb.10, 2019.

Wire services

Associated Press, Dec. 11, 1996.

NOTES

INTRODUCTION
1. *"I know nothing I say,* Frank Stanfield, "Ferrell Apologizes to victims' families," *Daily Commercial*, Nov. 20, 2019.
2. *"He was just a regular,* Florida v. Ferrell, Fifth Circuit, 35-1996-cf-001913-A, Vol. X, p. 1955.
3. *Oprah Winfrey famously,* XII, p. 2383.
4. *"There is genuine evil,* Stanfield, "Ferrell is sentenced to death," *Orlando Sentinel*, Feb. 28, 1998.

CHAPTER 1: "My parents have been killed"
1. *"I was late,* Jennifer Wendorf interview with Detective Ken Adams, Dec. 9, 1996.
2. *"My parents have been killed,* 911 tape, Nov. 25, 1996.

CHAPTER 2: "Is this for real?"
1. *"Without hesitation,* Detective Al Gussler, investigative report, Feb. 2, 1997.
2. *The Society of Professional Journalists,* spj.org/ethicscode.asp.
3. *"I thought you might,"* Frank Stanfield, *Vampires, Gators and Wackos, A Newspaperman's Life,* (Create Space, 2014), p. 394.
4. *Three days after,* Mary Murphy, "Murder warrants name all 5 teens," *Orlando Sentinel*, Nov. 28, 1996.
5. *"This is not,* Frank Stanfield, Mary Murphy, Lesley Clark, "Teens planned to kill," *Orlando Sentinel*, Dec. 5, 1996.

CHAPTER 3: "Dark and dreary things"
1. *"I thought that I was,* Jennifer Wendorf interview with Detective Ken Adams, Dec. 9, 1996.

CHAPTER 4: Mark of the clan
1. *"Are your parents alive?"* Lake Sheriff's Deputy Jeffrey Taylor deposition, July 2, 1997.
2. *Finding nothing,* Lake Sheriff's Lt. Christie Mysinger, Oxygen Presents, *"Vampire Clan, Deadly Cults,* Episode 1, Season 1, Feb. 10, 2019.
3. *"It was no wonder,* X, 1837.
4. *We searched,* Taylor deposition, Jan. 6, 1997.
5. *A French door,* Deputy Jeff Taylor, death investigation report, Nov. 25, 1996.
6. *"I found one,* Crime Scene Investigator Ron Shirley, deposition, Aug. 20, 1997.

CHAPTER 5: A warning too late
1. *"This just went,* Suzanne Leclaire deposition, March 21, 1997.
2. *"I never figured,* Shane Matthews, *Deadly Cults,* Oxygen.
3. *"I'm always trying,* Rick Badie, Lesley Clark, "Parents' murders: Ultimate shocker?" *Orlando Sentinel,* Nov. 27, 1996.
4. *Although she tried,* S. Leclaire deposition.
5. *Jennifer Wendorf had,* Interview with Detective Ken Adams, Dec. 9, 1996.
6. *"No, I can't,* S. Leclaire deposition.

CHAPTER 6: "No, you're not going to kill my parents"
1. *"Oh really?"* Jeanine Leclaire interview with Detective Ken Adams, Dec. 4, 1996.
2. *"So, Heather and I,* Jeanine Leclaire deposition, Oct. 14, 1997.
3. *"It was one of those,* Jeanine, Adams interview.
4. *"Be sure not,* Suzanne Leclaire deposition.

5. *Q: "What was in*, Jeanine deposition.
6. *Ferrell talked*, Jeanine, Adams interview.
7. *"He smelled bad*, J. Leclaire deposition.

CHAPTER 7: "A liar type person"
1. *"So, you're telling*, Stanfield, *Vampires, Gators and Wackos*, p. 273.
2. *"One girl was tall*, Shannon Yohe interview by Bill Gross, Detective Ron Patton, Nov. 27, 1996.
3. *"I didn't believe*, Frank Stanfield, Mary Murphy, Lesley Clark, "Friend: Teens planned to kill," *Orlando Sentinel*, Dec. 5, 1996.
4. *She was stunned*, Yohe, Gross interview.
5. *"And then*, Shannon Yohe deposition, March 25, 1997.
6. *He said if they had*, Yohe/Gross interview.
7. *"I want to be a part*, Yohe deposition.

CHAPTER 8: "Rod might kill her parents"
1. *"What has Heather*, Jeremy Hueber interview by Bill Gross, Nov. 26, 1996.
2. *That wasn't all*, Jeremy Hueber deposition, March 20, 1997.
3. *"I'm sure you must've*, Hueber, Gross interview.
4. *Scott Anderson's attorney*, Hueber deposition.
5. *"She didn't know much*, Mary Murphy, "Murder warrant names all 5 teens," *Orlando Sentinel*, Nov. 28, 1996.

CHAPTER 9: "Demure little girl"
1. *"You've got one wild*, Mary Murphy, Jerry Fallstrom, "5 sought in bludgeoning," *Orlando Sentinel*, Nov. 27, 1996.
2. *"She dressed differently*, Rick Badie, Lesley Clark, "Parents' murders: Ultimate shocker? *Orlando Sentinel*, Nov. 27, 1996.
3. *He had played golf*, Lesley Clark, "Grandpa hopes girl was taken, *Orlando Sentinel*, Nov. 28, 1996.

CHAPTER 10: Trapped

1. *Lake County investigators,* Don Fernandez, "Despite tips, teens sought in killings evade authorities," *Orlando Sentinel*, Nov. 29, 1996.

2. *Harrell Gibson said Rod,* Jerry Fallstrom, Lesley Clark, "Did girl want her parents dead?" *Orlando Sentinel,* Nov. 30, 1996.

3. *Charity told her grandmother,* Ken Adams deposition, July 7, 1997.

4. *"They were very,* William Clarida III deposition, Nov 3, 1997.

5 *"...he began to initiate,* Tommy Dewey deposition, Nov 3, 1997.

6. *One of the officers,* James Welborn deposition, Nov. 3, 1997.

CHAPTER 11: "Mentally disturbed"

1. *"I've lived more,* Rod Ferrell confession transcript with Baton Rouge officers, Nov. 28, 1996.

CHAPTER 12: "Don't worry about me"

1. *"Everything's okay,* Rod Ferrell, Charity Keesee videotaped conversation, Nov. 28, 1996.

CHAPTER 13: "I don't want to lose him"

1. *"Told me to tell,* Charity Keesee confession transcript, Nov. 29, 1996.

CHAPTER 14: "Jokes and stuff"

1. *"What I can tell you,* Dana Cooper confession transcript, Nov. 29, 1996.

CHAPTER 15: Heather: "I didn't know"

1. *She said she had asked,* Heather Wendorf transcript statement to Lake County investigators, Nov. 29, 1996.

CHAPTER 16: Killing was "a rush"
1. *"You still hanging,* Rod Ferrell confession transcript with Lake County investigators, Nov. 29, 1996.

CHAPTER 17: "I froze"
1. *Within a few minutes,* Scott Anderson confession transcript, May 29, 1996.

CHAPTER 18: Murky Mississippi
1. *"Did he actually,* Baton Rouge Officer Dennis Moran deposition, Nov. 3, 1997.

CHAPTER 19: "They're children"
1. *"She basically ran away,* Jerry Fallstrom, Lesley Clark, "Did girl want her parents dead?" *Orlando Sentinel,* Nov. 30, 1996.
2. *"It would be wrong,* Mary Murphy, Ines Davis Parrish, "Vampire cult teen to return to Florida," *Orlando Sentinel,* Dec. 3, 1996.
3. *She said she had talked to Rod,* Mary Murphy, "Teens to have day in 2 courts," *Orlando Sentinel,* Dec. 4, 1996.
4. *"I didn't understand,* Frank Stanfield, "Friend: Teens planned to kill," *Orlando Sentinel,* Dec. 5, 1996.
5. *Finally, after waiting for hours,* Jerry Fallstrom, "Vampire cult quit playing games, *Orlando Sentinel,* Dec. 1, 1996.
6. *The next day,* Lesley Clark, "Teens face court quietly, *Orlando Sentinel,* Dec. 8, 1996.

CHAPTER 20: Twisted sex
1. *"He hated it here,"* Jerry Fallstrom, "A Spooky Link – Vampirism," *Orlando Sentinel,* Dec. 3, 1996.
2. *"And I will be your bride,"* discovery records.
3. *"About two years ago,"* Psychiatric report, Robert B. Sively, Ph.D., Sept. 9, 1997.

4. *"I don't think that will fly,"* Associated Press, Dec.11, 1996.

5. *The boy's mother,* Penny Murphy sworn affidavit, Sept. 17, 1996.

CHAPTER 21: "Nothing to do with vampires"

1. *"I'm a little concerned,* Frank Stanfield, Mary Murphy," Cult angle attacked," *Orlando Sentinel,* Dec. 15, 1996.

2. *Florida law,* Frank Stanfield, "Vampire teens face grand jury charges today," *Orlando Sentinel,* Dec. 17, 1996.

3. *"I'm mad as a hornet,"* Frank Stanfield, "Grand jury indicts 4 teens," *Orlando Sentinel,* Dec. 18, 1996.

CHAPTER 22: "Interview with the vampire"

1. *"I know they did it,"* Jerry Fallstrom, Lesley Clark, "Interview with the Vampire," *Orlando Sentinel,* Dec. 19, 1996.

2. *"I've been practicing,* Frank Stanfield, "Officers don't buy remarks of 'vampire' leader Ferrell," *Orlando Sentinel,* Dec. 21, 1996.

3. *"It seems the only time,* John Douglas, *Mind Hunter,* (New York: Pocket Books, 1996, 351.

4. *She described going,* Stanfield, *Vampires,* 335.

5. *"It's humorous."* Jerry Fallstrom, Frank Stanfield, "Man accused by Ferrell must come up with alibi," *Orlando Sentinel,* Feb. 14, 1997.

6. *"It's the first time,* Jerry Fallstrom, Lesley Clark, "Officials: What rival clan?" *Orlando Sentinel,* Dec. 20, 1996.

CHAPTER 23: "Prince of the City"

1. *"He wore black"* Steven Murphy interview with Public Defender Investigator David Norris, Dec. 15, 1997).

2. *Twenty-two years later, Deadly Cults.*

3. *Murphy said he and Rod*, Norris.

4. *Murphy told the Sentinel*, Jerry Fallstrom, Lesley Clark, "Rival denies revenge," *Orlando Sentinel,* Dec. 21, 1996.

5. *"He just wanted to control*, Interview of Penny Murphy by David Norris, Sept. 17, 1997.

6. *He wanted people,* Steven Murphy interview in *Deadly Cults.*

7. *"We don't fit in,* Norris.

CHAPTER 24: "Nine-foot demon"

1. *"Mr. Ferrell told,* Calloway County Sheriff's Department Incident Report, Nov. 5, 1996.

2. *Ferrell told Joey,* David Norris interview with April Doeden.

3. *"He had several people,* David Norris interview with Steven Murphy, Dec. 15, 1997.

4. *"You become a murderer,* Norris.

CHAPTER 25: Destroying minds

1. *"Rod was a very good player,* David Norris interview with Matt Goodman, Feb. 15, 1997, court documents.

2. *The use of isolation boxes,* Laura Dorwart, "The Trauma of Coercion: Disabled Elementary School Students and Isolation Boxes," *Pacific Standard* magazine, March 1, 2018.

3. *A newspaper in Great Britain,* "Use of isolation booths in schools criticized as 'barbaric' punishment," *The Guardian,* Sept. 2, 2018.

4. *Months before the murders,* Norris.

CHAPTER 26: "It wasn't supposed to go this far"

1. *"The kids in the other,* Letter from Heather to Jennifer Wendorf, court documents.

2. *Back in Florida*, Letter from Heather to Jeanine Leclaire, court documents.

3. *Heather wrote to Jeanine again*, Dec. 15, 1996, court documents.

4. *"He still loves me,* Letter from Heather to Jeanine, Jan. 7, 1997, court documents.

5. *The verse in the NIV,* "Life Application Study Bible, (Wheaton: Tyndale House Publishers, 1991), 1135. Li.

6. *She apparently,* Tyndale, *Life Application,* 1150-51.

CHAPTER 27: "No more chains"

1. *"I've seen dead people,* Stanfield, *Vampires,* 374.

2. *"Is it possible,* 375.

3. *When she was asked,* 376.

4. *"I've got to win,"* 377.

5. *The man took the stand,* 379.

6. *"I knew some of her friends,* interview with Detectives Ken Adams, Al Gussler, Dec. 10, 1996.

7. *Sondra Gibson told the Sentinel,* Jerry Fallstrom, Lesley Clark, "Did girl want her parents dead?" *Orlando Sentinel,* Nov. 30, 1996.

8. *"I want to believe,* Frank Stanfield, Lesley Clark, "Heather blames Ferrell," *Orlando Sentinel,* Jan. 10, 1997.

9. *James Hope was undaunted,* Frank Stanfield, "Heather Wendorf to testify," *Orlando Sentinel,* Jan. 17, 1997.

10. *Prosecutors would later release,* Court documents.

11. *Heather was released,* Frank Stanfield, "Heather goes free," *Orlando Sentinel,* Jan. 29, 1997.

12. *"Ferrell's mother, in her polygraph,* Grand jury presentment, Jan. 28, 1997.

13. *"Hope said Heather,* Stanfield, "Heather goes Free," *Sentinel,* Jan. 29, 1997.

CHAPTER 28: What did Heather say?

1. *Grand juries operate,* Frank Stanfield, "May trial is set for 1 suspect in cult case," *Orlando Sentinel,* March 22, 1997.

2. *"Absolutely not,"* Frank Stanfield, Mary Murphy, "Heather's testimony in demand, *Orlando Sentinel,* Jan. 30, 1997.

3. *"This case is of compelling,* Frank Stanfield, "Sentinel sues for video of Heather's statement," *Orlando Sentinel,* Jan. 31, 1997.

4. *The Sentinel headline,* Frank Stanfield, "I want them alive," *Orlando Sentinel,* Feb. 5, 1997.

CHAPTER 29: "Will end in tragedy"

1. *"Where's your mama?"* Frank Stanfield, "Murder charge continues family's legacy of violence," *Orlando Sentinel,* Feb. 6, 1997.

2. *"I feel this case will end,* court discovery documents.

3. *In May of 1996,* Frank Stanfield, "Killers' pasts do not sway juries," *Orlando Sentinel,* April 5, 1998.

4. *"Hold on, hold on, "* Jerry Fallstrom interview with Frank Stanfield, March 16, 2020.

5. *In the days leading up,* Jerry Fallstrom, "Vampire cult quit playing games, *Orlando Sentinel,* Dec. 1, 1996.

6. *"I tried to hold off"* Frank Stanfield, "Jailed cultist tells his mom slaying suspect 'went crazy' *Orlando Sentinel,* June 12, 1997.

7. *"I just came."* Lauren Ritchie, "Jailed son sees strength of mother's love, *Orlando Sentinel,* June 15, 1997.

8. *Anderson told a fellow,* Mary Murphy, "Inmate: Cultist blames Ferrell," *Orlando Sentinel,* Jan. 4, 1997.

9. *"I could see him screaming,"* Ritchie, June 15, 1997.

10. **"People don't know the impact,"** Stanfield interview, *Daily Commercial,* April 1, 2017.

11. *"I thought my mom, Deadly Cults.*

CHAPTER 30: "Feisty"

1. *"She's feisty,"* Frank Stanfield, "May trial is set for 1 suspect in cult case," *Orlando Sentinel,* March 22, 1997.

2. *"I think anyone that,"* Rosemarie Dowell, "Mary Ann Plecas, 54, was 'go-getter' as Prosecutor, *Orlando Sentinel,* Dec. 19, 2002.

3. *"She doesn't want,"* Stanfield, "May trial."

4. *"No one wants,"* Frank Stanfield, "Blood lab is hot spot in cult case," *Orlando Sentinel*, Aug. 29, 1997.

CHAPTER 31: Constitutional clash
1. *"Only 70 days has elapsed"* Candace Hawthorne, Motion for Change of Venue, Feb. 7, 1997.
2. *"If the reporters,* Harold L. Nelson, Dwight L. Teeter, Jr., *Law of Mass Communications, Freedom and Control of Print and Broadcast Media,* Mineola, N.Y., 1978, The Foundation Press, 258.
3. *Anderson's attorney, Michael,* Frank Stanfield, "Reporters can hear cult tapes," *Orlando Sentinel*, Feb. 8, 1997.
4. *The Sentinel editorialized,* Lauren Ritchie, "Public the real winner in fight over slaying suspects' interviews, *Orlando Sentinel*, Feb. 16, 1997.

CHAPTER 32: Vampires don't suck
1. *Anne Rice, whose vampire,* Thecelebworth.com, May 30, 2018.
2. *Stephenie Meyers four-book,* https://stepheniemeyer.com/bio.
3. *"Feminine virtue is at stake,* https://www.melindadruga.com/hidden-means-in-dracula.
4. *"Well, of course,* Thomas C. Foster, *How to Read Literature Like a Professor* (New York: HarperCollins Publishers, 2014), 16.
5. *"Consuming human blood,* https://study.com/academy/lesson/blood-in-dracula-symbolism-imagery-significance.html.
6. *"The vampire has lasted,* Angela Hoover, "Immortality lecture: Vampires symbolic of society's fears, anxieties" *Arizona Daily Star*, Oct. 29, 2015.
7. *Buffy the Vampire Slayer,* Lynn Schofield Clark, *From Angels to Aliens,* (Oxford: Oxford University Press, 2003), 49.

8. *Margot Adler, the author*, https://www.patheos.com/blogs/johnbeckett/2014/03/vampires-are-us.html.

9. *Apparently, one of the,* Buckley, Kate, "The Evolution of the Vampire Other: Symbols of Difference from Folklore to Millennial Literature" (2016). *Honors Theses.* 504.https://egrove.olemiss.edu/hon_thesis/504

10. *"Here's what vampires,"* Alison Flood, "Stephen King explains how to make vampires 'scary again,'" *The Guardian*, Sept. 30, 2010.

11. *We have a need,* faculty.um.edu/bmarshall/Lowell/whywecravehorrormovies.pdf.

12. *In 2017, a blogger* https://www.quora.com/To-you-what-do-vampires-symbolize.

13. *The vampire hunter*, Bram Stoker, *Dracula,* (London: Arturus Publishing Ltd., 1956, 318.

CHAPTER 33: "This is not Rod"

1. *"Rod is a good boy,"* Frank Stanfield, "Rod is a 'good boy,' grandparents say," *Orlando Sentinel*, Jan. 11, 1998.

2. *"This is not Rod,"* Frank Stanfield, "Mom paints softer portrait of her son," *Orlando Sentinel,* Jan. 21, 1998.

3. *"She told me,* Janeann Turner deposition, Jan. 6, 1996.

4. *"...his mother was"* Norris.

5. *"Rod would never,* "Mom paints."

CHAPTER 34: "Opening the gates to hell"

1. *"Goodman stated,* Gussler supplemental report interview with Goodman on Feb. 19, 1997.

2. *Harrell Gibson told,* Lake County Sheriff's Detective Ken Adams Supplemental Report, Feb. 5, 1997.

3. *Months later,* Frank Stanfield, "Cultist: I saw blood on Ferrell," *Orlando Sentinel*, March 13, 1997.

4. *Brad King later asked Presson*, court transcript of proffered Presson testimony, Feb. 12, 1998.

5. *"When I arrived,* Murray Police Officer S. Galloway, Uniform Offense, Supplementary Report, Nov. 11, 1996.

6. *Gibson told the,* Frank Stanfield, "Mother, son caught in cult's web," *Orlando Sentinel,* Feb. 6, 1997.

CHAPTER 35: Shea: The "half-vampire"
1. *"She walks,* Frank Stanfield, "Diary details teen dreams, vampirism," *Orlando Sentinel,* July 26, 1998.
2. *"Rod, I bet,* Court documents, undated.
3. *"They don't just,* Court documents, undated.

CHAPTER 36: "Mental breakdown"
1. *I asked Brad,* Frank Stanfield, "Lawyers eager to question Wendorf," *Orlando Sentinel,* Oct. 13, 1997.
2. *"How many times,"* Frank Stanfield, "Attorneys grill girl in cult case," *Orlando Sentinel,* Oct. 15, 1997.
3. *Ferrell would later claim,* Frank Stanfield, "Ferrell blames Heather," *Orlando Sentinel,* Feb. 2, 1998.
4. *"I had a mental,* Heather Wendorf deposition, Oct. 14, 1997.
5. *There is a medical,* J. Gordon Melton, Ph.D., *The Vampire Book, The Encyclopedia of the Undead,* Third edition, Canton, Michigan: Visible Ink Press, 2011).
6. *"Some adolescents,* (https://www.aacap.org/AACAP/ Families_and_Youth/Facts_for_Families/FFF-Guide/ Self-Injury-In-Adolescents-073.aspx.
7. *"At some point, Heather* Deposition.

CHAPTER 37: "Hideous monster"
1. *Heather picked up,* Court documents.

CHAPTER 38: "I always wanted them alive."
1. *There was very little,* Heather Wendorf deposition, Jan. 14, 1997.

CHAPTER 39: Manson v. Ferrell

1. **When Keesee's attorney**, Vincent Bugliosi, Curt Gentry, *Helter Skelter, The True Story of the Manson Murders, New York:* W.W. Norton & Co., 1974), 641.

2. **One of the things**, Bugliosi, *Helter Skelter* 237.

3. **"Among ourselves**, Bugliosi, *Helter Skelter*, 239.

4. **A key characteristic**, Frank Stanfield, "Cult trials set for February, *Orlando Sentinel*, Aug. 31, 1997.

5. **FBI profiler**, John Douglas, Mark Olshaker, *Mind Hunter*, New York: Pocket Star Books, 1995, 115.

6. **"The more a person,** Sean Dolan, *Everything You Need to Know About Cults,* New York: The Rosen Publishing Group, Inc., 2000, 41-42.

7. **"One of the things**, *Deadly Cults.*

8. **It is not clear**, Bugliosi, *Helter Skelter*, 615.

9. **People often called**, Stanfield, "Cult trial."

10. **"After Rod came back**, *Deadly Cults.*

11. **One of Manson's tricks**, Bugliosi, *Helter Skelter*, 437-438.

12. **"Rod, me, Jaden**, *Deadly Cults.*

13. **"Contrary to popular**, Dolan, 41-42.

14. **Dolan also cited**, 54-55.

15. **"It would be like**, "Cult trial."

16. **It was certainly**, *Deadly Cults.*

17. **Manson said he had**, Bugliosi, *Helter Skelter,* 315.

18. **"To Charlie,"** Bugliosi, *Helter Skelter,* 319.

19. **Goodman also quoted**, Frank Stanfield, "Cult holds missing pieces in Wendorf murder puzzle, *Orlando Sentinel*, Nov. 23, 1997.

20. **"He wanted people**, *Deadly Cults*

21. **Fear wasn't the only**, Bugliosi, *Helter Skelter,* 317.

22. **Both Manson and Ferrell**, Bugliosi, Helter Skelter, 614-615.

23. **There were some**, Bugliosi, *Helter Skelter*, 534.

CHAPTER 40: Warming up the spotlight
1. *"I read with interest,* Judge Jerry T. Lockett, Fifth Judicial Circuit, "Judge: "I'm Not in Pocket," *Lake Sentinel,* Sept. 14, 1997.
2. *"What would she gain,* Stanfield, *Vampires,* 414.
3. *"I'll see you in your,* Stanfield, *"Vampires,"* 296.
4. *"To me, if there is,* Frank Stanfield, "Unanimous jury sets high bar for death penalty cases, *Daily Commercial,* Nov. 8, 2018.

CHAPTER 41: "Murder is not a private affair"
1. *Lockett was sympathetic,* Frank Stanfield, "Cultists can monitor blood tests," *Orlando Sentinel,* Sept. 11, 1997.
2. *King said he had a private,* Frank Stanfield, "Vampire trial judge vows to rule soon," *Orlando Sentinel,* Jan. 22, 1998.
3. *Two days later,* Frank Stanfield, "Judge: No delay in vampire cult trial," *Orlando Sentinel,* Jan. 24, 1998.
4. *Among the defense complaints,* Defense motion to declare Section 921.141 Florida statutes unconstitutional, Sept. 30, 1997.
5. *"I've always believed,* "Unanimous," *Daily Commercial,* Nov. 8, 2018.
6. *"I hate to sit up here,* Frank Stanfield, "Vampire case issue: Publicity," *Orlando Sentinel,* Dec. 10, 1997.
7. *"There were even,* Frank Stanfield, "Cult case stays open to public, *Orlando Sentinel,* Dec. 24, 1996.
8. *"This case has been,* Motion for closure of pretrial proceedings, Dec. 22, 1997.
9. *"Imagine a murder trial,* "Keep doors open, *Orlando Sentinel,* Dec. 28, 1997.
10. *"Rod Ferrell was not,* Frank Stanfield, "Ferrell's rights violated, attorney to argue today," *Orlando Sentinel,* Jan. 8, 1998.
11. *He said it had,* Frank Stanfield, "Jury can see Ferrell confession, *Orlando Sentinel,* Jan. 13, 1998.

CHAPTER 42: "They should all be sent to death row"
1. *One baffling question*, Jury questionnaires, court documents.
2. *"I am so convinced*, Frank Stanfield, David Damron, "Vampire jury stirs strong feelings, *Orlando Sentinel*, Jan. 16, 1998.
3. *"You would have had,* Frank Stanfield, "Cult case attorneys trim jurors," *Orlando Sentinel*, Feb. 3, 1998.

CHAPTER 43: "Disturbed," not insane
1. *Society is frightened*, Frank Stanfield, "Killers pasts do not sway juries," *Orlando Sentinel*, April 5, 1998.
2. *In Ferrell's case*, Stanfield, "Vampire jury," Jan. 16, 1998."
3. *"By 'evil,' we are not*, Dr. Michael H. Stone, M.D., and Gary Brucato, Ph.D., *The New Evil*, (Amherst, N.Y., Prometheus Books, 2019), 12.
4. *At the lower end*, Stone, *New Evil*, 14.
5. *Ferrell was mentioned,* Stone, *New Evil*, 172.

Chapter 44: The shocker
1. *Lackay interrupted,* Frank Stanfield, "I am guilty," Ferrell says. Surprise plea shocks court," *Orlando Sentinel*, Feb. 5, 1998.

Chapter 45: "Transformed"
1. *"We will not attempt,* Trial transcript, IX, 1779, Feb. 12, 1998.
2. *"And then, after,* IX, 1792.
3. *"I expect,* IX, 1792-1794.
4. *"Remember, you were,* IX, 1796.
5. *"What happened,* IX, 1797.
6. *The first thing he saw*, X, p. 1837.
7. *He said he saw Queen*, X, p. 1838.
8. *"Would you tell the,* X, 1958.

9. *Scott was walking*, p. 1960.
10. *"My understanding*, p. 1961.
11. *"We were both*, X, 1964.
12. *"Oh, we were both*, X, 1966.
13. *"He had gotten*, X, 1967.
14. *"Did he at any time*, X, 1969.
15. *"Right after Rod*, X, 1981.
16. *"On Mr. Wendorf's*, X, 1991.
17. *"Your honor,* X, 1993.
18. *King again used*, X, 1993-1994.
19. *"We have really*, Roger Roy, Amy Rippel, "Judge upholds law sealing autopsy photos," *Orlando Sentinel,* June 12, 2001.
20. *"There were nine*, X, 2000.
21. *"Dr. Hair, have you,* XI, 2020.
22. *The cause of death*, XI, 2023.
23. *"I do not believe so*, XI, 2053.
24. *"From the condition*, XI, 2055.
25. *"Now, on Miss Queen*, XI, 2057.
26. *She further reminded*, XI, 2059.

CHAPTER 46: Schizotypal vs. malingering

1. *"Malingering would,* XI, 2150, Feb. 13, 1998.
2. *One of those interviews*, XI, 2154.
3. *"His appearance changed*, XI, 2155.
4. *"She related a day*, XI, 2156.
5. *"For instance* XI, 2157.
6. *"...it involved*, XI, 2159.
7. *"As we were talking*, XI, 2164.
8. *"It was as though*, XI, 2172.
9. *"He also said things*, XI, 2173.
10. *Such a person*, XI, 2176.
11. *The disorder could be*, XI, 2178.
12. *"I believe that his*, XI, 2180.
13. *"And the reason*, XI, 2191.
14. *"Well, it is in*, XI, 2196.

13. *Krop said Ferrell*, XII, 2386.

14. *"That's correct*, XIII, 2431.

15. *"And part of that*, XIII, 2435.

16. *Ferrell told him*, XIII, 2436.

17. *King said, "He also*, XIII, 2441.

18. *Then, there was*, XIII, 2452.

19. *"Inmate Ferrell again*, XIII, 2532.

20. *"But if I don't get,* out, XIII, 2533.

21. *The things that were*, Hearing testimony of Desiree Nutt, Jan. 21, 1998.

22. *"Rod is both manipulative*, XIII, p. 2454.

23. *"Now, you discussed*, XIII, 2455.

24. *"But he said,* XIII, 2459.

CHAPTER 48: "Fantasy world" rage
1. *"He doesn't process*, XVI, 3188.

2. *"Now, does this mean*, XVI, 3189.

3. *She described it*, XVI, 3190.

4. *"There is also a*, XVI, 3191.

5. *Heather told Ferrell*, XVI, 3197.

6. *"I'm not going to*, XVI, 3199.

7. *"You don't internalize*, XVII, 3320.

8. *Both Ferrell and*, XVII, 3222.

9. *"I think the fact*, XVII, 3224.

10. *His "sire" became,* XVII, 3225.

11. *"He said that she,* XVII, 3228.

12. *She said she asked*, XVII, 3230.

13. *"I'm not saying*, XVII, 3232.

14. *"Beating him, and*, XVII, 3253.

15. *"I don't think he*, XVII, 3258.

16 *She conceded that*, XVII, 3259.

17. *"One gives rise,* XVII, 3269.

CHAPTER 49: "I didn't believe him"
1. *"You didn't take*, XIII, 2572.

2. *"Did you ever make*, XIV, 2631.

3. *"Your honor, I*, XIV, 2635.
4. *"Strike the reference*, XIV, 2636.
5. *"I had spoken with*, XIV, 2655.
6. *"Well, it's approximately*, XIV, 2683.

CHAPTER 50: The dead do tell tales
1. *"...I look at items*, XII, 2290.
2. **"What we do**, XII, 2312.
3. *Turning to another*, XIII 2492.
4. *She continued with*, XIII, 2493.
5. *The prosecutors then*, XIII, 2516.

CHAPTER 51: The horror movie
1. *"And in particular, judge*, XII, 2390.
2. *"I'm definitely not getting*, XII, 2399.
3. *But there was plenty*, XII, 2393.
4. *He also ruled against*, XII, 2396.
5. *The judge listened*, XII, 2394.
6. *King said it addressed*, XII, 2395.
7. *Odom asked: "Did you*, XIV, 2738.
8. *"So, it wasn't a planned*, XIV, 2739.
9. *"We didn't think anything*, XIV, 2761.

Chapter 52: Broken hearts
1. *"Now, would you please*, XV, p. 2831.
2. *"I'm Ricky's younger,* XV, 2835.
3. *"Ricky was really*, XV, 2837.
4. *"He had all the qualities*, XV, 2839.
5. *"Well, about a year*, XV, 2842.
6. *"Jennifer was looking*, XV, 2843.
7. *"Very rarely, if at all*, XV, 2864.
8. *"As I have mentioned* , XV, 2867.
9. *"One of the doctors*, XV, 2868.
10. *"I'm sorry about*, XV, 2953.

CHAPTER 53: Guts, no glory
1. *"Yeah, they both*, XV, 2875.
2. *"Well, of course*, XV, 2876.
3. *"She'd flirt with them*, XV, 2956.
4. *One letter caught*, XV, 2957.
5. *She said he called*, XV, 2962.

CHAPTER 54: A taste for blood
1. *Hawthorne began by having*, XV, 2966.
2. *Murphy described crossing*, XV, 2974.
3. *Murphy said becoming*, XV, 2975.
4. *He also talked about*, XV, 2977.
5. *Hawthorne pulled out a*, XV, 2982.
6. *"Yes, I do love Rod,"* XV, 2985.
7. *"We are supposed*, XV, 2986.
8. *Ferrell once told him*, Frank Stanfield, "Ferrell's past gets blame, *Orlando Sentinel*, Feb. 20, 1998.

CHAPTER 55: The inner circle
1. *"When Rod came back*, XVI, 3029.
2. *"No. That wasn't until he*, XVI, 3032.
3. *April Doeden testified*, XVI, 3035.
4. *Hawthorne asked Doeden*, XVI, 3036.
5. *"Did you ever*, XVI, 3038.
6. *"Well, it was originally,* XVI, 3037.
7. *"I believe I heard,* XVI, 3040.
8. *"April, you said*, XVI, 3045.
9. *He also got her to*, XVI, 3047.
10. *"But when we got into*, XVI, 3048.
11. *"How old were you,* XVI, 3051.
12. *She said she moved*, XVI, 3052.
13. *"No, I didn't. The* XVI, 3053.
14. *Hawthorne also asked if,* XVI, 3060.
15. *After the slayings,* XVI, 3061.
16. *She wore all black*, XVI, 3062.
17. *Rachel Cox, who,* XVI, 3068.

18. *The last time,* XVI, 3073.
19. *"She proceeded to talk,* XVI, 3074.
20. *Hawthorne asked if she,* XVI, 3075.
21. *King was subtle,* XVI, 3076.

CHAPTER 56: No 'goody two-shoes'
1. *"When he was born,* XVI, 3123.
2. *"Approximately, I would,* XVI, 3124.
3. *"And were you,* XVI, 3128.
4. *"Ecstasy, I did some,* XVI, 3129.
5. *"I was in the bathroom,* XVI, 3130.
6. *"Do you know if,* XVI, 3135.
7. *She said he would take,* XVI, 3136.
8. *"He (Rod) said they,* XVI, 3138.
9. *She said she didn't,* XVI, 3140.
10. *She said she was "pretty,"* XVI, 3144.
11. *She also admitted writing,* XVI, 3148.
12. *"I don't think I,* XVI, 3149.
13. *"Did you ever tell,* XVI, 3150.
14. *She said she went,* XVI, 3151.
15. *She said she approved,* XVI, 3159.
16. *"I heard him responding,* XVI, 3157.
17. *"I'm in love,* XVI, 3163.
18. *King began his,* XVI, 3164.
19. *King took a shot,* XVI, 3168.
20. *"That I'm not,* XVI, 3167.
21. *"Yes, it says that,"* XVI, 3169.
22. *King could have,* Jerry Fallstrom, Lesley Clark, "Did girl want her parents dead?" *Orlando Sentinel,* Nov. 30, 1996.
23. *"Yes, uh-huh,* XVI, 3171.

CHAPTER 57: The last hope
1. *"Now, there have been,* XVI, 3086.
2. *"Captain, are you familiar,* XVI, 3088.
3. *"My husband thinks,* 7:30, XVI, 3080.

4. *"Going to try to graduate,* XVI, 3091.

5. *"Would that be because,* XVI, 3092.

6. *"I don't quite recall,* XVI, 3109.

7. *"That she wanted,* XVI, 3115.

8. *"I cared about,* XVII, 3291.

9. *On Aug. 9, Turner,* XVII, 3315.

10. *"In regards,* XVII, 3319.

11. *"And in order usually,* XVI, 3320.

12. *"I thought Rod,* XVII, 3276.

13. *His response was,* XVII, 3277.

14. *Ferrell was given several,* XVII, 3283.

15. *"I could just slit,* XVII, 3287.

CHAPTER 58: It's unanimous: Death

1. *"In the Circuit Court,* XIII, 3469.

2. **"Richard and Ruth's honor were restored,"** Frank Stanfield, "Ferrell jury: Death 12, life 0, *Orlando Sentinel,"* Feb. 24, 1998.

CHAPTER 59: Ferrell blames Heather

1. *"...she knew Mr. Ferrell was threatening to kill,* XVIII, 3493.

2. *"He was like our only son,"* 3517.

3. *She also addressed the animal abuse,* 3519.

4. *"I truthfully would rather not discuss that,* 3536.

5. *"I really couldn't tell you.,"* 3537.

6. *"Demonology is a subtext,* 3541.

7. *"At that time I took it as a joke,"* 3543.

8. *He talked about Sondra's husband, Darren,* 3546.

9. *He said he told his mother,* 3552.

10. *"Not good. It's just, again,* 3557.

11. *He said he didn't feel,* 3558.

12. *By the summer of 1996,* 3560.

13. *He said she also told him,* 3574.

14. *"No, just from her demeanor,* 3565.

15. *"I told her that the Buick,* 3573.

16. *He said he asked her who was in the house*, 3574.

17. *"There is a lot about life in general*, 3594.

CHAPTER 60: "Disturbed" is no excuse

1. *"When I first agreed,* XIX, 3621.

2. *"It is the opinion of this court,* XIX, 3622.

3. *"We can know a few things,* XIX, 3623.

4. *"And when we have these,* XIX, 3624.

5. *"And I say to Rod,* XIX, 3625.

6. *"You stated it best to Baton Rouge,* XIX, 3626.

7. *After explaining that Ferrell,* XIX, 3630.

8. *"I'm a better mother than a lot,* Frank Stanfield, "Ferrell is sentenced to death," *Orlando Sentinel,* Feb. 28, 1998

CHAPTER 61: Dominoes

1. *"It was my choice to come,* Frank Stanfield, "Cultist won't see light of day," *Orlando Sentinel,* April 2, 1998.

2. *Just two months earlier, in May,* Frank Stanfield, "Cult trial will be moved to St. Augustine court, *Orlando Sentinel,* May 2, 1998.

3. *"I didn't really think he would do it,"* Kathryn Quigley, "Keesee's sentencing closes book on case, *Orlando Sentinel,* Aug. 14, 1998.

CHAPTER 62: Wrong, not criminal

1. *"Just like me,* Frank Stanfield, "Heather tells her side," *Orlando Sentinel,* Aug. 14, 1998.

2. *We find that the evidence identified,* Frank Stanfield, "Grand jury frees Wendorf," *Orlando Sentinel,* Dec. 19, 1998.

CHAPTER 63: Life, not death, or maybe….

1. *Juveniles are different from adults, Miller v. Alabama,* 2012.

2. *Prosecutors agreed,* Letter from Scott Anderson to Circuit Judge Don Briggs.

3. *The Queen family was okay*, Frank Stanfield, "Anderson to be released in 2032 for role in vampire murders, *Daily Commercial*, Dec. 3, 2018.

CHAPTER 64: Still a vampire?
1. *In 2003 he described vampirism*, "The Mind of a Murderer," Discovery ID, Season 2, Episode 6, 2003.
2. *In 2016, a different psychologist-interviewer*, Dr. Michelle Ward, "The Mind of a Murderer," Discovery ID.
3. *"I am 69 years old and it is heart-breaking*, Frank Stanfield, "Female groupies common, *Daily Commercial*, Nov. 18, 2019.
4. *"If you get a neuropsychologist*, Frank Stanfield, "Brain injury scientists play big role in death penalty cases, *Daily Commercial*, Aug. 12, 2017.
5. **"Every person has a story,"** https://lenamonortiz.com/terence-m-lenamon-esq/.

CHAPTER 65: From perfect life to "nothing"
1. *"The pain will never go away*, Frank Stanfield, "Wendorf asks judge to keep Ferrell behind bars, *Daily Commercial*, Nov. 18, 2019.

CHAPTER 66: "He's a different person"
1. *"As a survivor of domestic abuse*, https://www.crandall-isd.net/apps/news/article/1119684.
2. *How deep was,* Frank Stanfield, "Woman offers home, job to Ferrell if he's released, *Daily Commercial*, Nov. 19, 2019.
3. **"In a childish manner**, Post-conviction capital resentencing supplemental discovery exhibit No. 15.
4. *According to the report,* DOC Incident report, Feb. 2, 2010.
5. *"No discipline records for the incident,* Aug. 14, 2019 email from DOC spokesman, Rob Klepper.

CHAPTER 67: Sexual damage
1. *"She saw it as sticking up for her son*, Frank Stanfield, "Ferrell apologizes to victims' families," *Daily Commercial*, Nov. 20, 2019.

CHAPTER 68: "Truly sorry"
1. *"My name is Rodrick Ferrell,"* Videotaped testimony, Nov. 19, 2019.

CHAPTER 69: Sondra claims change
1. *"At first I was upset*, Frank Stanfield, "Mother of vampire cult killer: I've changed," *Daily Commercial,* Dec. 1, 2019.
2. *"I strongly object*, Frank Stanfield, "Sondra Gibson isn't welcome," *Orlando Sentinel* May 14, 1998.

CHAPTER 70: "Irreparably corrupt"
1. *"May I have a place that's not traumatized*," Frank Stanfield, "Wendorf asks judge to keep Ferrell behind bars," *Daily Commercial*, Nov. 18, 2019.
2. *"It is the court's responsibility*, Sentencing memorandum, Circuit Judge G. Richard Singeltary, Jan. 31, 2020.

CHAPTER 71: Heather
1. *"It's a very complex story*," Frank Stanfield, "Heather tells her side," Aug. 13, 1998, *Orlando Sentinel,* Aug. 13, 1998.
2. *"I regret that I was paralyzed*, Christine Delleret, "Heather Wendorf-Kelly was cleared in her parents' 1996 murder in Eustis, Now married and living out of state, she reflects on a tragic time," *Orlando Sentinel*, Dec. 17, 2006.
3. *"He was charming*, Stanfield, "Heather tells her side," *Sentinel*, Aug. 14, 1998.
4. *Jennifer testified*, Jennifer Wendorf interview with Detective Ken Adams, Dec. 9, 1996.
5. *April Doeden said she overheard*, XVI, 3040.

6. *Sondra Gibson, of course*, Fallstrom, Clark, "Did girl want her parents dead?" *Sentinel*, Nov. 30, 1996.

7. *Ferrell, of course,* Stanfield, "Ferrell blames Heather," *Orlando Sentinel,* Feb. 26, 1996.

8. *She said when the group arrived*, Keesee confession, Nov 29, 1996.

9. *"She knew her parents were home,"* Mike Graves, interview with Frank Stanfield.

10. *"I thought he was just*, Heather statement to detectives, Nov. 29, 1996.

11. *"Did you think you really*, Heather Statement.

EPILOGUE

1. *"I just can't do it anymore*, "Judge Lockett to step down after 15 years on the bench," Frank Stanfield, *Orlando Sentinel*, Oct. 30, 2001.

2. *In August of 1998*, Frank Stanfield, "Vampire cultist asks judge to shorten her sentence, Orlando Sentinel, Aug. 29, 1998.

3. *A Mayo Clinic online* https://www.mayoclinic.org/diseases-conditions/wolff-parkinson-white-syndrome/symptoms-causes/syc-20354626#:~:text=In%20Wolff%2D-Parkinson%2DWhite%20(WPW)%20syndrome%2C%20an,serious%20heart%20problems%20can%20occur.

4. *"She was seen kissing*, Karin Meadows, "Keesee drinks blood in prison, *Orlando Sentinel*, Dec. 11, 1998.

5. *"Based on inmate witness*, Fla. Dept. Corrections Disciplinary Report, Log # 314-990280.

6. *"She called up, and we didn't*, Christine Dellert, "Heather Wendorf-Kelly," *Orlando Sentinel*, 2006.

7. *"We just get sad,"* Frank Stanfield, "'Vampire Killer' keeps his life sentence, Daily Commercial, April 11, 2020.

INDEX

N

O

P

Q

R

S

**AVAILABLE FROM KEVIN SULLIVAN
AND WILDBLUE PRESS!**

VAMPIRE by KEVIN SULLIVAN

http://wbp.bz/vampirea